CW00740625

Intermediate

Business

Michael Fardon

John Prokopiw

OSBORNE BOOKS *GNVQ* SERIES

© Michael Fardon, John Prokopiw 1995

First published 1995. Reprinted 1995, 1996, 1998, 1999.

Published by Osborne Books Limited,
Unit 1B Everoak Estate, Bromyard Road,
St Johns, Worcester, WR2 5HN
Tel 01905 748071

Printed by The Bath Press, Bath

British Library Cataloguing in Publication Data
A catalogue record for this book is available from the British Library

ISBN 1-872962-26-2

contents

acknowledgements

The authors would like to thank the following people who have helped and advised in the preparation of this book: Cathy Fardon, Robbie Fardon, Mike Gilbert, Kay Kelly, Jason Orton and Rob Coward of NCVQ, Roger Petheram and David Singleton of Celtip Computers.

Thanks must also go to the following organisations for help and for providing material for use in this book: Barclays Bank Connect team, Barclaycard, BT, British Bankers Association, Broadheath Stores, The Controller of HM Stationery Office, Department of Employment (as was), the DTI, the European Commission, Harrison Clark, Marks & Spencer, Motronic Services, NCVQ, OECD, Prontaprint, Roger Straton Associates, Rover Group, Mick Ruff, Severn Trent Water, Times Newspapers Limited, W H Smith Limited, Vauxhall Motors Limited, Worcester Careers Centre, Worcester City Planning Department.

assignments

GNVQ *unit coverage*

The text and Activities in this book are referenced to NCVQ performance criteria throughout.

core skills coverage

Core Skills delivery has always been a difficult area. Some centres assess the Core Skills as an integral part of coursework, some deliver Core Skills as a separate 'subject' and allocate part of the timetable for skills development and some centres mix the two approaches. This book caters for all of these:

- through the formal extended Core Skill Activities at the end of the book (from page 266 onwards)
- through Core Skills being incorporated in the Activities and Assignments throughout the book, wherever you see these symbols:

 application of number    *communication*   *information technology*

The table below maps out the coverage of the Core Skills in the Student Activities and Assignments.

APPLICATION OF NUMBER		
Element 2.1	Collect and record data	26,60,172,178
Element 2.2	Tackle problems	47,129,178,222,223,241,248,249,254
Element 2.3	Interpret and present data	57,209,248

COMMUNICATION		
Element 2.1	Take part in discussions	15,71,97,145
Element 2.2	Produce written material	Many assignments require a report format , other formats can be found on pages 65,201,251,253
Element 2.3	Use images	51
Element 2.4	Read and respond to written materials	33,110,119,172

INFORMATION TECHNOLOGY		
Element 2.1	Prepare information	24,45,209,238,248,249
Element 2.2	Process information	24,45,66,209,238,248,249
Element 2.3	Present information	19,47,66,82,150,152,248
Element 2.4	Evaluate the use of information technology	209,251

to the tutor

the text

Intermediate Business has been written to cover the four mandatory Units of the GNVQ Intermediate Business Award and the Core Skills to the 1995 revised specifications.

Intermediate Business has been written with NCVQ requirements very much in mind. The authors have been careful to interpret the range and evidence indicators in accordance with NCVQ intentions.

As you will see if you used Osborne Books' *Introduction to Business*, the text has been extensively re-written to cover the revisions to the course specifications. The opportunity has been taken to expand the text to incorporate a new easy-to-read format, new activities and a series of practice multiple-choice questions.

Each GNVQ Unit is covered by a separate section of the book, and in most cases each chapter covers a *single* Unit Element. The performance criteria of each Element are printed below the chapter title, and are referenced within the text throughout the book. If the chapter covers only part of an Element, this is made clear in the chapter heading. Coverage of the GNVQ Unit Elements within the book is set out on page 6.

The text also covers all the range statements. Tutors should consult the index at the back of the book where they will find references to items in the range.

student activities

The Student Activities in *Intermediate Business* collectively cover all the performance criteria of the mandatory units. A reference to the relevant performance criterion (or criteria) is printed in the heading of each Activity.

The Student Activities are designed as learning activities to be used inside and outside the classroom – they are complementary to the Assignments which cover the Evidence Indicators. They also enable the student to cover the three main Core Skills – please refer to the table on page 7 which shows how this is achieved. The Core Skill symbols appear in the Activities with the Element reference to indicate tasks where the skills can be assessed.

assignments

Intermediate Business contains fourteen completely new full-length Assignments printed within the chapters (see page 5 for a list). These are designed to cover the Element Evidence Indicators set down in the course specifications. They are fully referenced to the performance criteria in each Element.

Osborne Books is well aware that most centres may have devised their own assignments based around schemes of work. The assignments in this book are therefore offered as ideas and material for development.

core skills

Teachers and lecturers have repeatedly asked us for a book which will enable them assess the Core Skills. *Intermediate Business* does this in two ways. The Core Skills are assessed and *referenced* in the Activities and Assignments throughout the book; they are also developed in the extended Activities at the end of the text (from page 266 onwards). For further details please see page 7. The Core Skills activities follow the 1995 revised specifications.

external testing

In order to help students prepare for the external tests, each chapter concludes with a summary, key terms and about half-a-dozen practice multiple-choice questions. In addition, the text itself uses terms from the range as subheadings.

If you want to comment on the book in any way, turn to page 285 – you can write your comments, tear the page out and send it to us.

Michael Fardon
General Editor
August 1995

to the student

some questions answered

what is a GNVQ?

GNVQ stands for General National Vocational Qualification. What is it? A GNVQ is a qualification which is recognised throughout the country – it is 'National'. It can lead to further qualifications or a job. The word 'Vocational' means that it relates to an area of work – in your case the business world. With a Business GNVQ you will be given the knowledge and skills you will need in a business job. A GNVQ means being able to 'do' a job as well as 'knowing' about it. A GNVQ qualification provides skills that employers like; it also enables you to progress to a further qualification.

Units? Elements?

When you do a GNVQ course you will find that it has a language all of its own: 'Units, Elements, portfolios, evidence, performance criteria etc etc . . .' – it can seem very confusing when you first start the course! Read on and you should be able to make some sense of all these terms.

Units

Units are areas of study which make up the course. For the Intermediate Award in Business you have to complete *at least* nine Units:

- four mandatory vocational Units (covered by this book)
- three mandatory core skill units (developed within this book)
- two optional units (your tutor will help you choose these)

Elements

Elements are areas of study within a unit. For example Unit 1 'Business organisations and employment' has three Elements:

1.1   Explain the purposes and types of business organisations

1.2   Examine business location, environment, markets and products

1.3   Present results of investigation into employment

You will have to do all three of these Elements to complete the Unit. In this book most chapters cover just one Element, although occasionally an Element may be covered by two chapters, as in the case of Element 4.1.

Performance criteria – what a student 'must do'

Each Element is in turn divided into statements of what you 'must do' to complete the Element. These are known as 'performance criteria' (abbreviated to 'pc'). They are listed at the beginning of each chapter, and also in section headings within each chapter. For example Chapter 1 is headed as follows:

The performance criteria are the numbered statements under the heading 'a student must'. They should all be covered in your coursework before you can complete the Element. The evidence that you collect for all these 'student must' items should be presented in a folder known as the 'Portfolio' which will be assessed by the Tutor. The work you do on the course is likely be taken from the Student Activities in the chapters of this book. Each Student Activity is headed with the relevant performance criteria reference. Look at the Activity heading below:

what is a business?

Core Skill 2.1

You will see that the performance criteria reference – '1.1.2 & 3' in theb arrow refers back to the 'student must' statements 2 and 3 at the start of the chapter. The other numbers '1.1' refer to the Element (Unit 1, Element 1).

You will also see a reference to the Core Skill of Communication (the telephone symbol). We will now explain the Core Skills.

what are Core Skills?   Core Skills are the job-related skills which you will develop during your course:

Application of Number

This skill involves the use of *numbers*: gathering them, making sense of them, using them to solve problems, and presenting them. The symbol for this skill is a calculator.

Communication

This skill involves taking part in discussions, being able to prepare written documents, using illustrations and images, and being able to understand and respond to them. The communication symbol used in the book is a telephone.

Information Technology

This skill enables you to become familiar with computers and to be able to use them for a variety of business tasks: word-processing, storing and handling data, and tackling business calculations. The symbol used is a computer.

your assessment

Portfolio

Your coursework folder – your 'portfolio' – will contain work covering all the Unit Elements and will be the evidence which forms the basis of your assessment. The grades you can get are Pass, Merit or Distinction. Your tutor will explain how the assessment is made of *what* you produce and *how* you produce it, and the forms that will have to be filled in to record your results for each piece of work.

External Tests

Part of your assessment involves you sitting external multiple-choice tests. These cover what is known as the 'range' of the GNVQ course. The 'range' is a series of topics which make up each performance criterion. Your tutor may or may not give you details of the 'range'. This text covers all the topics in the 'range'. To help prepare for your external tests you should:

- read and note the chapter contents carefully
- learn the 'key terms' at the end of each chapter
- do the practice multiple-choice questions at the end of each chapter
- ask your tutor for past papers

a message from the authors

We hope that you will enjoy the course and will make the most of getting out and seeing how businesses work in practice. We hope you will find the book useful. Good luck with the tests and good luck with getting a job or going on to do another qualification.

Michael Fardon and John Prokopiw

August 1995

**GNVQ UNIT 1
BUSINESS ORGANISATIONS AND EMPLOYMENT**

1 Types of business

what this chapter covers

This chapter explains the many different types of business that you will encounter. It looks at what they set out to do and how they link up with each other.

what you will learn from this chapter

- the division of business into different sectors – businesses that extract raw materials, manufacturing businesses and businesses that provide a service – and the changes that are occuring in these sectors

- the difference between the public sector (government controlled organisations) and the private sector (businesses in private hands) and the different sizes of business

- the different types of business ownership – sole trader, partnership, limited company, co-operative, franchise and state-owned businesses – who owns the business and who runs it

- the purposes of business – making a profit, increasing market share, providing customer service, providing a public service and operating as a charity

- the ways in which businesses operate together

what is a business?

When studying businesses it is essential to have a clear idea in your mind of how a 'business' is defined. This definition is often taken for granted, for example, when someone says 'I am going into business' or 'I want to start a business'. What precisely do they mean, and what are their aims?

STUDENT ACTIVITY 1.1
performance criteria 1.1.2 & 3

Core Skill 2.1

what is a business?

Divide into groups of three or four within the class and discuss whether the following organisations are businesses, and if so, what it is about them that make them 'businesses'. Ask questions like "What do they make or do? Who owns them? What are they in business for?" Appoint a spokesperson and report your findings to the main class group.
- The Post Office
- Nissan Cars
- your school or college catering services
- Oxfam
- a fruit grower

From looking at these you should be able to appreciate that business can involve:
- manufacturing a product (eg cars)
- growing a product from nature (fruit)
- providing a service (The Post Office, meals, charity relief)
- private ownership or state ownership (the Post Office)

Your discussions may also reveal that businesses
- employ staff (or use volunteers in the case of a charity)
- provide a product or a service to consumers

We will now look in more detail at these aspects of business, starting with the 'sectors' of business – often known as the 'industrial sectors'.

industrial sectors

pc 1.1.1

As we have just seen, businesses can be 'classified' according to what they *do*. The normal way to classify businesses is into three 'industrial sectors' ...

primary sector - extracting raw materials
This involves the extracting of natural resources, ie raw materials for use in the manufacturing process; examples of primary production are mining, agriculture, fishing and forestry.

secondary sector – manufacturing
This is the next stage of production; it involves the processing of raw materials into the manufactured product: fruit into pies or juice, wood into chipboard, metal into cars, and so on.

tertiary sector – services
This third classification involves a business providing a service rather than a manufactured item; examples include catering, shops, insurance, travel, and advertising.

STUDENT ACTIVITY 1.2
performance criteria 1.1.1 & 4

industrial sectors

task 1
Into which industrial sector would you classify the following?
(a) a china clay extraction company
(b) a bank
(c) a motor bike manufacturer
(d) a market garden
(e) a clockmaker

task 2
Look at the photographs on the next page.
(a) To which industrial sector do the businesses belong?
(b) In what ways do they link up or depend on businesses in *other* sectors?

developments in industrial sectors

You will know from reports in the press and on the TV that certain types of business are growing in number and other are declining. What are the recent trends and likely developments?

primary sector - extracting raw materials

This area of business is generally on the decline. Coal mining , once the pride of the UK is now carried out on a very small scale. Farming too, is seeing a drop in output as the European Common Agricultural Policy limits production, and actually pays farmers *not* to use land for growing crops in an arrangement known as 'set aside'. Another factor to consider is that as manufacturing industry declines, so too will the demand for raw materials. The outlook for the primary sector is one of little or no growth.

secondary sector – manufacturing

Manufactured goods can be:

- *consumer goods* – goods bought by consumers ; these goods can either be consumables (used straightaway, eg food) or durables (goods which will last, eg TVs and cookers)
- *producer goods* – goods which are not bought by consumers, but which are used by manufacturers in the manufacturing process, eg components in the car industry, machinery, fork-lift trucks

Manufacturing has seen an overall decline in recent years. Certain industries such as ship-building and engineering have shrunk dramatically. Car manufacturing in the UK, on the other hand, has fared better as Japanese companies such as Nissan and Honda have set up new manufacturing plants. Another growth area is the electronics industry where again foreign investment has created many new jobs, at Sony in South Wales, for example. The outlook is for a continued decline in the traditional manufacturing industries, but growth in the new 'high-tech' areas such as electronics.

tertiary sector – services

While the secondary (manufacturing) sector has declined in recent years, the tertiary sector (services industries) has grown. Business such as financial services (banking, insurance) and leisure and tourism have increased in number, offsetting the loss of jobs in the manufacturing sector. The recession in the economy in the early 1990s saw a temporary decline, particularly in the financial services industry, but the outlook is for further growth.

Now look at the table on the next page and the statistics in the Student Activity which follows.

the service industries

retailing
- independent retailers (eg corner shops)
- chain stores (eg Marks & Spencer)
- supermarkets (eg Asda, Tesco)

wholesalers
- distributors of specific goods (eg CDs, videos)
- general wholesalers (eg Makro)
- merchants (eg agricultural merchants)

financial services
- banks
- building societies
- finance houses

transport
- British Rail
- airlines
- bus companies
- holiday companies

professional services
- the law
- accountancy

insurance

advertising

entertainment
- TV and radio
- theatre
- concerts
- opera

education
- language classes
- music lessons
- driving lessons

healthcare
- doctor
- dentist

personal and household services
- electricians
- plumbers
- decorators
- gardeners
- window cleaners
- dry cleaning
- hairdressing
- photographic processing

STUDENT ACTIVITY 1.3
performance criterion 1.1.1

developments in industrial sectors

Core Skill 2.3

Percentage of people employed in the industrial sectors (000s)			
	1971	*1981*	*1991*
Agriculture	2	2	2
Manufacturing	41	35	29
Financial and business services	5	7	11

Source: Employment Department

tasks

1   From the figures shown above, produce a suitable graph or chart highlighting the trends in the three industrial sectors. Write short notes explaining what the graph or chart shows.

2   What evidence of these trends can you find in your local area?

private and public sector businesses

Businesses have traditionally been divided into what is termed the *private sector* and the *public sector*. What are they?

the private sector
The *private sector* includes organisations which are directly or indirectly owned by private individuals. This sector accounts for *most* businesses operating within the UK. Private sector businesses involve a wide range of means of *ownership* and *control*, including sole traders (one person businesses), partnerships (groups of people in business), limited companies, franchises and co-operatives. Also included in the private sector is the *voluntary sector*, which comprises charities and other non-profit making organisations.

the public sector
Part of your evidence gathering will involve you in identifying businesses that are state owned or controlled, ie those that are in the *public sector*. The public sector includes government owned or government controlled bodies such as:

• public corporations – eg the Post Office, the BBC and the Bank of England

• Government Departments (the Civil Service)

• local organisations – eg County, Metropolitan or District Councils

The table below shows the range of businesses in the public and private sectors. On the next page we will look at private sector businesses in more detail.

private sector businesses	**public sector businesses**
sole traders – shop owners, electricians, taxi cab drivers, restaurant owners	**public corporations** – eg The Post Office, the BBC
partnerships – doctors, dentists, accountants, builders, shop owners	**Local Authority enterprises** – leisure centres, local bus services, car parks
limited companies – manufacturers, supermarkets, chain stores, insurance companies, banks	
franchises – High Street stores, eg Benetton, Thorntons, Prontaprint	
co-operatives – eg Leos supermarkets owned by the Co-operative Retail Society	

sole trader

A sole trader is an individual trading in his or her name, or under a suitable trading name.

If you set up in business, you may do so for a number of reasons: redundancy, being fed up with your present job, or developing a hobby or interest into a business. The majority of people setting up in this way do so on their own. If you decide to do so, you become a *sole trader.*

If you are a sole trader you can use your own name, or adopt a trading name. You do not have to register a trading name, but you may find yourself in court if you use someone else's name or a name connected with royalty. You cannot, for instance, open a shop and call it 'Marks and Spencer' or 'Royal Designs'.

the sole trader and unlimited liability

In law a sole trader is an individual who is liable for all the debts of the business. He or she has what is known as *unlimited liability.* This means that if the business fails the sole trader will have to repay personally all the business debts, and may have to sell his or her personal belongings (house, car, TV, video) to pay off those debts. The sole trader may be taken to Court and be made bankrupt if the debts are not repaid.

advantages of being a sole trader

There are a number of advantages:

* *total control* – you are your own boss and control the business yourself

* *simplicity* – there is no 'red tape' (form filling) for starting to trade

* *money* – you are entitled to all the profit

disadvantages of being a sole trader

- *risk* – you are on your own, with no-one to share the responsibilities of running the business – you have *unlimited liability*
- *time* – you will need to work long hours to meet tight deadlines
- *expertise* – you may have limited skills in areas such as finance and marketing
- *illness* – if you are ill, you may have no cover to enable the business to carry on
- it is more difficult to raise *money* to expand the business
- liability for *debt* – as mentioned above, you have *unlimited liability* for the debts of the business – if it 'goes bust' then you 'go bust'

It is clear that setting up in business as a sole trader involves total commitment in terms of money invested, time, and the risk involved. If you are starting your business with other people or need to raise large sums of money, you may consider establishing a *partnership* or a *limited company*.

partnerships

pc 1.1.3

what is a partnership?

A partnership is a group of individuals working together in business to make a profit.

A partnership is simple to establish and involves two or more people running a business together. They *share control* of the business, and *own it between them.* In legal terms, the partners *are* the business. Examples of partnerships include groups of doctors, dentists, accountants, and solicitors.

A partnership – often known as a 'firm' – can either trade in the name of the partners, or under a suitable trading name. For example if M Smith & G Jones set up a glazing business, they could call themselves 'Smith and Jones & Co.' or adopt a more catchy name such as 'Classy Glass Merchants'. You should note that the '& Co.' does not mean that the partnership is a limited company. On the next page the photograph shows a sign displayed outside the premises of a firm of solicitors.

partners and unlimited liability

In law each partner is liable for *all the debts* of the partnership. Like the sole trader a partner has *unlimited liability.* This means that if one partner runs up a big debt, each or all of the other partners could be asked to pay it off. You therefore have to be careful whom you admit as a partner in your business!

The only exception to this principle occurs with the *limited partnership*, where the liability of one or more partners may be *limited*. These are uncommon.They may be established where one of the partners is a 'sleeping partner,' ie he or she contributes capital (money) but does not take any active part in the business.

Partnerships are regulated in law by the Partnership Act 1890. Most partnerships will operate according to the terms of a Partnership Agreement, a document usually drawn up by a solicitor, and known as the Articles of Partnership or Deed of Partnership (a more formal document). This document will set out matters such as the amount of capital (money investment) contributed by each partner, the sharing out of profit (and losses) by the partners, and what to do if there is a dispute. It must be stressed that a partnership does not *have* to draw up a partnership agreement; it is just that a written document sets out clearly each partner's rights and obligations, a useful factor in the case of a dispute.

advantages of being a partner

- you can raise more capital (money) – there are more people to contribute
- more expertise – one partner may be a technical expert, another a good salesperson, another a financial expert, and so on
- there is cover for holidays and sickness
- less 'red tape' than a limited company (see the next section)

disadvantages of being a partner

- you may be asked to pay off all the debts of the partnership if the business fails
- you are liable for the business deals of the other partners (this could be a problem if a deal went badly wrong)
- disputes among the partners – sometimes this can lead to the break-up of the partnership and the business

STUDENT ACTIVITY 1.4
performance criterion 1.1.3

Core Skill 2.1-2

sole trader or partnership?

A friend of yours asks you about the 'fors' and 'againsts' of setting up in business as a sole trader or as a partner. You are to set out on a word-processed sheet brief notes covering

(a) an explanation of who owns and controls each type of business

(b) what 'unlimited liability' means and how it affects the situation if either business 'goes bust'

limited company

pc 1.1.3

what is a limited company?

A limited company is quite different from a sole trader or partnership business.

A limited company is a business set up as a body which is separate from its owners.

limited liability

A limited company is different from a sole trader and a partnership in that it has a legal identity *separate* from its owners. The owners – the *shareholders* – are not personally liable for the business debts (the company's debts) – they have *limited liability*. If the company 'goes bust' they do not have to pay off all the debts; all they are likely to lose is the money they have invested in the company. A sole trader or partner, you will recall, have *unlimited liability*: if their business is bankrupt, so are they.

A company is managed by *directors* appointed by the *shareholders* (also known as members). In the case of many small companies the directors *are* the shareholders. The chief director is the *managing director*. A company must be registered at a central office known as Companies House. An annual return and financial statements must be sent each year to Companies House by the company. As you will see there is much paperwork and 'red tape' involved in establishing and running a limited company. Companies are regulated by the Companies Acts 1985 and 1989.

private and public limited companies

A limited company can be referred to as either:

- a *private limited company* (abbreviated to Ltd), or
- a *public limited company* (abbreviated to Plc)

Most small or medium-sized businesses which decide to incorporate (form a company) become *private limited companies*; they are often family businesses with the shares held by the members of the family. Private companies cannot offer their shares for sale to the public at large, and it therefore follows that their ability to raise finance for expansion is limited.

A private company may, however, become a public limited company if it has

- a minimum of two directors (a private limited company needs only one)
- a share capital (the money put in by the shareholders) of at least £50,000
- a Trading Certificate (which allows it to trade) issued by Companies House
- the words 'public limited company' or 'plc' in its name

A public limited company can offer its shares for sale on the Stock Market in order to raise money, but not all public limited companies do this.

control of limited companies

Shareholders *own* a limited company and appoint *directors* to control the management of the company and plan for its future. In the case of a *private limited company*, the directors often *are* the shareholders, and so the shareholders can be said to control the company. In the case of a *public limited company* the shareholders can only speak and vote at company meetings (often only once a year) and it is the directors who *control* the company.

the advantages of limited companies

- members (shareholders) have limited liability for the company's debts
- capital can be raised more easily, and in the case of plc's, from the public on the Stock Exchange
- expansion is made easier, because of the availability of finance
- continuity – the company continues, even if the shareholders and directors change

the disadvantages of limited companies

- the expense of setting up a limited company (solicitors' and accountants' fees)
- paperwork – the need to send an annual return and financial statements to Companies House
- the accounts have by law to be examined by a qualified accountant

STUDENT ACTIVITY 1.5
performance criterion 1.1.3

Note that this is an extended activity to run over the period of a term.

Core Skill 2.1

limited companies

In groups of three or four students choose a well-known public limited company.

(a) Write off for the Annual Report and Accounts and find out what its 'share capital' is.

(b) Prepare a display area on the wall of the classroom (or a scrapbook) for the company.

(c) Chart the share price (from the daily press) on a line graph (which could be pinned up on the classroom wall or stuck in the scrapbook).

(d) Collect press cuttings and other articles about the company and stick them on the display area or in the scrapbook

(e) At the end of the period give an oral presentation to the class about the performance of the company.

co-operatives

pc 1.1.3

A 'co-operative' is a general term applied to two types of trading body:

1. a retail Co-operative Society – a specific form of trading body set up under the terms of the Industrial and Provident Societies Acts

2. co-operative – a group of people 'clubbing' together to produce goods or to provide a service

We will deal with each of these in turn.

retail Co-operative Societies

Co-operative Societies date back to 1844 when a group of twenty eight Rochdale weavers, suffering from the effects of high food prices and low pay, set up a society to buy food wholesale, ie at the same price as it was sold to the shops. This food was then sold to the members at prices lower than the shop prices, and the profits distributed to the members in what was known as a *dividend*, the level of which depended on the amount of food they had bought. These self-help co-operatives grew in number until in 1990 there were around eighty in number. The best-known example of a retail co-operative is what is known as 'the Co-op', which now operates the 'Leo's' supermarket chain. The Co-op was founded as the Co-operative Wholesale Society in 1863.

A Co-operative Society is a separate legal body set up under the Industrial and Provident Societies Acts (unlike a company, which is set up under the Companies Acts). A person becomes a Co-operative Society member by buying a share; this confers rights such as voting at meetings and discounts at the Society's retail outlets (traditionally in the form of stamps) and use of other facilities (funeral services, for example).

At the time of writing, the retail Co-operatives, which have traditionally been regional, are declining in number, partly because of merger and rationalisation and partly because of the intense competition in the retail sector from public companies such as Tescos, J Sainsbury and Asda.

co-operatives

The term 'co-operative' also applies more loosely to co-operative ventures which are not registered as Co-operative Societies under the Industrial and Provident Societies Acts. At the time of writing there are around two thousand co-operatives which fulfil a number of different functions:

the trading co-operative

Groups of individuals, such as farmers, who do not have the resources in terms of capital and time to carry out their own promotion, selling and distribution, may 'club' together to store and distribute their produce. They may also set up co-operative ventures to purchase machinery and equipment.

the workers co-operative

A worker's co-operative may often be found where the management of a business is not succeeding and a shut-down is proposed. The 'workers' step in, with the consent of the management, and take over the ownership and running of the business with the aim of 'making a go of it' and at the same time safeguarding their jobs.

franchises

pc 1.1.3

what is a franchise?

The franchise system was first established in the USA and is now a rapidly growing business sector in the UK. A franchise is an operation which involves two separate parties:

- the *franchisor*, a person who has developed a certain line of business, such as clothes retailing, hamburgers, drain clearing, and has made the trading name well-known

- the *franchisee*, a person who buys the right to trade under the well-known trading name in a particular locality, and in return for this investment receives training and equipment

The photograph below shows a well-known printing shop franchise.

advantages of a franchise

- you are entering into a business which has been tried and tested in the market
- your business may well have a household name such as Benetton
- you are more likely to be able to raise finance from a bank for a franchise
- you should receive training, and in some cases, be provided with tried and tested equipment

disadvantages of a franchise

- the initial cost of going into the franchise – the payment to the franchisor
- a proportion of your profits also go to the franchisor
- you are less independent in that you cannot develop the business as you wish, – you cannot change the name or change the method of doing business
- in short, you are less independent and could be less profitable than if the enterprise were your own

STUDENT ACTIVITY 1.6
performance criterion 1.1.3

franchises

(a) Investigate sources such as your local Yellow Pages and shopping centre and make a list of franchises that you find.

(b) What type of products do they sell (a product can be an item or a service)?

(c) What are the benefits of a franchise to the person operating the franchise (the franchisee)? If you can, arrange an interview with a franchisee to help you with this task.

the public sector

Public sector organisations are directly or indirectly controlled by the government. They include:

- Public Corporations
- Central Government enterprises
- Local Authority enterprises

public corporations
Public corporations are bodies established by Act of Parliament, and owned and financed by the State, for example the Post Office, the Bank of England and the BBC. There used to be more public corporations, but Conservative governments *privatised* a number of them – in other words they sold them off to the public by turning them into public limited companies, eg BT. Public corporations are run by a Board of Management headed by a chairperson appointed by the Government.

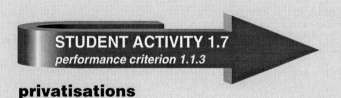

STUDENT ACTIVITY 1.7
performance criterion 1.1.3

privatisations

The photographs above show two organisations which the government has at one time or another wanted to privatise.

(a) Find out individually the latest situation about the two possible privatisations.

(b) What benefits or problems can you see coming from privatisation? Discuss in class.

central government enterprises

These fall into two categories:

- an enterprise run as part of a government department – a Government Minister has ultimate responsibility, and the day-to-day operations are run by Civil Servants; the Inland Revenue (the 'taxman') is an example

- a public limited company in the private sector in which the Government has a shareholding

local authority enterprise

Local Authority is a term applied to local governing councils which operate both in the county areas and also in urban areas. Local Authorities taken as a whole have a wide range of services to administer. These include education, environmental health, planning, refuse collection, social services, transport, fire services, libraries and recreational facilities. They finance these from three main sources:

- Central Government Grants

- local taxation (currently the Council Tax)

- income from local authority enterprise (see below)

Local authority enterprises include a wide variety of commercial activities, including, for example:

- leisure – swimming pools, golf courses

- transport – local bus services

- car parks

- lotteries

Not all of these are actually carried out by the Local Authorities: in recent years Local Authorities have engaged in Compulsory Competitive Tendering (CCT), the system whereby services such as waste collection and catering have been offered for tender to private businesses.

STUDENT ACTIVITY 1.8
performance criterion 1.1.3

local authority enterprise

Investigate what local authority services are provided

(a) at your school or college

(b) at your nearest sports/leisure centre

To what extent are these services provided by outside businesses? Do you think this brings benefits to most people?

the purpose of business organisations

pc 1.1.3

All businesses have purposes – reasons for operating – and the larger the business, the more defined those purposes are likely to be. Examples include:

- making a profit
- increasing market share – selling more than your competitors
- commitment to employees – providing them with benefits
- providing a quality service to customers
- providing a service to the public
- giving to charitable causes
- looking after the environment

mission statements

Many business organisations set out their main purposes in a public 'mission statement'. The mission statement of BT is shown below.

> BT's mission, our central purpose, is to provide world-class telecommunications and information products and services, and to develop and exploit our networks, at home and overseas, so that we can:
> - meet the requirements of our customers
> - sustain growth in the earnings of the group on behalf of our shareholders, and
> - make a fitting contribution to the community in which we conduct our business

the profit motive

Profit is probably why most people go into business in the first place. There are a number of basic principles relating to profit:

- profit-making businesses create wealth in the economy
- sole traders and partners are entitled to the whole of the business profit
- limited company profit is due to the shareholders and distributed in the form of dividends
- the profit of a co-operative is due to the members
- part of the profit made by a franchisee has to go to the franchisor, the rest is retained by the franchisee
- profits made by public sector organisations go to the government (and therefore indirectly back to the public)

It is important for the owners of private sector businesses to remember that it is good business practice not to take out all the profit, but to retain a proportion of it in the business, to invest in expansion, new equipment and research. It is all very well for the managing director to drive around in a Mercedes, but if no profit is re-invested in the business, the business will probably fail.

market share

Businesses like to see their market share growing at the expense of their competitors. In other words they want to see a steady rise in their percentage of total sales of a product. Sometimes the competition can be very fierce, as for example between Virgin and British Airways, Coca Cola and Pepsi, or competing daily newspapers. Sometimes prices are cut in 'price wars', and this may, of course, reduce the levels of profits made.

customer service

Many businesses pride themselves on customer service, and spend a lot of money on staff training and 'customer care' schemes. Customer service will help the business in terms of what the public thinks about it, but it will also be a drain on profit because of the cost of training.

public service

Public service means providing a product which provides *benefits for the public*. In the pubic sector this includes health and education services, and in the private sector involves a wide range of activities which benefit both people in general and also the environment in which they live. Examples include:

environmental policies

It has become a prime aim of business organisations to publicise the measures they are taking to avoid damage to the environment. In fact, care for the environment has become a 'selling point' for many businesses.

sponsorship

Many businesses give to causes which benefit society, for example

- sponsorship of sporting events
- sponsorship of artistic events: music, theatre, literature

The support given by businesses is usually widely publicised, as it promotes the name of the business in the eyes of the public.

charities

Whereas a business may be seen as an organisation which may care for society, a charity is often an organisation which has social responsibility as its prime aim, and which will use business methods to pursue that aim. Charities include:

- organisations which aim to alleviate hardship and suffering both at home and abroad; these include national bodies such as Oxfam, Mencap and Cancer Relief, and also local bodies which raise money for local schemes

• other non-profit making organisations which are run for educational and artistic reasons, eg many independent schools and historical preservation societies

Charities are run by trustees, individuals who administer and manage the funds raised for charitable purposes. Charities are registered under the terms of the Charities Act 1992. The money raising methods of charities can be very businesslike, and the profits made will help to boost the money devoted to charitable aims. Oxfam, for example, was founded in 1942 as the Oxford Committee for Famine Relief to provide relief for famine and sickness.

STUDENT ACTIVITY 1.9
performance criterion 1.1.2

Core Skill 2.4

the purpose of business

task 1

Collect and compare 'environmental' statements and literature from a range of businesses in your locality (eg leaflets from food supermarkets). Analyse and compare:

(a) the environmental issues with which they deal

(b) the ways in which 'going green' may conflict with other business aims such as making a profit

(c) their success in making you want to buy that company's products

Present your findings to your tutor in the form of a short written report. Remember that it is what you say about your findings rather than the number of leaflets collected which will determine your assessment.

task 2

Read and analyse the 'Corporate Statement' of The Royal Bank of Scotland which is reproduced on the next page. (This statement is taken from the bank's Report and Accounts to Shareholders).

Write down all the business aims which you can identify from this statement. To what extent do these aims correspond with those set out in the text above? Can you identify any further aims?

The Royal Bank of Scotland Group is an independent financial services group, with its headquarters in Edinburgh, operating throughout Great Britain and in certain overseas markets. We regard our reputation for integrity and financial stability earned from over two hundred and fifty years of serving our customers as the foundation upon which we will build our future.

Our overall objective is, through the excellence of our service, to satisfy the needs of our customers, the requirements of our shareholders and the aspirations of our staff.

We will seek to use our skills and capital in markets where we can give special value to our customers through superior service thus achieving higher returns for our shareholders while expanding the Group. We recognise that our most important resource is our people, their skills and their commitment to our customers.

Communication is a priority as is personal development. Our people will participate in success through a system which rewards initiative, effort and performance and which accords with the practice prevailing within their particular business area. We will maintain our commitment to innovation and technology in order that our customers will benefit from new services and lower costs. We are fully aware of our social responsibility to the communities in which we live and work, national and local. At each level we will play our part in creating a good business environment and in participating in the wider aspects of the fabric of community life.

The achievement of these objectives, year on year, will contribute to our Group retaining the independent status which we firmly believe is in the best long-term interests of our customers, shareholders and staff.

EVIDENCE COLLECTION ASSIGNMENT 1

investigating types of business

Element 1.1

introduction

This assignment will enable you to gain an overall view of the different types of business that exist and the differences between them in terms of their products, their size, ownership, and overall purpose.

tasks

pc 1.1.1

1   **Find** an example of a business from the primary, secondary and tertiary sectors. **Write** short notes on the present trends in these three sectors. Use as evidence the material in this chapter, interviews with the businesses and statistics from libraries and resource centres.

pcs 1.1.2 - 3

2   **Investigate** SEVEN business organisations (including if you like the three from Task 1). They must include at least

• one public sector organisation

• a small, medium-sized and large business organisation (eg a sole trader, a private company and a PLC)

Compare all seven in terms of

• their purposes (obtain a mission statement if you can)

• their product

• their legal status (ie whether sole trader, partnership, franchise etc)

• who owns and controls them

• what happens to their profit

You can present this comparison either in the form of short notes or in the form of a matrix – a table with the types of organisation running across the top and the points of comparison down the side.

pc 1.1.4

3   A short report presenting an in-depth description of one of the chosen businesses explaining its location, what it produces, its ownership and how it links up with other businesses (eg suppliers, customers, lenders). Illustrate your report with product catalogues if available.

Note: you are recommended to use this same organisation as the basis for the next Assignment (page 51), so make sure that you obtain all the information you need at the same time.

chapter summary and key terms

■ The three industrial sectors are the primary (extracting from nature), secondary (manufacturing) and tertiary (services). The primary and secondary are in decline while the tertiary is growing.

■ Public sector business are government-owned or controlled; private sector businesses are owned by private individuals.

■ Public sector businesses include public corporations and local authority enterprises; private sector businesses include sole traders, partnerships, limited companies, co-operatives and franchises.

■ Private sector businesses differ in terms of ownership, control, and use of profit.

■ Business organisations also differ in their purposes; these can include profit, market share, customer service, public service and charity.

key terms

industrial sector	the division of businesses into primary, secondary and tertiary (see above)
public sector	organisations that are government owned or controlled
private sector	organisations that are owned by individuals
sole trader	an individual in business on his or her own
partnership	2 or more individuals in business together
limited company	a business which is separate from its owners, the shareholders
private company	a limited company, the shares of which are not bought and sold by the public
public company	a limited company, the shares of which can be bought and sold by the public
co-operative	a business set up and owned by its members and operating for their benefit
franchise	a business where the franchisee sets up using the trading name of the franchisor

multiple-choice questions

1   A group of solicitors normally trades as a
    A   private limited company
    B   public limited company
    C   partnership
    D   co-operative

2   One advantage of being a sole trader is that
    A   you get a lot of holiday
    B   you pay no tax
    C   you are your own boss
    D   you have unlimited liability

3   An estate agent is an example of a business in the
    A   primary sector
    B   tertiary sector
    C   public sector
    D   secondary sector

4   The public sector comprises
    A   public limited companies
    B   businesses in which the public can buy shares
    C   organisations which are state owned and controlled
    D   brewery companies

5   A sole trader will NORMALLY
    A   spend all his profit on himself
    B   retain some of the profit in the business
    C   lose all his profit in paying tax
    D   pay all the profit to the shareholders

6   The main purpose of a charity is to
    A   make a profit
    B   provide a public service
    C   appear on TV
    D   promote a special cause

2 Business location and markets

GNVQ SPECIFICATIONS

Element 1.2

Examine business location, environment, markets and products

performance criteria – a student must:

1 explain the reasons for location of businesses

2 explain influences of the business environment on business organisations

3 describe markets for businesses' products based on demand

4 identify products provided by business organisations

5 explain activities undertaken by businesses to improve their market position

6 propose products which would meet market demand

---

what this chapter covers

This chapter explains the outside influences which affect what businesses do – where they are located, the influence of other organisations and the need to provide products that their customers want.

what you will learn from this chapter

- many factors influence where a business is located – resources in the area and assistance from governments – local, central and European Union

- businesses are also affected by external factors such as other competing businesses, regulations such as Health & Safety and public pressure groups

- businesses need to be very aware of the potential markets for their products – both within the UK and also abroad

- 'products' include manufactured items and services

- markets are created by demand – what customers want and need and have the money to buy

- the marketing function within a business enables it to assess consumer demand, to provide the products that are needed and to promote and deliver them effectively to the people that want them

factors influencing the location of business

the personal factor

In this section we look at the main factors affecting the decision of where to set up business. It must be appreciated that this decision is not a form of scientific calculation; there are also many personal factors involved. In the first place, many businesses are already based in a particular location, and any expansion or relocation may well be in the same area, because that is where the workforce lives and the commercial contacts are established. Secondly, the owner of a business may well want to set up in a certain location because he or she happens to like it!

natural resources

If a business is dependent on natural resources, it is likely to be sited near to the source of the materials it needs. Brick manufacturers, for example, concentrate in areas where suitable clay is to be found. Scotch whisky is highly dependent on the peaty quality of Scottish water and is therefore distilled on site in Scotland.

transport

Some businesses need access to the transport system – major motorways, airports, railway stations; this is particularly important if the business has a sizeable and active salesforce travelling in the UK and overseas.

The transport system is also needed to transport raw materials and finished goods. This may be a critical factor for siting the business. If a manufacturer relies on the use of heavy and bulky raw materials which are expensive to transport, and the finished product is less bulky and cheaper to transport, the factory will locate nearer to the source of raw materials. If, on the other hand, the finished product is bulkier than the raw materials, the production plant will be located nearer to the purchaser in order to save transport costs. A ship, for example, is built next to the sea or a river rather than next to the inland foundry where the steel is produced, and for obvious reasons!

labour factors

Labour is more readily available and wage levels are lower in some areas of the UK than in others. Generally speaking, labour costs are higher in urban areas and in the South East, reflecting the higher costs of living in those areas, although the trend in the 1990s is for a levelling off of the North/South divide. If a business is *labour intensive* (ie it employs many people), this argument will carry more weight. Expertise is another important labour factor. Certain areas are well-known for particular skills: for example the Cambridge area and the M4 'corridor' for advanced technological skills.

markets

Some businesses do not need to be 'near' their markets, because their markets do not have a specific geographical location. Car manufacturers, for example, distribute to dealers throughout the UK and abroad; their decision of where to locate rests on other factors (land, amenities, communications). Mail order companies, too, serve a nationwide market, and can locate anywhere within easy reach of the road transport system. Some markets, however, have a very precise geographical location. Small businesses such as a sandwich-making service must be in the area it serves. On a larger scale, the City of London is the geographical base of the UK financial services industry and centre for banking, insurance and stock-broking, all of which need to be in the City.

other businesses in the area

Many industries are traditionally based in certain areas because of the availability of raw materials: coal, steel, china clay. Many businesses are located in certain areas because they serve other businesses: the City of London provides all the necessary support for the financial services industry – large firms of specialist accountants, solicitors, insurance brokers, export agencies. Fiat, the Italian motor manufacturer, has taken this principle to the extreme by building a car plant with all the component manufacturers on the same site in Melfi, Southern Italy.

Government incentives – the 'Enterprise Initiative'

The Government, in order to alleviate the social, economic and political problems brought about by sustained unemployment in certain areas (the North East, the North West, and South Wales for example) provides financial incentives to businesses setting up in those areas. These incentives – grants, cheap rents, free and subsidised advice – are administered though the Department of Trade and Industry, and are known as the 'Enterprise Initiative'. Details of these incentives can be obtained from your local office of the Department of Trade and Industry (or the Welsh Office in Cardiff and the Scottish Office in Glasgow.) The areas given assistance are known as the *Assisted Areas*. These were redefined in 1993 by the UK Government in negotiation with the European Commission. Look at the map on the next page: the Assisted Areas are divided into two 'bands':

- *Development Areas* (dark shading)

  These are the areas of greatest need and cover approximately 16% of the working population of Great Britain. They include many of the urban areas in the North and the West.

- *Intermediate Areas* (lighter shading)

  These cover approximately 18% of the working population of Great Britain

You will be able to find out about the status of your own locality by contacting your nearest DTI office or Business Link.

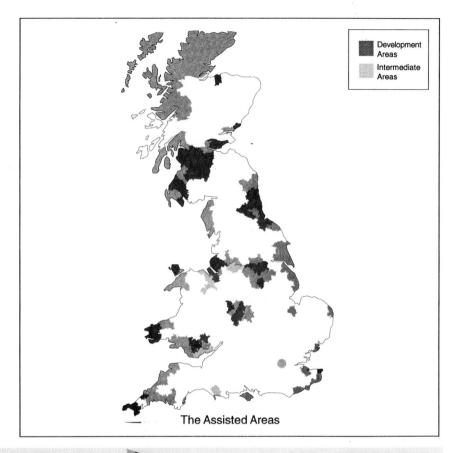

The Assisted Areas

STUDENT ACTIVITY 2.1
performance criterion 1.2.1

location of business
task 1

Where would you locate the following businesses? What factors would affect your decision?

(a) a saw-mill

(b) a sandwich bar

(c) a firm of solicitors

(d) an electronics research company

(e) a mail order company

(f) the sales division of a national company manufacturing and selling garden furniture

(g) a cider making company

(h) a company setting up for the first time, and needing inexpensive premises; it plans to employ 50 people, and will manufacture specialist bicycles

(i) a firm needing a warehouse for storing wine imported from the EC

task 2

The map on the right has been drawn up by the Worcester City Planning Department.

(a) What benefits can you see will be gained by setting up business in the Worcester area?

(b) If you have a business which runs a fleet of delivery vans, on which side of the city would you locate?

(c) What benefits can you see for a business which exhibits at trade fairs?

(d) What benefits to tourism firms can you see in the area?

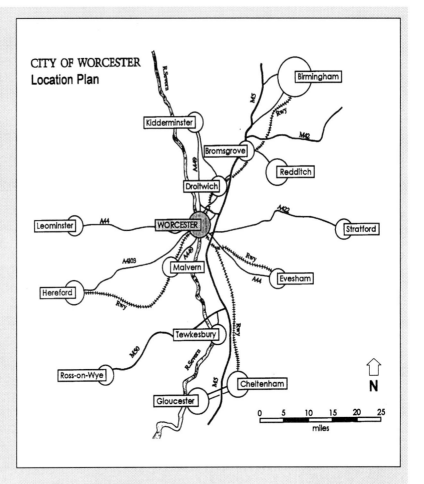

CITY OF WORCESTER
Location Plan

task 3

The article below is a press release from the European Commission.

(a) Where is the money coming from and how much is it?

(b) What geographical areas will benefit?

(c) What type of businesses do you think this will attract to the area?

(d) How will they be helped?

Aid for UK Coalfields

Former coal-mining areas in North-East England will receive 51m ECU under an aid programme adopted by the European Commission. This programme will help improve the economic and social position of the coalfield areas in Northumberland, Durham, and Tyne and Wear. It will support projects to develop degraded and derelict land, boost economic development, encourage tourism, small businesses and retraining programmes. The EU is contributing 23.45m ECU from the Regional Development and Social Funds, the remainder coming from central and local government and the private sector.

influences of the business environment

The operation of businesses is very much affected by *outside influences*. The business which just does what it wants, regardless of anything will soon come unstuck. What are the factors that influence businesses?

the competition

No business can afford to ignore competing products in terms of

- price
- design
- packaging

The result is often that similar products *look* very similar and are *priced* at a similar level. Look at products like family cars, baked beans, jeans, package holidays – where there is a degree of competition, products tend to become indistinguishable. Occasionally a brave business challenges the competition by being *different* – The Body Shop, for example – and wins. But few people remember the failures: the C5 electric car, hedgehog crisps. Pricing is also critical: too high a price and nobody will buy, too low a price (it can happen) and people will think the product is cheap and nasty.

legal influences

Businesses are constrained by a wide range of laws covering areas such as:

- Health & Safety
- product safety

You are not required to know about these laws in detail, but you should be aware that they regulate business activities.

environmental pressures

Businesses are affected by the need to care for the environment. As we saw in the last chapter (page 32) many businesses have a environmental policy which they turn to commercial advantage. Consumers favour environmentally friendly businesses – hence the immense success of The Body Shop which uses environmentally friendly raw materials. In addition, businesses need to abide by legislation which protects the environment, the Clean Air Act for example.

public influences

The public, particularly when whipped up by the media, can exert a considerable pressure on business operations. When Shell wanted to dump an oil platform in the open sea, their sales of petrol in Germany dropped by 20% and a number of their filling stations were set on fire. The influence in this case was largely that of Greenpeace, the environmental group. A more subtle and steady public influence is also exerted by consumer pressure groups. The Consumers Association has influenced many buying decisions through their magazine *Which?*

influences on business

Conduct a survey into one of the topics suggested below. The suggested topics (which you can amend as you wish) are:

- child safety in cars
- lead-free petrol
- the sale of high-priced fashion clothes
- price wars (ie price cutting by competing businesses such as newspaper publishers, supermarketrs, holiday firms)

Word process your findings in the form of short notes setting out both

(a) the influences on the businesses involved and the benefits (or otherwise) to the business

(b) the benefits (or otherwise) to the consumers

businesses and demand

pc 1.2.3

demand

Businesses sell their products because there is a demand for them. *Demand* can be defined simply as:

the amount of a product that consumers want over a period of time

needs and wants

A business selling a product will need to be sure there is a *demand* for it. Demand can be for

- a consumer's *needs* – items that are essential, eg lavatory paper, bread
- a consumer's *wants* – items that the consumer can be persuaded to want to buy, eg luxury biscuits, a video

It is straightforward enough for a business to sell products that are needed. The skill lies in a business promoting products which the consumer can be *persuaded to want* and to buy. Many advertising campaigns can turn a want into a purchase: the expensive luxury ice cream Haagen-Dazs, promoted in a series of sensual adverts, is an example.

effective demand

Look at the definition of demand again:

the amount of a product that consumers want over a period of time

Clearly not all consumers can *afford* to buy all that that they want or need over a period of time, so the *wish to buy* is not always matched by the *ability to buy*. The amount of a product that a consumer can actually afford to buy is known as *effective demand*. Sometimes producers can increase effective demand by offering credit terms (ie buy now, pay later).

consumers and customers

It is important to sort out the meanings of certain terms that we are using. The *consumer* mentioned in the definition is strictly-speaking the *user* of a product. The word *customer* is used to describe the person who actually buys the product. The difference is easily seen if you look at the purchase of disposable nappies: the parent is the *customer* who buys them, the baby is the *consumer* – the person who wears them!

Normally, of course, the consumer *is* the customer. Businesses can sometimes increase sales by convincing the consumer to persuade someone else to buy the goods. This is particularly the case with products for children – examples include sweets by checkouts, adverts for toys on the TV on Saturday mornings when all the family are at home, and so on.

STUDENT ACTIVITY 2.3
performance criterion 1.2.3

Core Skill 2.1-2

businesses and demand

tasks

1   Compile two lists on a word processor:
     (a)   a list of products you have bought over the last week which are essential 'needs'
     (b)   a list of products you have bought over the last week which could be described as 'wants'
     Note: a 'product' can be an item or a service.
2   Write down in a few sentences the difference between 'needs' and 'wants'.
3   Write down any products you have bought which you consider you have been persuaded to buy through advertising pressure. Are you happy with your decision?

businesses and markets

what is a market?

What is a market? This may seem an obvious question.

A market provides buyers of goods and services with their needs and wants

A street market, the local newspaper, a mail order catalogue and a department store are all *market places* for many different products. The market price of a product will depend on the *demand* for that product in relation to its *supply*. If a product is very much in demand (eg computer games) the manufacturers can charge a high price and get away with it. On the other hand you will know that if a shop wants to create demand for old stock that it wants to get rid of, it will do so by having a sale and by slashing its prices.

types of market

Markets can be classified in a number of ways – one classification is by *size*. The type of market a business enters will depend on the type of business. Here are some examples:

local market – sole traders
- a market gardener selling vegetables
- a sandwich bar selling 'butties' in the town centre
- a plumber operating in one locality

national (domestic) market – public limited companies
- banks – NatWest, Abbey National
- shops – Marks & Spencer, Tescos
- power companies – Powergen, British Gas

international markets – multinationals*
- car manufacturers – Ford
- drinks manufacturers – Pepsico
- oil companies – Shell

* a multinational is a business which owns operating companies worldwide

market share

The success of a company can be measured by its market share, ie the percentage share of the total market for the goods which it sells. Producers can look at market share in terms of its product and similar products, and also in terms of other 'bestsellers'.

Look at the soft drinks industry, for example: Coca-Cola is recognised as being the market leader. It can be compared in terms of sales with other soft drinks; it can also be compared with other 'brands', ie well-known goods other than soft drinks. The two tables below illustrate recent figures for the market share of Coca-Cola.

bestsellers in the soft drinks market		top UK brands	
drink	*percentage of worldwide sales*	*brand*	*£M per year*
Coca-Cola	15	Coca-Cola	242
Diet Coke	7	Persil detergents	236
Pepsi	5	Ariel detergents	231
Diet Pepsi	4	Nescafe instant coffee	228
Tango	4	Andrex toilet roll	183
Schweppes mixers	3	Silver Spoon sugar	152
R Whites lemonade	3	Whiskas cat food	142
		Flora margarine	133
		PG Tips tea	130
		Walkers crisps	127

STUDENT ACTIVITY 2.4
performance criterion 1.2.3

Core Skill 2.3

Core Skill 2.2

measuring market share

Set out below are recent circulation figures for daily newspapers.

1 Calculate the total number of newspapers read.
2 Calculate the market share percentage for each newspaper.
3 Use a computer (if possible) to construct a pie chart showing the market share.

average daily sale of newspapers (April 1995)			
Daily Telegraph	1,061,230	Daily Mail	1,794,964
The Times	631,638	Daily Express	1,292,944
The Guardian	400,921	Today	549,459
Financial Times	305,928	The Sun	4,134,571
The Independent	290,360	Daily Mirror	2,476,746
		The Star	741,550

products and consumers

pc 1.2.4

Before investigating the products and the consumers of a business for your Portfolio (see Assignment 2 on page 51), you will need to be able to distinguish between the different types of product and customer. The term 'product' refers equally to manufactured *goods* and to *services*.

goods
Goods can be:

- *consumer goods* – goods bought by consumers; these goods can either be *consumables* (used straightaway, eg food) or *durables* (goods which will last, eg TVs and cookers)

- *producer goods* – goods which are not bought by consumers, but which are used by manufacturers in the manufacturing process, eg components in the car industry, machinery, fork-lift trucks

services
The service industries are traditionally divided into two areas:

- *direct services*, which provide assistance directly to consumers, eg health care, hairdressing

- *commercial services*, which provide assistance to businesses, eg insurance, wholesaling

consumers
These include members of the public, organisations in the public sector and other businesses

STUDENT ACTIVITY 2.5
performance criterion 1.2.4

types of product

Classify the following products, stating whether they are consumer goods (distinguish between durables and consumables), or producer goods:

(a) cigarettes

(b) fish and chips

(c) a CD player

(d) a lathe

(e) silicon chips

marketing activities

what is marketing?

The successful business is the business which

* finds out what products consumers want
* produces a well-designed product
* advertises the product effectively
* gets the product to the customer efficiently

Much of this activity is undertaken by the *marketing function* in a business. People sometimes think that marketing is the same as selling. It is a lot more than that – it is the job of the marketing function of a business to create *demand* among consumers. Marketing has been humourously defined:

Marketing is selling goods that don't come back to people who do.

A more serious definition is:

Marketing is a series of activities which satisfy customers needs and wants through selling a product.

Marketing is dealt with in depth in Chapter 8of this book . We will give here a brief introduction to the way marketing works.

the marketing mix

The marketing process has traditionally been categorised into four functions, known as the '4 P's', the marketing mix:

Product	deciding on the range of products that a business offers to the market, eg the Ford Fiesta, Escort, Mondeo, Scorpio, Galaxy, Frontera and Probe
Price	setting the right price for the product range – arranging promotional price cuts, discounts, special offers
Promotion	making the consumer aware of the product (eg through advertising, packaging, publicity) and persuading the consumer to buy it
Place	deciding how far afield the product is to be sold (locally? nationally? or internationally?), choosing the outlets for the product, arranging for distribution

the marketing process

Marketing' is not the same as 'advertising'. In order to market a product a business should proceed through a number of stages. Study the diagram shown below.

the marketing process

marketing research
Finding out through consumer surveys and looking at statistics what consumers' needs and wants are – finding out if there is a demand for a product.

product design and production
Getting the product 'right' from the design point of view (this may involve a trial run of the product) and setting up production. Remember a 'product' can be a service as well as an item.

marketing communications
Telling the consumer about the product through a wide range of techniques: advertising in various ways, using sponsorship, publicity (mention on TV or in the press), special promotions.

selling the product
Getting the product to the customer – organising the sales force and setting up a timed sales campaign, deciding on outlets and geographical spread (local sales? national? international?)

after-sales
Making sure that there is back-up for the product – providing customer service (eg desks in shops) and guarantees; it also involves monitoring sales – seeing how successful the product is.

A number of the subjects mentioned in this diagram are covered in more depth later in the book. So that you can carry out the assignment on the next page, you should also read the following:

- Chapter 8 'Consumers and customers' pages 140 to 157 to give you more information about how customers are targeted

- Chapter 9 'Promotional Material' pages 158 to 175 to show you how a business uses advertising and other techniques to promote a product

EVIDENCE COLLECTION ASSIGNMENT 2

the location and markets of a business

Element 1.2

introduction

This assignment asks you to choose a single business for investigation (it may be the business looked at in Assignment 1). You will analyse its location and the markets for its products and see how it promotes them. You will also suggest ideas for new products and markets. The assignment will take the form of a report, preferably produced on a word-processor.

tasks

Core Skill 2.3

1   **Choose** an example of a business in your locality. **Obtain** a map of the area (try your local information office, planning office or estate agents). Identify and mark on the map (which you should scan iin if you can):
   • the location of the business
   • any *relevant* natural resources in the area (eg land for agriculture, mines for raw materials)
   • transport links (eg motorways, railways, airports, ports)
   • other businesses in the area (major local customers, suppliers)
   Write short notes explaining the items you have marked on the map and explain *why* the business is located where it is.

pc 1.2.2

2   **Investigate** the business and summarise under headings
   • the competition it faces
   • legal or other regulations which affect its operation
   • environmental issues it may have to face (eg packaging, fumes)
   • any public pressure groups with which it may be involved

pcs 1.2.3 - 5

3   Developing the theme of competition in Task 2, you are to **analyse its products** in detail and write notes on
   • the market in which the business operates (the range of customers)
   • the demand for its products (whether increasing or decreasing)
   • the marketing communications it uses (advertising, sponsorship), and how effective they are in maintaining or increasing its market share
   If possible, you should compile this task with help from the marketing and sales staff of the business you are investigating.

pc 1.2.6

4   Having investigated the business, think of one **new product** which the business might be able to market. Write down your proposals and discuss them with staff from the business. Note down their comments.

chapter summary and key terms

■ A business will locate in a particular place for a number of reasons: natural resources, transport links, labour availability, other businesses in the area and because of government grants and incentives.

■ Businesses are affected in their operations by external factors in the business environment: these include their competitors, requirements set down in law, environmental issues and public pressure groups.

■ Businesses will provide products to meet demand in various markets: local markets, domestic and international markets – it will all depend on the business and the product.

■ Products are classified as goods or services; goods can be durables (which last) and consumables (which do not last).

■ Businesses successfully promote their products through marketing activities: marketing research, marketing communications, and sales.

key terms

demand	the amount of a product that consumers want over a period of time
needs	essential products that a consumer cannot go without
wants	products that a consumer can be persuaded to buy
consumer	the person who uses a product
customer	the person who buys a product
product	a manufactured item or a service
market	where buyers of goods and services can obtain their needs and wants
marketing	activities which satisfy customer needs and wants through selling a product
marketing research	finding out customer needs and wants through surveys and analysis of statistics
marketing communications	telling the consumer about the product through advertising, publicity and sponsorship

multiple-choice questions

1   A sawmill is MOST likely to locate near
    A   its customers
    B   its raw materials
    C   a motorway
    D   its competitors

2   A business needs to be aware of its competitors in order to
    A   keep its prices very high
    B   keep its prices very low
    C   to match its prices to its competitors
    D   to qualify for government grants

3   A business with an environmental policy is likely to
    A   deter consumers from buying its products
    B   reduce its tax bill
    C   attract consumers to buy its products
    D   break pollution control regulations

4   Demand is normally defined as
    A   the amount of a product that consumers want to buy over a period
    B   the total market share of a business over a period
    C   the needs and wants of the sellers of goods and services
    D   the amount of a product that suppliers can supply over a period

5   Market share is
    A   the percentage of total sales of a company contributed by a product
    B   the percentage of total sales of a product made by a company
    C   the percentage of products which are similar to competitors' products
    D   the percentage of sales made by one sales representative

6   Marketing communications involve
    A   advertising, publicity and sponsorship
    B   advertising, production and sponsorship
    C   advertising, marketing research and sponsorship
    D   marketing research, faxes, video-conferencing and memos

3 Investigating employment

GNVQ SPECIFICATIONS
Element 1.3
Present results of investigation into employment
performance criteria – a student must:
1   describe and give examples of types of employment
2   collect, analyse and explain information about employment in different regions
3   compare working conditions for employees in different organisations
4   present results of investigation into employment, or comparison of working conditions

what this chapter covers

This chapter investigates the different types and patterns of employment – eg full-time, part-time, and how they are changing. It also looks at regional differences in working conditions, both in the UK and in the European Union.

what you will learn from this chapter

- there are a number of different types of employment: full-time and part-time, permanent and temporary, skilled and unskilled, self-employed

- the trend in employment is away from permanent full-time jobs towards temporary part-time jobs – a factor which reflects the decline in manufacturing industry and the growth of the services sector

- a further trend is the steady increase in the number of women in employment, particularly in part-time and temporary jobs

- working conditions for employees in different organisations vary widely; the differences relate to factors such as travel to work, physical conditions and safety, use of new technology, pay levels, job security, training and promotion

self-employed or employed?

the scope of self-employment

The self-employed worker is the individual who is his or her own boss, either in a full-time business, or in a part-time venture. The full-time self-employed aim to support themselves (and their families) out of the profits of their business; the part-time self-employed usually aim to supplement the family income. Examples of self-employment include:

- professionals – accountants, physiotherapists, architects
- shopkeepers
- craftsmen, artists, writers
- providers of services – taxicab drivers, plumbers, electricians, hair stylists

You will no doubt be able to add to this list. These occupations are normally carried out full-time. Examples of part-time self-employment include an unemployed wife or husband using skills (eg cake-making, computer programming) to earn extra cash, or the less well paid person doing evening work to supplement their income.

what it takes to be self-employed

The individuals who decide to become self-employed do so for a number of reasons:

- they may have been made redundant
- they may be dissatisfied with their current job
- they are encouraged to do so by Government incentive schemes
- they are independent self-starters who want to make money

Whatever the reasons for becoming self-employed, the individual must have very specific personal qualities – motivation and good health probably being the two most important. We will look at these qualities in detail in Chapter 7.

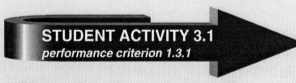

STUDENT ACTIVITY 3.1
performance criterion 1.3.1

Core Skill 2.3

self-employed or employed?

Official statistics for the UK reveal the following figures:

	1983	1994
Self-employed workers	2,310,000	3,280,000
Employed workers	20,420,000	21,444,000
Unemployed	2,865,000	2,493,000

Source: *Social Trends 1995*, No 25. © Crown Copyright.

please see next page

tasks

(a) add together the total number of workers for each year (include the unemployed)

(b) work out the percentage of each of the three categories for each of the two years

(c) draw up pie charts showing the three categories for each of the two years

(d) comment on any trends which you can detect

full-time or part-time?

what is full-time?

A full-time employee works the normal working week set down by the employer. The officially accepted minimum is 30 hours, but the normal full-time week is from 37 to 40 hours. Many professionals work far in excess of this figure: junior hospital doctors, for example, who have to carry on through the night on occasions, may work for 60 or more hours a week. Part-time employees work for part of the working week. There is no strict definition of 'part-time', but it is sometimes interpreted to mean less than 16 hours a week.

the advantages of part-time employment

The current trend, as you will see from the Student Activity on the next page, is for more people to work part-time.

- *advantages of part-time work for the employer*
    - it is cheaper because wage rates are often lower and the employer may not have to pay National Insurance Contributions to the Government
    - it is more flexible because employees can be called in as and when the employer becomes busy
- *advantages of part-time work for the employee*
    - flexibility of hours, eg for mothers who have to take and collect children from school, full-time students who have to supplement their grants
    - a valuable source of money for a family where the wife (or husband) can supplement the main income earner by going out to work

job-sharing and job 'doubling'

Another way in which a job may become part-time is through *job-sharing*. Here a full-time post is shared between two part-time employees. This might come about when an organisation is cutting back on staff but wants to reduce redundancies to a minimum. Part-time jobs are also on the increase because people are increasingly doing more than one part-time job, they are job 'doubling' eg 'temping' in the day, working in a bar in the evening.

STUDENT ACTIVITY 3.2
performance criterion 1.3.1

Core Skill 2.3

full-time or part-time?

The statistics set out below show the trends for full-time and part-time work in the UK. Study them closely.

	Full-time (millions)			Part-time (millions)		
Year	men	women	total	men	women	total
1984	13.0	5.3	18.3	0.5	4.3	4.8
1986	13.0	5.5	18.5	0.6	4.5	5.1
1988	13.5	5.8	19.3	0.7	4.7	5.4
1990	13.9	6.4	20.3	0.8	4.8	5.6
1992	12.9	6.1	19.0	0.8	4.9	5.7

Source: Employment Department

tasks

(a) Draw a line graph showing full-time employment in the UK for the years 1984 to 1992. Draw three lines, one for men, one for women, and one for the total.

(b) Draw a line graph showing part-time employment in the UK for the years 1984 to 1992. Draw three lines, one for men, one for women, and one for the total.

Now write down your comments on the graphs:

(c) What does the full-time employment graph show in the years 1988 to 1992? What do you think is the reason for this trend?

(d) What does the part-time employment graph show? How does it differ from the full-time employment graph?

(e) How do the figures for the employment of men and women differ on the two graphs. Why do you think there is this big difference?

permanent and temporary employment

A further distinction to be drawn is that between permanent and temporary employment ...

Permanent employment is where the employee is taken on for an indefinite period of time. Of course the employee is free to resign or can be dismissed or made redundant, often according to the terms of a contract of employment (explained in Chapter 5).

Temporary employment, on the other hand, is as you would expect, for a limited time period. Examples of temporary employment include:

- temporary office staff – 'temps' – often employed by an agency to fill vacancies caused by illness, holidays or resignation by permanent office staff
- casual workers required for seasonal work, eg fruit and hop pickers, holiday workers at seaside resorts and other tourist attractions, Christmas workers

Temporary employment can be full-time or part-time, depending on the circumstances of the job.

skilled and unskilled employment

What do the terms 'skilled' and 'unskilled' mean? Most people would probably accept that *skilled workers* are in jobs which require a relatively long period of training. In the past young people wishing to learn a craft such as carpentry, plumbing, hairdressing and bricklaying would be taken on as apprentices. Today most young people wishing to become craftspeople start their careers under the YT scheme whereby the government subsidise the costs of training by paying firms for each trainee they take on. For those hoping to join the ranks of the professions the normal route is A-levels or GNVQ followed by a degree course at a university and a period of specialist training which normally includes the need to pass further examinations. Training continues during an employee's career.

By contrast *unskilled workers* may receive no more than a few hours training and even less in some cases. They are forced to accept lower wage rates than skilled workers who often find their services in considerable demand when the economy starts to recover from a recession. Unskilled workers are amongst the first to be laid off when sales start to fall and career prospects are often non-existent. They are more likely to be asked to work unsocial hours including shift work and their working environment tends to be less attractive.

employment trends

pc 1.3.2

the decline of manufacturing

The decline of British manufacturing industry is probably the most important feature of the UK labour market over the past twenty years. This trend was responsible for the loss of over two and a half million jobs between 1971 and 1990 (from 8.2 million to 5.5 million workers).

At the same time industries in the *service sector* were expanding rapidly. Employment in banking, finance and insurance, for example, doubled during 1971 to 1990 increasing employment in this sector by 1.6 million. The growth of banking, finance and insurance was particularly rapid during the 1980s. Other services including education, business services and retailing also expanded considerably over the same period.

STUDENT ACTIVITY 3.3
performance criterion 1.3.2

changes in sectors of industry

Percentage Change in Employment in the UK by Industry

Industrial Sector	percentage change	
	1971-80	1980-90
Agriculture, forestry and fishing	- 13.0	- 10.4
Energy and Water	-10.0	-37.5
Manufacturing	-13.7	-22.8
Construction	+ 4.5	+ 11.7
Distribution, hotels, repairs	+ 12.6	+ 13.4
Transport and communications	-1.8	-1.9
Banking, finance, insurance	+ 24.8	+ 68.8
Public admin and defence	+ 5.0	- 5.3
Education and health	+ 25.7	+ 10.4
Other services	+ 30.9	+ 41.8

Source: Employment Department

Select two significant items from the table of statistics and construct bar charts (using both sides of the 'x' axis) which show the trends for *manufacturing* and *service* industries. Write short notes analysing the charts and explaining the trends.

more women in employment

The increasing importance of female employment is another striking trend in the UK labour market. The idea that the male full-time worker makes up the backbone of the workforce is rapidly going out-of-date. As recently as 1990, there were more than 14.1 million men in full-time employment, half of all the people in employment. In 1994 the figure had shrunk to 12.8 million.

reasons for the trend

*   businesses are cutting their costs by employing more part-time staff
*   the growth of Sunday trading has provided part-time employment opportunities for women
*   the falling birth rate (ie women having fewer children) has resulted in more women being free to work – for example between 1971 and 1993 the employment of women aged between 25 and 34 rose by 25%
*   the growth of the service industries at the expense of the manufacturing sector – service industry businesses are a rich source of jobs for women

STUDENT ACTIVITY 3.4
performance criterion 1.3.2

Core Skill 2.1

women in employment

what the statistics say

In 1994 12.8 million men were in full-time employment and 1 million had part-time jobs; in the same year 6.1 million women had full-time jobs and 5.3 million had part-time jobs

Source: Employment Department

1   Conduct a survey among students at your school or college and discover what percentage of women in their households are:

(a) in employment

(b) in part-time employment

(c) in full-time employment

Do your findings reflect the national picture? If not, suggest reasons why this might be the case.

2   Write short notes on why women may prefer part-time to full-time employment.

working conditions

pc 1.3.3

physical conditions
All jobs are different, and the factors that cause a person to choose one job rather than another may well have much to do with the *physical* working conditions involved, ie the level of comfort and cleanliness offered by the occupation, and the care taken over the *Health & Safety* aspects. Expectations will differ widely. You will not find the same level of comfort in a coal mine as in a travel agency. There are a number of different types of physical environment and choices that can be made:

indoors or outdoors

quiet or noisy

clean or dirty

sitting down' job or 'moving about' job

travel to work and teleworking
The time and money spent travelling to work will affect a person's quality of life. The millions of people who spend two or more hours daily travelling to and from jobs in London, often in crowded conditions, may be attracted by the idea of teleworking, ie working from home or away from the office, in touch with work through a telephone, computer and modem. The picture below, reproduced by kind permission of BT, says it all.

teleworking – a BT impression

pay

Probably one of the most important aspects of a job for the employee is the amount of money received. Pay can be calculated and paid in a number of different ways:

wages

This is the term normally applied to pay which is received weekly, often in cash. Many workers – factory, shop, public service – are paid a flat rate for so many hours per week and are given overtime payments for excess time worked.

salary

This is the term normally applied to pay which is received monthly, often paid direct into a bank or building society account. A salary is usually paid to more senior staff, eg managers and supervisors.

commission

Sales representatives often work 'on commission', ie their pay is based on the number of items they sell. Pay can either be worked out as a flat percentage of the amount of money a sales representative brings in, or more commonly as a flat salary plus a percentage of sales. Commission is not only paid to the traditional sales 'rep'; many industries are now introducing 'performance related pay' for their top managers. Even bank managers' pay is often related to the number of new mortgages they sign up or credit cards that they sell.

technology in the workplace

Technology affects working conditions in a number of ways:

- the increasing use of *robots* in the manufacturing process reduces the number of jobs available (see illustration)

- modern *telecommunications* – eg mobile phone, fax, video-conferencing (holding a meeting through computer link-up; see illustration) – have made the operation of a business much more flexible and convenient

- the use of *computers* in business has meant that many routine tasks can be done by machine rather than by an employee – this will *reduce* the number of jobs. At the same time computers, through efficiencies in the workplace, give the business more opportunity to achieve sales and expand – this can *increase* the number of jobs

job security and career progression

An employee will naturally be concerned about the level of job security in a particular job. Some jobs are seen as 'safer' than others, but often the 'safer' jobs are also seen as the less interesting or challenging ones! Another factor threatening job security is the trend for organisations to offer *short-term contracts* to employees, rather than taking them on indefinitely. This has serious implications for career progression: many employees progress up the job 'ladder' by moving from job to job rather than staying in the same organisation.

using new technology – video-conferencing

using new technology – electronic checking of new cars

training and qualifications

In the past most people expected to enter a job, possibly by means of an apprenticeship, and then to remain in that job for most of their working life. Things have changed: people now expect to change occupation several times in a lifetime, often switching to completely different types of work. The significance of this is that training is much more central to peoples' lives as an ongoing process rather than just something they do at the start of their careers. In all organisations there are several types of training required:

- initial training for new employees
- 'on the job' training – internal courses
- multi-skilling training – employees are trained to do several jobs
- external training courses

vocational and professional courses

Training often has to be reinforced by courses provided by local colleges and universities. These courses provide the essential *knowledge* to support what is learnt in the workplace and on internal courses. College courses include vocational courses and professional courses:

- *vocational courses* provide training in job-related skills, eg office-skills; the National Council for Vocational Qualifications (NCVQ), established by the Government, sets standards for workplace competences which can be assessed both in the workplace and at College by examining bodies such as BTEC, RSA and City and Guilds

- *professional courses*: all the professions operate professional training schemes which enable people to acquire qualifications for their career development; these include the various Accountancy Institutes, the Law Society, and the Institute of Personnel Management; colleges are given permission to run these courses and the students sit exams which are usually set by the professional bodies

STUDENT ACTIVITY 3.5
performance criterion 1.3.3

working conditions

Decide on

(a) the job you would *most* like to do

(b) the job you would *least* like to do

Give a short oral presentation to the rest of the class describing the reasons for your choice in terms of the working conditions of the two jobs. Base your decisions on the factors set out on the last few pages.

EVIDENCE COLLECTION ASSIGNMENT 3

investigating employment

Element 1.3

introduction

This assignment will involve you in an investigation of working conditions of individuals in your area, and also an analysis of figures showing the differences in employment trends in different regions in the UK and in the EU. You will be asked to give a presentation of some of your findings.

 ## tasks

pc 1.3.1

1   **Investigate** SEVEN different types of employment in your area and write a brief description of each. The types of employment are:

- a full-time employee
- a part-time employee
- a person with a permanent contract
- a person with a temporary contract
- a skilled worker
- an unskilled worker
- a self-employed person

The description should briefly cover what the person does, the hours worked, the pay (take care here – it may be a sensitive issue), and what the physical working conditions are. Write about half a page on each.

Note: it would be best to approach a number of large organisations for your investigation, as there will be a greater range of jobs and more information available about working conditions. Remember that your own school or college will have full-time and part-time teachers, some on permanent contracts, some on temporary contracts. School or college support services will employ both skilled and unskilled workers.

pc 1.3.3

Core Skill 2.2

2   **Investigate** TWO of the jobs in different organisations in greater depth (you can include the self-employed person) and write a short report comparing them in detail in terms of their working conditions: travel to work (time and cost), physical working conditions (including safety), hours of work, pay (including any overtime or bonuses or pension), job security and career opportunities, training opportunities and the use of new technology.

pc 1.3.2

Core Skill 2.2-3

3 The chart set out below shows employment patterns in three sectors of economies within the European Union : the agricultural sector (primary), manufacturing industry (secondary), services (tertiary).

Set up a summary of the table on a computer spreadsheet ...

Follow the format of the table with *columns* for the *totals* of Agriculture, Industry, Services, and an overall total, and *rows* for *all* the countries. Do not enter the male/female figures.

Using the charting facility, extract charts to show the breakdown of employment by sector in all of the countries. Comment on the figures.

Choose two countries, including the UK as one of them, and set up a computer spreadsheet ...

This should show the full range of figures, including the male/female split. Using the charting facility, extract charts to show the breakdown of employment by sector and sex in the two countries. Comment on the figures. Try to choose a country which is different from the UK, such as Greece or Italy, and explain why the differences exist.

Support your comments for this task if you can by investigating other statistical sources, eg *Social Trends, Labour Force Survey* and *Eurostat.*

Employment by Sector in the EC (000's)

	AGRICULTURE			INDUSTRY			SERVICES		
	male	*female*	*total*	*male*	*female*	*total*	*male*	*female*	*total*
Belgium	82	29	111	879	213	1092	1251	1030	2281
Denmark	117	27	154	532	191	723	806	985	1791
Germany	654	549	1203	8260	2682	10942	7541	7314	14855
Greece	537	435	972	715	213	928	1127	629	1756
Spain	1229	442	1671	3185	629	3814	3697	2527	6224
France	1014	533	1547	4858	1568	6426	6475	6961	13436
Ireland	156	15	171	245	66	311	337	268	605
Italy	1377	694	2071	5175	1621	6796	7491	4742	12233
Luxembourg	4	2	6	40	5	45	56	46	102
Netherlands	217	69	286	1324	239	1563	1283	1858	3141
Portugal	477	467	944	1080	460	1540	1050	911	1961
UK	471	131	602	6415	1946	8361	7770	8788	16558

Source: OECD

pc 1.3.4

4 Make a presentation of your findings in *either* Task 2 *or* Task 3, using visual aids such as handouts, OHPs or flipcharts.

chapter summary and key terms

■ There are many different types of employment: full-time and part-time, permanent and temporary, skilled and unskilled, self-employed.

■ There are a number of trends in employment which are affecting the way people work, eg from full-time jobs to part-time jobs, permanent contracts to temporary contracts, manufacturing jobs to service jobs.

■ A significant trend is the steady increase in the number of women in employment, particularly in part-time and temporary jobs.

■ Working conditions for employees in different organisations vary widely; the differences relate to factors such as travel to work, physical conditions and safety, use of new technology, pay levels, job security, training and promotion.

key terms

self-employment	working for yourself as opposed to working for an employer
full-time	officially 30 hours or more a week, normally 37 to 40 hours a week or more
part-time	working less than 16 hours a week
permanent employment	the employee is taken on for an indefinite period of time
temporary employment	the employee is taken on for a limited period of time
skilled worker	a worker who has been given extended training
unskilled worker	a worker who has been given little or no training
teleworking	working away from the office using a telephone, computer and modem
multi-skilling	being trained to do more than one job

multiple-choice questions

1   Which of the following is MOST likely to self-employed?
     A   A company director
     B   A wages clerk
     C   A teacher
     D   A window-cleaner

2   A person who works in a supermarket at the weekends is
     A   full-time
     B   self-employed
     C   unemployed
     D   part-time

3   Temporary staff are normally used because they are
     A   easy to train
     B   better qualified
     C   easy to replace
     D   very young

4   The meaning of teleworking is that a worker
     A   is working for BT
     B   researches what people watch on TV
     C   works away from the office
     D   works on a computer

5   A sales representative is normally paid
     A   on a commission basis
     B   on a flat rate basis
     C   on an income tax basis
     D   on a mileage basis

6   The main reason for the rise in female employment is
     A   there are more women than men
     B   the rise in the birth rate
     C   the increase in part-time working
     D   new laws passed through Parliament

GNVQ UNIT 2
PEOPLE IN BUSINESS ORGANISATIONS

4 Structures and functions of businesses

GNVQ SPECIFICATIONS
Element 2.1
Examine and compare structures and working arrangements in organisations
performance criteria – a student must:
1 describe organisational structures
2 produce organisational charts showing departments
3 describe the work and explain the interdependence of departments within business organisations
4 identify and explain differences in working arrangements
5 explain and give examples of reasons for change in working arrangements in one business organisation

what this chapter covers

This chapter looks at the ways in which businesses are organised in terms of their structure (who does the managing) and the way their functions are divided up (eg production,sales, finance).

what you will learn from this chapter

- there are a number of different shapes of organisational structure – flat, hierarchical and matrix (these will be explained in the text)

- organisations are divided up into functions such as production, sales, finance, for example; in large organisations these functions will be carried out by departments, in small organisations they will be shared out by individuals

- functions and departments within an organisation can be illustrated by means of structure charts

- there are wide contrasts in working arrangements within business organisations, they include teamwork and rigidly structured departments, rigid hours/flexible hours, fixed contracts/temporary contracts, working from premises/working from home

organisational structures

sole trader – flat structure

Let us take as an example Asaf, the owner of a small shop. He is a sole trader who employs four part-time shop assistants. The structure of the business will look like this:

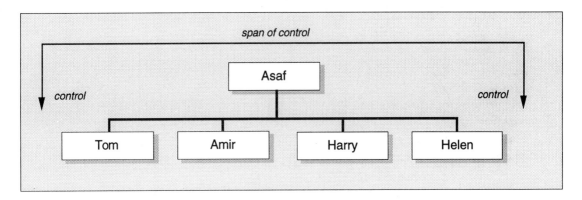

You will see from this diagram that:

- the structure is *flat* in shape; there is only one level of command – Asaf himself tells the assistants what to do

- Asaf has a span of control which extends over the four assistants; if he had more assistants, it would extend over those as well

- there is no indication as to who carries out what *function* in the business, ie 'who does what'

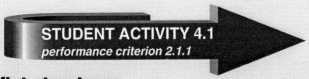

STUDENT ACTIVITY 4.1
performance criterion 2.1.1

flat structures

Core Skill 2.1

Look carefully at the flat organisational structure shown above.

(a) Who do you think carries out all the functions of the business, ie raising the money, paying the wages, ordering and controlling stock, advertising?

(b) What problems might this cause for the business?

(c) Asaf expands his business and opens another shop. He has to take on another six assistants. What would be his span of control, and what problems could this cause?

(d) Hold a class discussion to find a solution to the problem.

other examples of the flat structure

The flat structure is not confined to sole traders. Your own class is a flat structure with many students and one tutor in charge! A current trend in large business organisations is for each operating area to be independent, to take its own decisions, and be answerable to a managing function. 'Operating areas' could include regional divisions or product divisions.

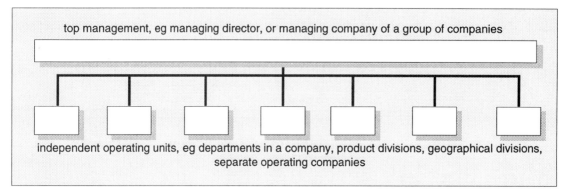

top management, eg managing director, or managing company of a group of companies

independent operating units, eg departments in a company, product divisions, geographical divisions, separate operating companies

hierarchical structures

A *hierarchy* is a series of levels, each responsible to and controlled by the level above. Most limited companies, and particularly public limited companies may have hundreds or even thousands of employees. They therefore have a more elaborate and 'tall' organisational structure which is characterised by:

- more levels of hierarchy
- more specialisation, ie division into functional areas such as sales, finance, human resources

The structure chart set out on the next page is that of a manufacturing company. Each horizontal level represents a step in the level of importance and responsibility of the staff:

- the managing director is responsible for directing company policy
- the other directors are responsible for policy in their defined areas (eg sales, finance, production)
- the company secretary is the director responsible for the administration of the company; in some companies the managing director is the company secretary
- managers are in charge of the departments, they implement policy and liaise with the directors
- supervisors are in charge of the day-to-day running of the departments and normally work alongside the production and administrative staff; sales representatives and design staff are also on this level
- production, administrative and support staff carry out the day-to-day work of the company

Each horizontal level represents a level of authority which must be respected and used in cases of:

- *instructions* – passed down the line of authority
- *problems* – referred to a higher level
- *disciplinary matters and complaints* – referred in the first instance to the next level up

functions in the organisation

You will see from the structure chart that the company is subdivided into vertical columns, each representing a particular *function* or group of functions, eg sales and marketing, finance, production and distribution. Generally speaking the larger the business, the more specialised each function becomes. At the other extreme the sole trader who runs a 'one-man' business carries out all the functions, from deciding on new products to making the tea.

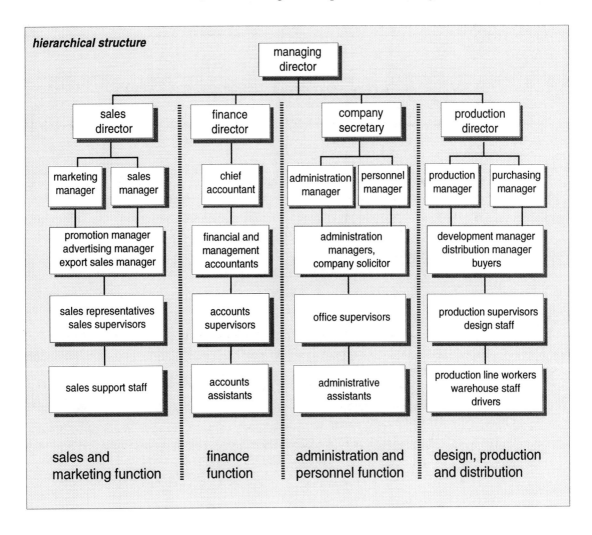

matrix structure

Another form of structure which needs to be examined is the *matrix* or 'project team' structure. Sometimes in an organisation it is necessary to take people out of their specific function areas – finance, sales, production – to form teams to work on specific projects. The 'matrix' concept originated in the aerospace industry where new projects were essential to keep manufacturers in business. The word 'matrix' means a 'rectangular grid of quantities and symbols'. The matrix concept involves a different form of organisational structure chart. Look at the example below which sets out a traditional functional 'flat' structure extended to show two project teams.

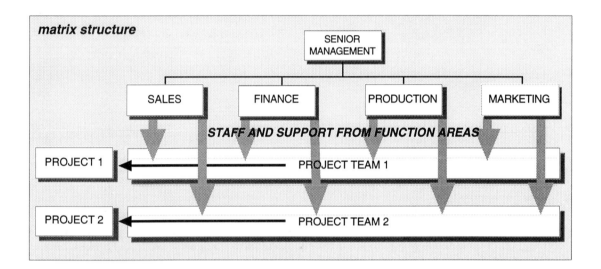

matrix structure

STUDENT ACTIVITY 4.2
performance criterion 2.1.1

hierarchical and matrix structures

tasks

1   Investigate the levels of authority in your school or college and draw up a structure chart. What type of structure is it?

2   Tangerine Limited manufacturers computers. It wants to set up a project team for a new design of laptop computer, the Pip. The company is divided into finance, sales, marketing and production departments. Draw a suitable matrix structure chart showing how the project team can be set up.

departments and functions

So far in this chapter we have concentrated in looking at the *shape* of the organisation, ie whether it is flat, hierarchical or matrix. It is also important to appreciate that the organisation can be viewed in terms of *function*, in other words by what it *does*. The diagram below shows the functions which one would expect to find as separate and specialised departments within a large manufacturing company.

It must be stressed that not all manufacturing companies have *departments* exactly the same as those in the diagram – they will all have those *functions*, but they may be organised differently. Marketing, sales and customer service, for example may all be within one department. Also, the departments will vary according to the *nature* of the business. A business in the services industry, eg a travel firm, will clearly not have a production facility!

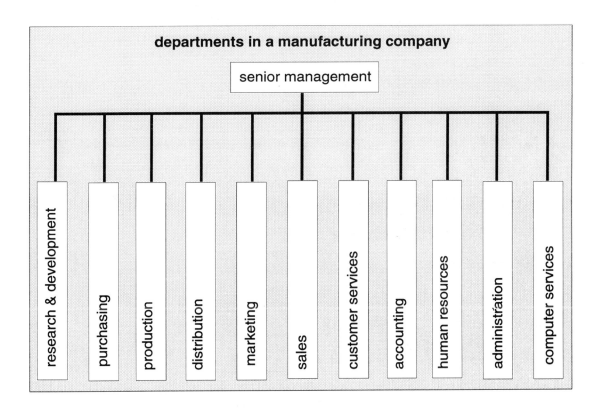

departments in a manufacturing company

senior management

research & development

purchasing

production

distribution

marketing

sales

customer services

accounting

human resources

administration

computer services

Now read the text which follows – it explains the functions and the departments

research and development

Research and development (often referred to simply as 'R&D') looks into the design and production of new products. A car manufacturer, for example, will use its R&D Department to investigate new materials, aerodynamics, car safety, and design shapes. Computers are being used increasingly in design since CAD (Computer Aided Design) programs have become widely available.

production

If a business is manufacturing a product, the manufacturing process will have to be strictly controlled in order to maintain quality and keep to production targets. The business must also monitor the efficiency of production methods and research and develop new techniques in line with modern technology.

Production is normally by one of three methods:

- *job production* is used by a business which produces a series of 'one-off' items to special order, eg ships
- *batch production* is used by a business which produces groups of identical items in the manufacturing process; when the group of products is complete the process starts all over again; a simple example of a batch is a tray of sausage rolls baked together
- *flow production* is the process whereby each item is constructed, one after the other without interruption, the components being added to the item, normally on a production line, until it is completed; many modern car plants involve flow production

The term mass production means 'large scale' production and can apply to any of the above methods, although it is most commonly applied to flow production.

purchasing

A closely controlled purchasing policy is also an important aspect of efficient production and will have a direct effect on profitability. The purchasing function must ensure that it obtains raw materials from the right supplier, at the right price, at the right time, and of the appropriate quality.

accounting

The Accounting or Finance department of a business is responsible for financial record keeping. This involves keeping records – either in manual form, or on computer file – of money received and paid out. Linked with this function is credit control, the monitoring of how well the customers pay up. The financial records maintained will be used to produce the financial statements of the business. This function of the Finance department is known as *financial accounting*. The Finance department is also responsible for the *management accounts* of the business. These are figures produced for the management of a business showing how well the company is performing in terms of income and expenditure in comparison with budgets prepared in advance. This function of the Finance department is known as management accounting. Cost accountants work out how much it costs to produce individual products.

The Finance department normally also oversees the payment of wages and the handling of cash by the cashiers. Full and accurate wages records are a legal requirement.

The Finance Director of a limited company, together with the Managing Director, will decide on how the business is to raise finance from outside sources such as the banks, and how it is to invest its spare funds. The Finance department will help to compile a document known as a Business Plan. This will contain financial details of the business and aims to 'sell' the business to outside lenders.

human resources

The personnel function, commonly now called the 'Human Resources' department fulfils a number of needs within the organisation. It is responsible for the 'hiring and firing' of employees, for staff training and development, and for dealing with matters relating to industrial relations. It also looks after the welfare of the workforce. In service industries in particular the personnel function is responsible with senior management for the 'customer care' programme which will be critical in winning new business and satisfying existing customers.

sales and marketing

Marketing is involved with satisfying customers' needs at the right price. It means researching what the customer wants, and investigating how the business can satisfy that need. Selling, on the other hand, involves persuading the customer to buy the products the business has already produced. Normally the marketing and selling functions are closely linked. The danger lies in the business becoming product orientated – ie the business believing that its products are best for the customer – rather than believing that 'the customer is king' and finding out exactly what the customer actually wants.

The sales function will co-ordinate the selling programme, using a variety of techniques – travelling sales representatives, telephone sales, mailshots and a follow-up schedule (ie contacting people who have made enquiries in order to try and turn the enquiries into sales.)

customer services

Customer Services is the area of the business which deals with its customers. Sometimes incorporated as part of the Sales department, Customer Services deals with customer enquiries about products and prices, complaints and all aspects of after-sales service. Now that 'the customer is king', Customer Services has become the 'shop window' of a business; if the department (or section) functions well and provides good service, customer loyalty can be maintained.

distribution (logistics)

Efficient distribution (logistics) means that the customer gets the product on time and in perfect condition – everything must be in the right place at the right time. Distribution involves warehousing and storage, packing, despatch and transport. Businesses will vary in their distribution methods, but the most successful businesses will always ensure that

- the goods arrive quickly and on time
- the goods arrive in excellent condition

administration and computer services

The administration and support services are essential in keeping the 'wheels' of the business turning. They include maintenance of the business premises and equipment, reprographics (photocopying), in-house printing (forms, stationery, newsletters), catering and computer services, mail handling and data storage. Nowadays many of these functions are being subcontracted to service companies which specialise, in what is known as 'facilities management'. Computer services are often part of the administration function of a business; again they are often contracted out to specialist companies.

STUDENT ACTIVITY 4.3
performance criteria 2.1.2 & 3

departments at work

1   Draw up a structure chart of a business which has departments for: production, customer services, sales and marketing, finance, human resources and administration.

2   Investigate how the following transactions affect different departments of a camping equipment manufacturer. List the departments that will be involved, and write down what they will do.

(a) a customer telephones to find out the price of a tent, she orders it, and it is delivered by van to her home address

(b) the production department takes on two more production line workers

different patterns of working

pc 2.1.4

No two businesses are identical in the way in which they organise their functions (departments) or in the way the employees are organised. We have already seen in Chapter 3 when looking at employment trends that working patterns in the UK are changing significantly. Read through the table shown below.

decentralised working	organisations are giving staff in regional offices more authority to make decisions on their own – they no longer have to refer to a centralised head office for everything they do
flexitime	organisations are increasingly setting a weekly or monthly number of hours for employees and then allowing them to choose the hours they work within those limits – this is more flexible than *shifts* where different employees work a series of set hours, eg 'night shift', 'day shift' so that production keeps going 24 hours a day
annualised hours	this is where the annual (yearly) hours are set, and the employee works to a flexible timetable – this is useful where a business is seasonal, ie busy at some times of the year and not at others
contracts	employment contracts are becoming increasingly short-term rather than permanent – it is cheaper and more flexible for the employer, but provides less security for the employee
place of work	because of the advances in information technology and communications employees are becoming less tied to the workplace; in the case of teleworking (see page 61), employees can even work at home

developments in teamwork

The traditionial hierarchical structure, with its many levels of authority and decision making and its rigid division into departments, has its disadvantages:

- departments tend not to communicate with each other
- employees at the bottom of the structure – production workers and clerical staff – often feel undervalued and ignored: their comments and ideas in many cases do not count for much

Major changes in working practices – largely the result of ideas imported from Japan – have involved the introduction of the works 'team'. Car manufacturers in particular have benefited greatly by involving designers, production staff and suppliers in the development and production of new cars. Read the comments below from Rover Group's report on the building of the Rover 800.

INVESTMENT AND INVOLVEMENT IN PEOPLE

The culture within Rover has changed significantly. Rover sees employees as its major asset, and is investing heavily in employee development.

Devolution of authority and accountability down to the people doing the job will increase. The well-established 'team structure' is the focus for this.

Right from the start of the project, a team of production employees with long experience of car manufacture was seconded to the project team. They worked alongside the process and production engineers, bringing to the team their hands-on knowledge of actually building cars.

Some of these employees were sent to visit equipment manufacturers in various countries during the evaluation of possible assembly techniques. Some went to Japan and the United States as part of their studies

STUDENT ACTIVITY 4.4
performance criterion 2.1.4

changes in working practices – teamwork

1   Read through the extracts from the Rover Group Report.
    (a) What does 'devolution of authority and accountability' mean, and how does it show that Rover is getting away from the traditional hierarchical structure?
    (b) Who were the team members?
    (c) Why did some of the employees go abroad as part of the project?
2   Investigate your resources centre and local manufacturers. What evidence can you find of teamwork in production?

reasons for change in working arrangments

The changes in working arrangements described so far – the greater flexibility of hours and contracts, the introduction of teamwork – have occured for a number of reasons ...

increasing productivity

Productivity is the value of the output of a business (ie the sales income) related to the cost of producing that output. In other words:

greater sales income and lower costs = greater productivity

How does achieving greater productivity affect employees?

* employers can *cut costs* by offering more part-time work and shorter contracts
* employers can achieve *more output* and a *high quality output* by introducing teamwork

quality assurance

Businesses can be certified for the quality of their systems and output through the government's Quality Assurance scheme – BS EN ISO 9000. Some businesses like their suppliers to be certified in this way – it ensures a quality product. The effect on the *employees* of the supplier is to stipulate a high standard of quality. Again, the teamwork approach, with its encouragement of employees' sense of responsibility, is helpful here.

competition

Competition keeps businesses 'on their toes' and ensures that management keep the workforce efficient and productive. They will review their working practices so that they can maintain a competitive edge and beat their competitors.

technology

We have already seen in Chapter 3 (page 62) how technology is changing working practices:

* the increasing use of *robots* in the manufacturing process reduces the number of jobs available
* modern *telecommunications* – eg mobile phone, fax, teleworking have made the operation of a business much more flexible and convenient
* the use of *computers* in business has meant that many routine tasks can be done by machine rather than by an employee – this will *reduce* the number of jobs. At the same time computers, through efficiencies in the workplace, give the business more opportunity to achieve sales and expand – this can *increase* the number of jobs

EVIDENCE COLLECTION ASSIGNMENT 4

business structures and working arrangements

Element 2.1

introduction

In this assignment you can *either*

(a) investigate two businesses with departments, one business with a flat structure and one with a hierarchical structure

or

(b) carry out the tasks on the basis of the Case Studies on the next page

Note: if you choose option (a) the two businesses investigated could also provide the evidence for Assignment 6.

 tasks

| pcs 2.1.1-2 | 1 | **Draw** an organisational chart for the two businesses. Use a computer drawing package if you can. |

| pc 2.1.3 | 2 | **Write notes** describing the work in each department, and giving examples of how the departments link up together in their work. |

| pc 2.1.4 | 3 | **Compare** in a **short report** the working arrangements in the two organisations. Where possible comment on the use of teamwork, and the reasons for its introduction. |

| pc 2.1.5 | 4 | **Write a summary** explaining how one of the following has brought about changes in working arrangements in ONE business organisation:
 • productivity
 • quality assurance
 • competition
 • new technology |

Core Skill 2.3

BUSINESS 1: MARLEY PRINTERS LIMITED

Marley Printers is an old family company, founded in 1850 and situated in a factory unit on the outskirts of Oldbury. It is headed by a board of directors and has separate departments for production, sales, administration, and finance. Each department has a departmental manager, a supervisor and assistants. All other functions of the business such as personnel work, are carried out by Jean Marley, the Company Secretary. The business employs 15 full-time and 20 part-time workers.

The work of the company involves printing small runs of items such as leaflets, forms, booklets, wedding invitations and so on. The instructions for each job are taken from the customer and the work is typeset and produced on the printing presses in the factory, and delivered by van or by post.

The financial performance of the company is giving the Marley family some sleepless nights. They are facing increasing competition from small computerised printing bureaux in the High Street who are able to do the same sort of work at lower cost. The production director, Jim Marley is very traditional in his outlook and is suspicious of computer technology.

BUSINESS 2: DYNASET

Dynaset is a partnership which operates a printing bureau in the centre of Oldbury. It is run by Meg Hann, a Desk Top Publishing computer expert , Ray Phillimore, who oversees the printing machinery, and Luigi Costello the sales and marketing partner. They employ five full-time assistants who help with computer input, printing and packing. Between them they process the same type of order as Marley Printers, but because of lower costs they can afford to undercut Marley's prices but still make more profit. They use a courier service to deliver the completed work.

The partners are great believers in teamwork. They hold regular meetings – with all staff present – and discuss the work in hand, technical problems, customer relations, and financial matters. Because of this they can make decisions quickly and run the business efficiently. They have a firm policy of continual product improvement. They are not certified for Quality Assurance at present, but they are looking at the possibility. They reckon they have cornered 35% of the market in Oldbury.

The five assistants are well motivated. Because of the teamwork attitude they can take many decisions without referring to the partners. They have been put on flexitime – they agree the hours amongst themselves – and are given productivity bonuses when the sales figures reach specific targets.

chapter summary and key terms

■ Organisational structures can be flat (simple), hierarchical (many levels) or matrix (project team).

■ Business organisations divide their work into functions. In large businesses the functions are carried out by departments; in smaller businesses they are normally shared out by the owners.

■ The functions include research & development, production, purchasing, accounting, human resources, marketing, sales, administration, computer services, customer services and distribution.

■ There are contrasts in working arrangements within business organisations, they include teamwork and rigidly structured departments, rigid hours/flexible hours, fixed contracts/temporary contracts, working from premises/working from home.

■ Changes in working arrangements are brought about by a number of factors, including the need for productivity, the introduction of quality assurance, competition and technology

key terms

hierarchical structure	a series of levels, each with authority over the next level down
flat structure	a simple organisational structure with few levels of authority
matrix structure	literally a grid of figures, a matrix structure illustrates how project teams are taken out of function areas
team working	where all levels of employee work together with a common purpose
decentralised working	an organisation where decision-making is taken away from the central office and given to regional managers or function areas
productivity	the relationship between the level of sales income and the cost of those sales
quality assurance	business systems given government certification (BS EN ISO 9000) for quality

multiple-choice questions

1   Which of the following is MOST likely to have a flat structure?

A   A sole trader business

B   A public limited company

C   A local government department

D   A public corporation

2   A matrix structure plan can be used to illustrate

A   levels of management

B   product teams

C   decentralised teams

D   flexitime

3   Recruitment of staff is most likely to undertaken by

A   the Company Secretary

B   the Finance Department

C   the Advertising Department

D   the Human Resources Department

4   Flexitime means

A   working when you want to while your children are not yet at school

B   choosing your hours, but working a set number per week or month

C   working and being paid by the amount you produce

D   working from home and being in touch with the office by 'phone

5   Productivity means

A   working as hard as you can

B   designing new products

C   relating sales income to the cost of those sales

D   reducing output by cutting down on hours

6   Businesses like to deal with firms with quality assurance certification because

A   they are cheaper

B   they are more expensive

C   they have quality systems

D   their goods are guaranteed for ten years

5 Employers and employees

Element 2.2
Investigate employee and employer responsibilities and rights
performance criteria – a student must
1   explain the benefits of employer and employee co-operation
2   describe ways to resolve disagreements
3   explain employer rights and responsibilities
4   explain employee rights and responsibilities to their employers

what this chapter covers

In this chapter we will look in detail at the rights and responsibilities of employees and employers. We then examine some of the ways in which employers and employees can resolve disagreements that they may have (over pay rises for example). Finally we see how employers and employees benefit when they co-operate with one another.

what you will learn from this chapter

- Employers have many responsibilities to their staff, such as providing safe and healthy working conditions, paying them fairly and treating them all equally regardless of sex, race or disability.

- Methods of resolving disagreements between employer and employees include the use of trade unions and employer associations, ACAS, Industrial Tribunals and the European Court of Justice.

- The survival and success of a business depend more than ever before on co-operation between the employer and the employees.

- There are many ways in which employees and employers can co-operate and these will benefit both in the longer term.

rights and responsibilities

pcs 2.2.3 & 4

rights and responsibilities and disputes

When an employer takes on staff, the employee has:

- *rights* – things he or she can expect the employer to do
- *responsibilities* – standards of work and behaviour expected of the employee

You can easily see from this that the rights of the employee are also the responsibilities of the employer! What we are saying is that employers and employees can expect to be treated in a certain way. If they are not, a dispute can arise – either the employer or the employee will have a grievance – and the dispute will have to be resolved, as we will see later in the chapter.

We will first look at the rights of the employee.

employee rights

pcs 2.2.3 & 4

The main employee rights are ...

to be given a statement of terms and conditions of employment

A *contract* is a legal agreement which is enforceable in a court of law. If you buy a TV, book a holiday, or get a job, there is an agreement – a *contract* – which is created. If anything goes wrong with the TV, holiday, or job, you (or the other person) can take the matter to court if a dispute cannot be settled in any other way.

All contracts have terms and conditions. For example, different types of train ticket have different terms and conditions: some are more expensive, some restrict the times of travel. Similarly, all jobs – 'contracts of employment' – have terms and conditions.

When you get a job you will be given *either*

- a formal signed written contract (see page 89), *or*
- a written *statement* of the terms and conditions of employment

Since 1975 it has been a legal requirement to give employees working more than 16 hours per week a *written statement* of terms and conditions. This must be done within 8 weeks of the employee being appointed, and in practice most employers will provide them much more quickly than this. Since March 1994 even those people working for under 16 hours per week will now be entitled to one of these statements.

what does this statement include?

1 The *names* of the employer and the employee

2 The *date* when the employment begins – this is important because entitlement to certain legal rights only applies after specific lengths of service, eg protection against unfair dismissal by the employer only applies after exactly two years service.

3 The *job title* – employee must take care that the title accurately reflects what they have to do!

4 The *pay rate* and how payment is made (weekly, monthly, credit transfer, by cheque, BACS etc) and details of paid overtime and the rate of overtime.

5 The *hours of work* – the number of hours required eg 37 per week, and the times of starting and finishing work each day, and any variations on those times.

6 *Holiday pay* entitlement – currently at least 4 weeks a year plus public holidays is very common.

7 *Sick pay* entitlement (eg 3 months full pay and 3 months half pay).

8 *Pension entitlement* (many employers make a contribution to employees' pensions).

9 The *length of notice* required if you decide to leave or if the employer decides to get rid of you.

10 Details of where to find the *grievance procedures* (employee complaints) and *disciplinary procedures* (employer complaints).

formal contract of employment

Many employers, particularly larger ones such as public limited companies and local authorities, issue a formal written contract of employment to employees setting out the terms and conditions of employment (see opposite page). These contracts are *not* in any way different from the statement of terms described above, it is just that the law now says:

an employer that does not issue a formal contract must issue a statement of terms and conditions.

CONTRACT OF EMPLOYMENT

Particulars of Terms and Conditions of Employment pursuant to the Employment Protection (Consolidation) Act 1978

Employer............. Osborne Electronics Limited ....

Employee.......... Helen Cassidy ....

1. **Continuous Employment**
   You are on a fixed term contract of ....2.....................years

   Your continuous service dates from.... 21 January 1996 ....

2. **Job Title**
   You are employed as........ Computer operator ....

3. **Salary**
   The rate of your salary is....£8,400........................per annum, paid monthly

4. **Hours of Work**
   Your normal hours of work are ...35....... hours a week, worked over a five day period (Mondays to Fridays inclusive)

5. **Leave**
   You are entitled to....22...........days paid holiday per annum in addition to statutory holidays. The leave is to be taken at a time convenient to the employer.

6. **Sickness**
   Notification of absence should be made on the first day of sickness, in writing or by telephone.
   If you are absent for a period in excess of five working days, a doctor's certificate must be submitted to the employer.
   Regulations for payment during periods of sickness or injury may be inspected on request in the Administration Manager's Office.

7. **Notice**
   The length of notice for termination of employment required from employer or employee is.....4.........weeks, subject to statutory requirements.

8. **Grievance Procedure**
   In cases of dissatisfaction with disciplinary procedure you are to apply in the first instance to the Manager of the Sales Department. Details of the rules of the Company and disciplinary procedures may be obtained from the Administration Manager's Office.

9. **Pension Scheme**
   Details of the contributory Company Pension Scheme, for which you are eligible, may be obtained from the Administration Manager's Office.

Signed this....21st.....day of...January...19..96....

T J Hardy

T J Hardy, Managing Director and Company Secretary

other employee rights

Although the statement or contract of employment will not state them, there are other employee rights which can be assumed or 'implied'. There are also employee rights set down in law.

to pay employees fairly

An employer has a duty to pay you according to the terms in your contract of employment. If your employer suddenly decides to alter your pay without you agreeing to such a change then you may complain to an Industrial Tribunal. It should be noted that there is no law in Britain to ensure employees are paid at least an "adequate" income for their work (or a "minimum wage").

to allow employees to join a trade union

Trade Unions will be dealt with in more detail later in the chapter (page 99).

to have equal pay

Since 1970 employees of both sexes have been entitled to equal pay. Before this it was legal for an employer to pay women less than men (or vice versa!). The Equal Pay Act 1970 (Fair Employment [NI] Act in Northern Ireland) meant that, for example, a restaurant would have to pay all its waiters and waitresses exactly the same rate of pay. In 1983 an Equal Value Amendment was added to the 1970 Act. This European Community ruling enabled women to improve their pay by comparing their jobs with particular 'mens jobs' and showing that their jobs are of 'equal value'.

no discrimination in the workplace – sex, race or disability

The Sex Discrimination Act in 1975 and the Race Relations Act in 1976 made it illegal to discriminate on sexual or racial grounds when offering jobs, advertising for applicants for jobs, determining pay and conditions in jobs, and when promoting employees. The employer would also be liable if it let employees discriminate against other employees.

Both Acts include a small number of exceptions where discrimination can still occur but these only cover a small proportion of the workforce (for example, the Act includes a 'Chinese Restaurant clause' which enables ethnic restaurants to discriminate in favour of particular ethnic groups when filling jobs as waiters or waitresses).

In addition employers may not discriminate against people with registered physical or mental disabilities (under the 1944 and 1959 Disabled Persons Acts). Government money is available to help organisations to modify buildings and buy special equipment for the use of disabled employees.

Health & Safety at Work

The Health and Safety at Work etc Act 1974 sets down the regulations for employers providing a safe working environment for their employees. The Act covers both premises and systems of work. To comply with the Act, employers should provide and maintain:

- safe and healthy plant and systems of work – and maintenance of the equipment

- a safe and healthy working environment and adequate welfare facilities and arrangements

- safe and healthy premises with adequate amenities, access and exits

- safe methods for handling, storing and transporting materials

- adequate instruction and training for employees, and adequate supervision

- information to employees concerning health and safety

In addition, most organisations must issue a written *safety policy* covering the health and safety arrangements in the workplace and appoint safety representatives and form a safety committee.

STUDENT ACTIVITY 5.1
performance criteria 2.2.2 & 3

employee rights

task 1

Write down what your rights are in the following situations, and what you would do:

(a) You are offered a job, but your employer says she can only pay you £1.50 an hour.

(b) You are given a job doing 15 hours a week at the local supermarket. The employer at the end of the first week says "I won't be giving you anything in writing because you are only part-time."

(c) You find out that someone of the opposite sex (who joined the business at the same time as you) is being paid more than you, even though you are doing the same type of work.

task 2

Look at the Contract of Employment on page 89. Suppose Helen is unhappy with the way she is being treated by her supervisor.

(a) Where would Helen have to go to find out about the grievance procedure?

(b) How much notice would she have to give if she wanted to leave?

(c) What would be her position if she spent most of her time filing letters?

(d) What would be her position if the supervisor says "You've only got three days holiday left – we count bank holidays as holiday entitlement you know."

employer responsibilities

explaining business objectives to employees

Employers increasingly realise the importance of keeping all employees fully informed about every aspect of their organisation – its performance, its prospects, its plans for the future and its financial position. It is also increasingly common for employers to set up systems to ask their employees their opinions about how to run the organisation more successfully. Consultation with employees has been very popular in Japan and it has become more popular in the UK because of the Japanese companies that have opened UK factories. The main types of employee consultation include the following:

joint consultative committees

These consist of employee and employer representatives who consider a wide range of issues which affect the workforce eg health and safety matters, provision of welfare services. Through these the employer can tell employees about business performance, sales, profitability, and any future plans.

team briefings

This is where employees meet in their work groups about once every two weeks and they are briefed by management about the important issues affecting the organisation.

quality circles

This is where employees meet regularly in their work groups and consider ways in which the quality of their work can be improved.

suggestion schemes

This is where employees can hand in their suggestions (usually placed in a box fixed on a factory or office wall) on all kinds of matters. Often they are technical suggestions – how a production process might be improved,for example. If they are used and they save the organisation money then the employee will get a prize or a cash sum.

offering training to all employees

All jobs require some basic skills and an employee is expected to be 'skilled up' to the level required to do the job he or she has been given. In addition to basic training, more and more employers now offer staff development opportunities such as job rotation, internal and external courses and the opportunity to study for further qualifications. Many employers encourage able employees to study for advanced qualifications which improve their knowledge and skills for use at work

pay and deductions

An employer has a duty to pay an employee according to the terms of the contract of employment. In addition to the wage or salary paid to an employee there are often other payments added such as commission (eg to sales reps), bonuses (payments if the organisation does really well) and profit sharing (a payment based specifically on the profit of the organisation).

The employer is also required to take from an employee's weekly or monthly pay certain deductions and show them on a payslip (see below).These include:

- income tax (a tax on earnings)
- National Insurance Contributions (abbreviated to N.I.) – a tax to provide state benefits
- pension (superannuation) payments, if the employee is contributing to a pension scheme

STUDENT ACTIVITY 5.2
performance criteria 2.2.2 & 3

the payslip

WCC Wyvern County Council	Pay Statement May		
	£		£
Pay	1200.00	**Tax**	214.75
Overtime	0.00	**N.I. Non-Contr Out**	100.34
		Superannuation	72.00
TOTAL GROSS PAY	1200.00		
		TOTAL DEDUCTIONS	387.09
		NET PAY	812.91

CUMULATIVES		EMPLOYEE DETAILS
Taxable earnings	1818.50	
Tax to date	429.50	Miss D Penny
NI to date	200.68	Staff No 0178653425
Superannuation	144.00	NI No YT 77 77 01 A
		Tax Ref 792/W1
NET PAY	1625.82	Payment via BACS

Identify on the payslip:

(a) the pay before deductions (gross pay) and pay after deductions

(b) the deductions made

(c) the pension payment and the percentage of gross pay it represents

employee responsibilities and employer rights

pcs 2.2.3 & 4

You will remember that at the beginning of the chapter we saw that the responsibilities of the employer are also the rights of the employee. We now look at the situation from the other point of view – employer rights and employee responsibilities. What should the employer expect from the employee?

employees must be available, willing and capable to work

When someone has agreed to work they must be *available* to do the job agreed. The employer will set out specific times for starting and leaving each day in the written statement of terms and conditions provided to all employees when appointed. They will expect them to stick to these conditions. Being "capable" means that staff will be physically and mentally able to do the job and that any training required will be provided.

the employee must take reasonable care and skill

An employer should expect employees to be reasonably careful in doing their job. The rule is that one can expect them to be as careful as any 'reasonable' person would be. Where an employee makes a genuine mistake the employer would normally be expected to give them one more chance to do the job properly. A mistake caused by fooling about is another matter entirely and might result in instant dismissal. Employees should also comply with the Health & Safety regulations and COSHH (control of substances hazardous to health) requirements.

an employee must take proper care of premises and equipment

An employer can expect employees to look after business property as they would their own. If they intentionally damage or destroy it this would certainly be a just reason to dismiss them from the job they hold.

the employee must obey any reasonable order given

The key word is "reasonable". An employer can require a person to do any work which is covered by their contract of employment and which an average person would find reasonable to do. The order must be legal. The business owner who asks a seventeen year-old (who has got her driving test the following week) to drive a van should get a firm refusal! Also if the order is dangerous, it could be refused – for example if you had a holiday job in a factory you could refuse to clean the skylights on the roof!

employees must act in good faith

"Good faith" means that an employee must always behave in a honest and fair manner in respect of the employer. An employee is not acting in good faith if he or she gives confidential details about the employer's business to other people.

STUDENT ACTIVITY 5.3
performance criteria 2.2.2 & 3

employer rights

Write down what you think are the employer's rights in the following situations? You do *not* have to say what action would be taken.

(a) Maisy Grace is persistently late for work. She says "It's my car, it just won't start."

(b) Jo Green is persistently late for work. He says "I'm sorry, but I have been on anti-depressant drugs this last month. I am not so well."

(c) A production line worker complains that she cannot work a new machine because she was off sick when the training sessions were held.

(d) Des Aster has crashed the fork-lift truck for the second time in a week. This time he has hit the Managing Director's Mercedes.

(e) You overhear an employee talking to a stranger in a pub about a new "hush hush" secret project your company is developing.

disciplinary action against the employee

pc 2.2.2

There are two possible situations which involve the employer and the employee 'falling out' with each other:

• the employer considers it necessary to discipline the employee

• the employee can have a grievance against the employer – sometimes because the employee considers that he or she has been unjustly disciplined

We will deal first with the *disciplinary procedure*.

reasons for disciplining an employee

An employee can be disciplined for:

• being unable to do the job

• being frequently late or absent

• fighting or swearing or being drunk at work

• stealing from the employer or from workmates

• doing private work that is competing with the employer's business

• having a long term(chronic) illness which means you cannot work properly

There is a laid-down disciplinary procedure which is followed by most employers. It is designed to ensure that everyone is treated as fairly as possible.

the disciplinary procedure

Suppose you are being disciplined: the disciplinary procedure you will go through will follow a number of distinct stages:

stage 1

informal discussion
At this very informal stage your manager or supervisor will explain that he/she is unhappy with your work and will ask you what the problem is. At this stage you can request that the organisation gives you extra training, or a simpler, lower-grade job, or you might want to tell him/her about recent illnesses or personal problems that have affected your work.

If this does not lead to an improvement in performance there will be a formal verbal warning.

stage 2

verbal warning
In most cases this formal 'telling off' is enough to get you to work harder . However, it will be formally recorded in your employment records in case you do not improve.

If the quality of your work has still not improved you will receive a formal written warning.

stage 3

formal written warning
You will get a formal letter from the Personnel Department (or whoever deals with staff management) which will give details of your performance, stating what is wrong with it, and threatening dismissal if the poor performance continues. Some employers give you a second written warning but it is not strictly necessary.

If the problem continues, you are likely to receive a notice of dismissal.

stage 4

notice of dismissal
The final stage is to issue you with a letter stating you are dismissed with one week or one month's notice and giving full details of the reasons why you have been dismissed. You are entitled to an interview with the personnel manager and you may be represented by a trade union official to ensure that you have been fairly treated.

gross misconduct – instant dismissal

If the disciplinary matter is extremely serious then the earlier stages of the procedure may be missed out. For example, theft from the organisation or from fellow employees, or assaulting someone at work, is often dealt with by the "instant dismissal" of the employee concerned for "gross misconduct."

employee grievances

pc 2.2.2

All organisations will inevitably have disagreements between the owners or managers and the people who work for them. Here are some examples ...

examples of disagreements – comments from employees

unfair treatment at work	*My supervisor is picking on me, giving me all the rubbish work – it's because he doesn't like me!*
discrimination	*I will never get promoted, its because of my colour and because I am a woman.*
working conditions	*I am not working on that machine any more, it's so unsafe, it's only fit for the scrapheap!*
victimisation	*My fellow employees pick on me – they call me names and have sprayed paint on my car.*
pay	*Our pay rise is pathetic; the management is getting 5% more than us.*
redundancies	*I don't like the way they are bringing in the redundancies; its always the production line workers that get the raw deal.*
working conditions	*It's not fair to expect us to do two jobs where we used to do one – we are not getting any more money!*
dismissal	*I've been sacked for being late again – I'm sure they can' t do that to me*

STUDENT ACTIVITY 5.4
performance criterion 2.2.2

Core Skill 2.1

problems in the workplace?

Discuss each of the above problems in class and decide:

(a) who is at fault

(b) whether the problem affects one or a number of employees

(c) who is responsible for the problem

(d) who should do something about it

the employee grievance procedure

For the employee the main way of dealing with complaints he or she has about the job (or anything relating to their job) is the *grievance procedure*. Many employees currently complain officially about how they are treated. All employers with more than 20 staff must by law have some kind of written grievance procedure. Many smaller organisations also understand the wisdom of having one. This is because if the employee is still dissatisfied he or she can takes the complaint to ACAS (the Advisory, Conciliation and Arbitration Service) or to an Industrial Tribunal – see below. The officials in those organisations will be highly critical of any employer who does not have a written grievance procedure.

how a grievance procedure works

A standard type of grievance procedure should:

- Be in writing so all staff can have a copy of it.
- Specify to whom the employees should go in the first instance with a grievance. As with disciplinary procedures this should start off very informally so that, if possible, it can be sorted out with the minimum of fuss and bother.
- State to whom to go at a higher level (eg the Managing Director) if the employee is still not happy with the treatment received.
- State specified time limits within which staff can expect to be told what management is going to do about the complaint.
- Ensure that all meetings to discuss the complaint are properly recorded in writing.

the next stage? – the Industrial Tribunal service

If an employee is not happy with the outcome of a disciplinary procedure or a grievance procedure he/she can pursue the case through an Industrial Tribunal. Industrial Tribunals were established by Act of Parliament as a form of informal court – a panel of experts – to offer employees the chance to get themselves quick, cheap and efficient justice, with none of the legalistic language and procedures which many people find rather offputting (and expensive). They operate in several large regional centres (eg Bristol, Birmingham, Manchester). A tribunal consists of one representative from the local branch of the Trades Union Congress and one from the local branch of the Confederation of British Industry (which represents employers). The chairman will be a full time post held by a barrister or a solicitor. Tribunals deal with disputes about:

- equal pay
- sex discrimination
- race relations
- contracts of employment.

Trade Union negotiations

pc 2.2.2

Approximately 8 million employees in Britain belong to legally recognised Trade Unions (associations of workers) because they believe that this is the most effective way of dealing with their employers. As a group employees can threaten to "take industrial action" to get what they want whereas an individual employee's threats to strike would not worry an employer very much. Taking industrial action can take several forms:

strike action

Employees 'on strike' do not turn up for work until the employer agrees to give them what they want. If the strike stops an organisation from operating normally, this will eventually force the employer to give in – for a business with no sales there can be no profit.

overtime ban

Many organisations rely very heavily on employees doing overtime to complete production orders, to replace or cover for staff who are on holiday or away sick. A ban on overtime hits such organisations very badly. The advantage to the employee is that they still earn their basic pay so they can carry on an overtime ban longer than they could a strike.

Trade Unions use the methods listed above to try to resolve the disagreements outlined earlier. Improvements in pay and better working conditions have traditionally been won by Trade Unions through industrial action.

Trade Union involvement in disputes

Trade Union officials may be called in:

* to help sort out a dispute in the workplace – officials will talk to employees and employers
* officials will assist at Industrial Tribunals, and the Union will pay the costs of the Union member

STUDENT ACTIVITY 5.5
performance criterion 2.2.2

Go to your local library and find out the names of at least ten trade unions. For each one:

(a) Find out how many members they have.

(b) Find out which groups of employees they represent.

What trends can you discover about trade union membership?

ACAS and disputes

`pc 2.2.2`

ACAS (the Advisory, Conciliation and Arbitration Service) is a government-financed organisation set up in 1974 to provide a range of services to employers and employees. The aim was to create an organisation which would make it quicker and easier to sort out problems between employers and employees. In Northern Ireland the body equivalent to ACAS is the Labour Relations Agency.

the functions of ACAS

an advisory service to employers and employees
ACAS can help companies with all kinds of legal advice (particularly useful for small businesses which cannot afford their own legal advisors) and they provide the same kind of help to employees.

advising employees applying to an Industrial Tribunal
If the employee does decide to make a claim against his employer (or ex employer) both parties will be visited by an ACAS official who will try to get both of them to sort out their problems *without* a Tribunal hearing. If the ACAS official feels that the employee has little chance of winning in a tribunal hearing then he will tell both employee and employer that this is the case.

other ACAS services
Apart from dealing with individual cases, ACAS also intervenes, where necessary, to sort out problems between employers and employees as a group. If a pay deal or a planned redundancies programme cannot be agreed then ACAS may asked to help to achieve an agreement.

the European Court of Justice

`pc 2.2.2`

This organisation acts as the supreme court of the European Union. If an argument between an employer and employees has not been resolved inside the UK court system, it may be referred to the European Court for a decision. The decision of the 15 judges (one for each EU member country) is final and a UK court may not challenge that decision.

It is important to stress that such referrals to the European Court of Justice are very rare.

employer and employee co-operation

There are a number of important benefits which arise from co-operation between employers and employees.

business survival

Nowadays business organisations operate in a highly competitive environment. In order to survive they have to be productive, efficient and competitive. This requires full co-operation from employers and employees. Read the Case Study below.

The UK car industry - a success story

In the 1970s UK cars could not compete in Europe – they had inferior designs,poor quality workmanship,and higher prices. UK firms had to change their ways of working, which required co-operation from employees. Gradually the UK car industry improved and,although it has reduced in size, it now attracts far more foreign investment in car making than any other European country. Investments by Honda, Nissan, Toyota, Peugeot, BMW and Ford, all prove that the UK is now an attractive place for car manufacture.

The BMW takeover of Rover Cars and Ford's investment in Jaguar Cars are particularly relevant – Rover and Jaguar only survived by changes in the ways in which they operated. This required the co-operation of employers and employees.

---

areas where employers and employees co-operate

We will now look at these areas of co-operation. Remember that what is true for car making is equally true for other UK businesses ...

co-operation over job reductions

Co-operation comes about because good employers try to make people redundant in the least painful way, asking firstly for volunteers and for early retirements coupled to generous redundancy payments. Some companies, Rover Cars for example, now have "jobs for life" policies which guarantee people a job until they retire so long as they co-operate over where they work and what they are prepared to do

co-operation over methods of working

A competitive manufacturing business often needs the most modern production machinery – robots, for example, to build car bodies. This requires staff to retrain and be more flexible in what they do. For example, at one time in many British factories, employees would only carry out one job whereas now people are required to do a variety of work. Co-operation has come about because employees understand that it is the only chance of survival for the business – and their own jobs.

co-operation over where people work
More and more people are expected to move about the country to new factories. Employers offer generous help to find employees new homes and in helping them to sell their existing ones.

improved employee commitment to the business
Measures to improve co-operation will usually help employee commitment as well. Let us look at some examples …

good management
When an organisation improves by taking on better managers, it is likely to increase sales and enhance the reputation of its products. Employees will feel more confident and more committed to the business.

new equipment
New equipment combined with new methods of working (eg quality circles, team working) should convince employees that the future is better for the organisation and for them.

improved efficiency
The co-operation of employees and employers will also increase efficiency. By "improved efficiency" we mean that the output per employee is increased. To raise output per employee in factories there must be new methods of working and new equipment. The same applies in the service industries – the banks and building societies increased efficiency through installing cash machines and reducing the number of branches. Both required the co-operation of employees.

STUDENT ACTIVITY 5.6
performance criterion 2.2.1

the benefits of co-operation
Prepare on a word processor a list of the benefits of workplace co-operation for:
(a) an employer
(b) an employee

EVIDENCE COLLECTION ASSIGNMENT 5

Employers and employees

Element 2.2

introduction
Read the case study below and then carry out the tasks following it .

In 1993 Ledbury Soft Toys Limited,established by William Ledbury in 1959, negotiated a new "flexibility" agreement with its employees. In return for a flat one-off payment of £1,000 all employees agreed that they could be required to carry out a wider range of jobs in the factory or offices than before. This meant, for example, that skilled staff who previously only did skilled maintenance and repair work could now be required to do jobs like toy stuffing and sweeping up if they had nothing else to do.

John Smith,an electrician since 1964 at Ledbury's, took his £1,000 like everyone else in 1993 but had never really approved of the agreement. In fact, since 1993, he very rarely got asked to do tasks away from his normal duties.

However, in 1995,due to big overseas orders, he was asked by a supervisor to help pack the 'Yogi Bear' output. After three days on this work he damaged two 'Yogi Bears', walked off and swore at the supervisor.

Smith decided to bring a grievance procedure against the company because he felt he was being 'picked on' by the supervisor (who just happened to be his ex-wife's brother...) since no other fitters or electricians had been expected to do this work for more than one day at a time. Mr Ledbury knew about the swearing incident but, so far, had done nothing about it. Smith had always been a good employee with a first rate record in all respects and he had known him for 31 years.

tasks

1   Outline in note form how flexibility agreements benefit both employees and employers.   `pc 1`

2   Explain how you could persuade John Smith that he might benefit.   `pc 1`

3   Advise him in a series of steps how he must prepare his grievance complaint against the company.   `pc 2`

4   Prepare a set of points for and points against his going on with this action.   `pc 2`

5   Explain to him about the possible involvement of ACAS and the Industrial Tribunal service assuming he gets no satisfaction from the company.   `pc 2`

6   Since John is a member of the Amalgamated Electrical & Engineering Union explain to him how they might also help.   `pc 2`

7   Although the company have so far said nothing, tell him there is a possibility that they might decide to discipline him. Explain how this would work and what might happen to him.   `pcs 3-4`

chapter summary and key terms

■ Employers and employees have certain duties to each other, some of these are set down in law and in the contract of employment, others are assumed.

■ If the employer is unhappy with the employee, the disciplinary procedure can be followed; if the employee has a dispute with the employer, the grievance procedure can be followed.

■ The grievance procedure can involve Trade Unions, ACAS (the Advisory, Conciliation and Arbitration Service), taking the case to an Industrial Tribunal, or even in very rare circumstances, the European Court of Justice.

■ The most important aim of business organisations is to remain competitive in a harsh business environment where there is more and more competition for customers. This means employers should try to gain the support of their employees rather than upsetting them with unpopular measures. The main benefits of co-operation between employers and employees are business survival, improved employee commitment to the business and greater efficiency.

key terms

contract of employment	the legal relationship between an employee and an employer which is set out in the Written Terms and Conditions of Employment or Contract of Employment
equal opportunities	a situation where everyone has the same opportunities within an organisation
disciplinary procedures	rules set out by a business which ensure that if an employee is disciplined he/she is fairly treated by management
grievance procedure	rules setting out the steps to be followed by an employee who is in dispute with the employer
employee consultation	ways in which employers encourage a better relationship with their employees
collective bargaining	the method by which employees bargain, as a group, for better pay and conditions

multiple-choice questions

1   Written Terms and Conditions of Employment are
   A   given to employees who do not have a written contract of employment
   B   given to every employee who has a written contract of employment
   C   given only to trade union members
   D   given only to employees who want to go to an industrial tribunal

2   An employee's duties to the employer include
   A   taking professional exams
   B   being available to work at all times
   C   taking care of the employer's property
   D   paying National Insurance

3   The court to which an employee can take a dispute with the employer is
   A   ACAS
   B   the trade union
   C   the European Council
   D   an industrial tribunal

For questions 4 to 6, match the problems listed at the bottom of the page to the regulations listed below

   A   Sex Discrimination Act
   B   Equal Pay Act
   C   Race Relations Act
   D   Health & Safety at Work Act

4   an employee is injured by a dangerous piece of machinery

5   an employee complains that someone doing the same type of work is being paid more

6   a woman complains that she is being passed over for promotion and that the men are getting all the better jobs

6 Job roles

what this chapter covers

This chapter examines various job roles performed at different levels in an organisation and looks at the benefits gained from working as a team.

what you will learn from this chapter

- what the key jobs are in an organisation – director, manager, supervisor and assistant – and how they depend upon each other

- how people work far more effectively as a team and how this benefits them and the organisation

- the main functions of the most important departments in a typical business organisation, and how they differ according to the level of the person involved

- that all employees have to perform routine tasks (planning, decision-making, setting and achieving targets) and non-routine tasks (eg dealing with emergencies).

job roles at different levels in an organisation

In all except the smallest organisations there will be a variety of job roles which are tied to particular job grades. For example, if you are studying your Intermediate GNVQ in a college or a school at the present time, you will find that there is a graded structure of management to run the organisation. The typical management structure for a college or school, for example, looks like this...

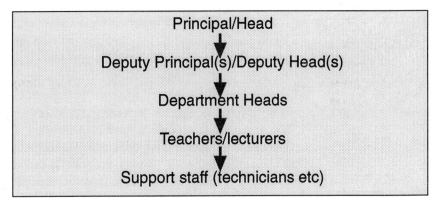

It is quite likely that the management structure in your college or school is slightly different to this one. Draw a diagram of the structure in your college or school (refer to the prospectus for details).

In a limited company the equivalent job roles and grades would be these:

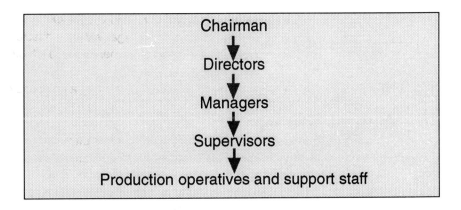

We will now examine each of these job roles in more detail.

the chairman and the board of directors

You will remember from your study of limited companies that there are two classifications of company:

- private limited company – a small company, often a family business
- public limited company (plc) – a large company in which the public can buy shares

There is no major difference between the two apart from *size*. The law requires that all public and private limited companies are run by a *board of directors*. In a public limited company the directors will be elected and employed by the shareholders (the owners) of the company. The board is normally headed by a *chairman* (male or female!). The managing director (sometimes called the Chief Executive) is in charge of the operation of the company. In private companies, a small family company for example, the managing director is often the chairman and the directors are the shareholders.

In public limited companies directors are sometimes part-time but there will always be full-time directors as well – these are known as "executive" directors. They often have a specific area of responsibility, eg "finance director". A more recent development, which is more common elsewhere in Europe than in the UK, is the election of "worker directors" to the boards of companies. They are elected by fellow employees to represent the interests of the workforce as a whole. If you study at a college which has been incorporated (ie become a company) you may find that it has a student on the college governing body.

---

the role of directors in a company is to ...

1   plan the long term strategy of the organisation.
2   appoint the right management team to ensure that this strategy is put into effect
3   oversee all major financial decisions.
4   ensure that shareholders interests are always protected
5   ensure that the company always operates within the law

---

managers

In each department there will be a team of managers. They are required to carry out the policy of the board of directors, to ensure their own department works efficiently and to supervise the work of all of their departmental staff. Good managers will employ a range of management techniques to ensure that their staff are not only effective but also highly motivated.

The main roles of the department manager will be as follows – these roles are more or less the same whatever kind of organisation it is ...

the role of a manager is to ...

1 carry out the instructions of the directors

2 ensure his/her departmental staff work effectively

3 ensure they reach their targets, eg sales figures

4 ensure staff are motivated so that they do their jobs properly

5 carry out the administration of the department – this will include the appointment and dismissal of staff

6 allocate the work between the members of the department – this will call for some sensitivity and tact to keep everyone as happy as possible

7 ensure all staff know what is going on – this is not as easy as it sounds!

8 ensure that departmental staff use systems such as suggestion schemes which encourage them to contribute ideas of their own

supervisors and 'the team'

Under each manager there will be a *team* of staff. The size of this team will vary considerably. In a factory the team under a Personnel manager will be very much smaller that the team under the Production manager. The members of this team will include *supervisors*, *operatives* (people who work machines) and *support staff*.

supervisors

Supervisors are often known as "first line managers". This is because they manage groups of employees on behalf of the manager who is their boss. The job of supervisor has changed considerably in recent years and this has meant that the characteristics of the modern supervisor are very different to the old style supervisor (traditionally called a "foreman"). The modern supervisor is more like a manager; the older type of supervisor was more 'one of the lads'. In some organisations, supervisors have been replaced by managers.

the role of a supervisor is to ...

1 take responsibility for 'operatives' (production workers in manufacturing businesses) and 'support staff' (employees in service industries or administrative functions in manufacturing businesses)

2 ensure that the staff are meeting their production targets and identify people who are not doing so

3 work closely with the manager to identify ways of improving efficiency and introducing change

production operatives

Production operative is a broad term which describes someone who operates machinery and equipment or who takes part in a production process – eg assembling electronic components, making up hamburgers in a fast food outlet.

support staff

These are the people who make sure that production employees and their managers have the right conditions in which to work. These include caretaking staff, security officers, cleaners, canteen assistants and"odd-job persons" who deal with repairs, maintenance work etc. More and more of these jobs are now carried out by other companies who provide these services under a contract in return for a yearly fee, eg Group 4, Sketchleys and Compass.

---

the role of production operatives and support staff is to ...

1 carry out the day-to-day work as instructed by supervisors or managers

2 achieve targets – these include reaching set output levels

3 achieve the required quality standards

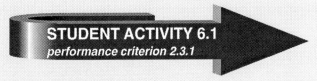

STUDENT ACTIVITY 6.1
performance criterion 2.3.1

Core Skill 2.4

job roles and levels

Study the text on the last few pages and the chart on the opposite page and answer the questions set out below. You could also make use of evidence gathered from work experience, work shadowing and visits to businesses. Produce your answers on a word-processor.

1 What are the three levels on the chart, and which job roles are in each of them?
2 What is the difference between a Finance director, a Managing director and a Chairman? When might there be no difference at all?
3 What is the difference between a manager and a supervisor? What is the recent trend for the role taken by supervisors?
4 Give five examples of a production operative and five examples of support staff.
5 What teams are shown on the chart, and what job roles do they involve?
6 What advantages can you see from team working? (Note: this is the topic covered in the next section of the chapter).

JOB ROLES IN A LIMITED COMPANY

senior level

board of directors
(headed by a Chairman and Managing Director)

middle level

managers
(in charge of the Departments)

supervisors

junior level

production operatives
support staff

departmental teams for
Finance, Production, Sales & Marketing,
Administration, Human Resources

the benefits of team working

pc 2.3.2

Under each manager or supervisor there will be a team of staff, and obviously the size of this team will vary considerably. In a factory the team under a Personnel manager will be very much smaller that the team under the Production manager.

Let us look at a typical personnel department. How is it structured?

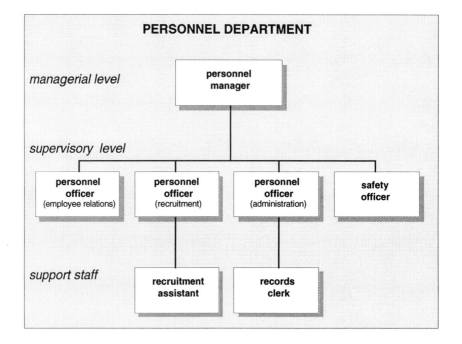

PERSONNEL DEPARTMENT

managerial level — personnel manager

supervisory level — personnel officer (employee relations) | personnel officer (recruitment) | personnel officer (administration) | safety officer

support staff — recruitment assistant | records clerk

working as a team

The department will only work effectively if it works as a team. The Personnel manager will call regular meetings to discuss performance and efficiency and to invite supervisory level and support staff to contribute with suggestions and comments.

what are the main benefits of working as a team?

For the reasons listed below it is easier for a department to achieve its objectives and targets when people work as a team ...

1   If you work in a team there is a friendlier atmosphere in the workplace which encourages staff to perform better.

2   You can get jobs done more quickly.

3   It means that everyone supports everyone else and if the need arises each team member is capable of doing other people's work.

4   A team also provides a career structure because staff at the bottom can see that there is a career "tree" to climb. This is important for staff motivation and it increases their commitment to the organisation.

qualities needed for team-working

For any team to work effectively the team members need certain qualities. Read through the following list:

1   They must be able to listen to one another

2   They must only criticise constructively (helpfully)

3   They must be able to accept helpful criticism – they must not take it personally.

4   They should make suggestions to help one another work more effectively – they must not selfishly guard ideas as "their own".

5   Where a team member has a problem it should be recognised that it is the team's problem for them all to help sort out.

6   A team must be led by somebody who understands all the members and knows them well on a personal level. When he or she gives team members their roles he or she should know what they like to do, what they are good at and what they are most useful for.

If it has all or some of these features a team can:

1   solve problems by sharing ideas

2   encourage creativity and new ideas

3   motivate people because they do things together

4   discipline its members and make sure they are all 'pulling their weight'

STUDENT ACTIVITY 6.2
performance criterion 2.3.2

the benefits of team working

Examine situations where people work in a team.

For example:

(a) a group of students working together gathering evidence as part of a college project

(b) a sports team

(c) a couple in a car, one driving, the other reading the map and giving directions

Give a list of the *benefits* of working in a team and also *reasons* why teams like these may not always work well together.

activities in business organisations

pc 2.3.3

In this section we will look at the main activities of people working in the principal departments of an organisation. For this purpose we will look at the main departments in a manufacturing business. However, most of the departments covered here are also found in service industries too.

The main departments are:

- Finance
- Human Resourcing (or Personnel)
- Production
- Administration
- Sales and Marketing

In Chapter 4 we looked at the *functions* of these and similar departments. If you are not familiar with these functions, please look back at pages 75 to 78. In this chapter we will concentrate on the *activities* undertaken by different job roles in these departments.

The company we will be looking at is Carcare Limited, a manufacturer of car accessories. The jobs we will be looking at are shown below on the structure chart and are described in more detail on the four pages that follow.

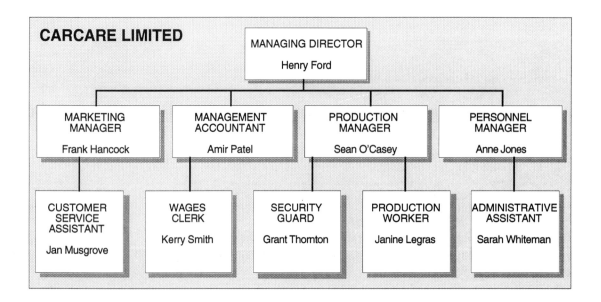

Henry Ford – managing director

"I am in charge of the whole business. My job is to see that the company runs efficiently. I head the board of directors, each of whom is in charge of a department. I must make sure that the shareholders' interests are looked after. I help to plan the future of the company both short-term and long-term, and aim to keep it profitable.

I like to mix with staff at all levels and hear their views and complaints – that way I can get the feel of how the business 'ticks'. I always keep an 'open door' – any employee can always come and see me, if they want to."

Frank Hancock – marketing manager

"I am in charge of the marketing department. I report directly to the marketing director, who is in charge of sales and marketing. I work with Rick Brunson, the sales manager. I also talk regularly with other departmental managers.

Selling our products is obviously important, but we would never sell any goods without proper marketing. I have twenty assistants in my department. They look after areas such as market research and advertising."

Amir Patel– management accountant

"I work in the finance department and at the same level of authority as a departmental manager. I report to the board of directors and have twenty five staff working under me.

My work involves supervising *costing* – the process of finding how much it costs in terms of materials and labour to produce a product. I am also in charge of *budgeting* – working out how much each department can spend, and making sure that they don't overspend! As you can see, I have to work with all areas of the business – which makes it interesting."

Sean O'Casey – production manager

"I am in charge of the production lines of the business. I report directly to the production director. I also work with Rick Brunson, the sales manager, who lets me know about any problems. I also talk regularly with other departmental managers – particularly the purchasing manager who buys in my raw materials and components.

I am in charge of sixty production line workers. We are a fairly happy bunch – we rarely have any disputes. Carcare is a good employer and looks after its workforce."

Anne Jones – personnel manager

"I am in charge of the personnel department. I report directly to Henry, the managing director. I am mainly responsible for the recruitment and training of staff, so I have to work closely with the other departmental managers. I have six assistants working for me altogether.

The job involves dealing with people, which makes it very interesting, as you very often feel that you are being a positive help in difficult situations – we had a case of sexual harrassment the other day which required very delicate handling – it involved someone senior in the company."

Jan Musgrove – customer service assistant

"I work in the Customer Services section of Sales Department. I take telephone calls from our customers and deal with sales enquiries, orders and complaints. There are five assistants in the office altogether, and our supervisor who deals with the important customers and any major problems. We also have typists and computer operators.

The work is never boring – I am dealing with customers all the time, and get a lot of satisfaction from helping people. Of course you get the occasional awkward one – but that's life. We do get a thorough training in telephone technique."

Kerry Smith – wages clerk

"I work as a wages clerk in the finance office. There are ten clerks altogether, and our supervisor.

Although we occasionally have to work out wages manually, most jobs are computerised now – all we have to do is to enter the hours worked by each employee on the computer, and it automatically works out the pay and prints out a payslip. Some employees still get paid in cash – and I have to work out a cash analysis and get the right notes and coins from the bank. More and more employees now get paid direct into their bank account. I find the work interesting because I like working with figures."

Janine Legras – production worker

"I have worked on the production lines here at Carcare for two years now. At the moment I make the covers for car seats. They like women on this job because you have to be nimble-fingered. There are twenty of us on this line, and a supervisor who keeps her eye on us and the work we do.

They treat you well here at Carcare. They change what you do now and again, and they pay well, particularly the Christmas bonus. We all have a good laugh from time to time – you need to when you do work like this – the work can be very boring otherwise!"

Sarah Whiteman – administrative assistant

"I work in the administration department on a part-time basis. I work with fifteen other assistants and a supervisor.

The work is certainly varied. I do mostly word processing, filing and photocopying. We deal with all the paperwork involved with the running of the company, so we get to see what all the other departments are up to. I like working here, the atmosphere is good – the supervisor is strict, but has got a broad sense of humour!"

Grant Thornton – security guard

"I work part-time as a security guard for Carcare. I used to work for Securesafe, but some of the jobs were a bit rough, and I even got beaten up once. They treat you well here. I report to the Administration Manager, and he tells me all that he wants done. My main job is to work at nights patrolling the premises, making sure that everything is OK. I have got my own little room with heating and a kettle, so I am well looked after".

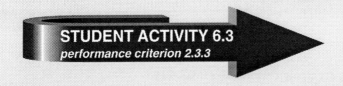

Core Skill 2.4

analysing job roles

Study the ten employees on the previous four pages and then answer the following questions. Write (or word process) your answers on a sheet headed "Jobs – activities and responsibilities"

1. List three of the main duties of a managing director. Why is it so important that he keeps an 'open door' to his employees? What could happen if he did not?

2. Who are the two people that the marketing manager deals with most? Why is a marketing department important to a business?

3. To whom does the management accountant report, and what level of seniority is he? Why does he need to deal with the other departments in the business?

4. Who are the three people that the production manager deals with most? Why does Carcare rarely have any industrial disputes?

5. To which director does the personnel manager report? What are her areas of responsibility? What type of person do you think she will have to be in order to do her job?

6. What type of work does the customer services assistant carry out? She is at the bottom of the promotion ladder, but her job is very important . Why?

7. What work does the wages clerk carry out? How do you think this job has changed in recent years?

8. How does the security guard's job differ from all of the other jobs described so far?

9. How does Carcare ensure that the production worker's job does not become too boring?

10. What type of employee is the administrative assistant – full-time or part-time? Out of the 6 million part-time workers in the UK, how many do you think are women – 3 million? or 4 million? or 5 million?   (the answer is on page 60)

tasks in job roles

pc 2.3.4

This final section examines what tasks employees carry out in their day-to-day work. There are firstly *routine tasks* involving:

- planning and decision making
- problem solving
- setting and achieving targets.

Secondly, there are non-routine tasks such as dealing with emergencies or accidents.

routine tasks – planning and decision making

Activities at work often involve making decisions. Normally the more senior you are, the more you have to make decisions, and the more serious the consequences will be.

In a small organisation with a few staff the owner looks after everything (eg in a corner shop) and he/she has to make all the decisions. Because the owner is responsible for everything it may make him/her a better decision maker.

In a large organisation like a public limited company or a County Council decision-making is far more complex. Junior and middle managers are left to make day-to-day decisions and the top managers only make the most important ones - the "strategic" ones which affect the long term future of the organisation.

STUDENT ACTIVITY 6.4
performance criterion 2.3.4

decision-making

Jabba Jehangir owns "Excelsior Motorways", a small bus and coach business based in Bristol. He owns six coaches of varying ages which he uses on a mixture of bus services (mainly school services from surrounding villages) and day trips to the seaside and tourist attractions like Stratford-upon-Avon and London. He employs a supervisor, seven full-time and one part-time driver, an office clerk and a mechanic.

Set out below is a series of decisions which have to be made by his business. Identify the decisions which

- only Jabba can make
- his supervisor can make
- drivers and other staff can make

1 When to order spare parts for coach maintenance work?

2 Whether to give a refund to a day trip passenger who complained about the driver's rudeness?

3 Whether to ask a mother to control her unruly child on one of the company's bus services?

4 Whether to apply to the Department of Transport for permission to run a new bus service?

5 Whether to buy a new coach costing £106,000?

routine tasks – problem solving

Making decisions is much easier if you can solve problems. Many decisions are really problems, sometimes fairly simple in nature and sometimes more complicated.

How do you solve problems?

1 Define the situation – what is the problem?
2 What caused the problem?
3 Collect all the facts.
4 Analyse the facts – pick out the relevant ones.
5 Identify the true cause of the problem.
6 Consider what to do about the problem – sometimes there will only be one solution, but usually there are several. Which is best?
7 Make a decision after weighing up all the possibilities.

routine tasks – setting and achieving targets

The setting and achievement of targets is usually associated with production and sales departments. A sales target for one salesman might be 5,000 cases of baked beans a month, or 800 teddy bears, or 25 new cars ...

Teamworking in organisations involves the whole team – managers, supervisors and production workers – in target setting and monitoring. Sometimes pay is linked to meeting targets. Targets can be:

- *positive*, where the employee aims to increase something, eg sales, or
- *negative*, where the employee aims to reduce something – eg the number of faulty products, the number of customer complaints, the time taken to make one unit of a product

Individual targets must support the achievement of a higher level target. For example, each baked bean salesperson will have an individual target, but the sales department as a whole will also have a well-publicised target. This motivates staff because they then feel they are working together towards a common goal and their personal performance is vital to the overall target.

There must be positive rewards for the achievement of targets. This should be just as true for staff in personnel or finance as it is for salespersons. As mentioned earlier, some employees are paid according to whether or not they reach or exceed targets, either in the form of commission (for sales staff) or 'performance-related pay' for managers.

non-routine tasks

A non-routine task could be virtually anything which an employee could have to deal with on a "once in a lifetime" basis. Here are a few examples.

You are the supervisor in the production department and one Monday morning are told that your immediate superior, the Production manager, has been taken seriously ill and will not be at work for at least 2 months.

You are the purchasing manager. The supply of parts which are used to make the organisation's products has stopped because of a sudden strike at the parts supplier. The organisation has only got 4 weeks stock of parts.

You are the marketing manager. A college orders 10,000 prospectuses to send to households in its catchment area. A fire at the printers means they will be at least four weeks late. Classes start in a fortnight.

You are a supervisor in the accounts department. One of the wages clerks is celebrating her engagement and comes back after lunch very drunk and unfit for work.

You are an assistant in the administration department; your colleague puts a heavy-duty staple through her finger.

You are not required to provide solutions to all these problems, but you will at least appreciate that there *is* a problem. Generally speaking the more senior you are, the more difficult the non-routine tasks become.

EVIDENCE COLLECTION ASSIGNMENT 6

investigating job roles

Element 2.3

introduction

This assignment, which looks at three job roles in one organisation, may be carried out as an extension of Assignment 4 on page 82.

 task 1 `pcs 1-3`

From your own work experience and from library sources you should choose three jobs from one organisation, preferably from different departments. You should try to get to talk to people who hold these jobs, if you can.

One of the jobs must be at a junior level, one at supervisory level and one at a management level.

Write a summary on the day-to-day activities carried out in each job. One approach you could adopt is to write a diary of the day's events, setting down the activities for each job and commenting on what happens.

You should include in each case a paragraph stating to what extent *team membership* played a part in helping each job holder to perform his or her duties.

 task 2 `pcs 3-5`

Prepare a presentation, including OHPs and an A4 word-processed handout, on "the role of the Personnel Manager". It would be helpful to talk to a personnel manager in a business with which your school or college has a link. Otherwise rely on library sources and this book. Your presentation should include a description of :

(a) how the personnel manager recruits and selects new employees

(b) your ideas of how he/she would handle the situation described below

On Monday afternoon, a large number of employees at Ledbury Soft Toys Ltd, which has its own works canteen, started to feel ill. A doctor was called and diagnosed food poisoning. Out of 88 production workers, 54 were hit by the outbreak and were ordered to stay off work for at least five days. Explain what the personnel manager must do to keep teddy bear production going and to prevent another outbreak.

chapter summary and key terms

■ The main job roles in a business organisation are the chairman, the directors (including the managing director), managers, supervisors, production operatives and support staff.

■ The best way of working effectively together is in properly organised teams from which the organisation and all the team members benefit.

■ The main departments in a business organisation are finance, production, human resources (personnel), administration, and sales and marketing.

■ The main tasks of employees are either of a routine or non-routine nature. Routine tasks include decision making, problem solving, setting and achieving targets. Non-routine tasks include dealing with emergencies.

key terms

director	senior employee of a limited company, appointed and employed by the shareholders; directors sit on a committee known as a board
Managing Director	the chief executive of an organisation, responsible for overall control of the business
manager	an employee with overall responsibility for a function of a business, normally a department such as finance or production
supervisor	an employee with specific responsibility for an area of work, eg production line, computer input
production operative	an employee who works machinery or assembles a product
support staff	staff who support the internal working of an organisation or who support its external operations, eg sales and customer service
team working	where employees work in groups so that they benefit from each others ideas and support
target setting	organisations set targets for areas such as sales and production, and quality of products and systems

multiple-choice questions

1   The managing director of a company is
     A   appointed by the chairman to manage the directors
     B   in charge of the operation of the company
     C   the workers' representative on the board
     D   employed by the government to safeguard employee rights

2   The role of the supervisor is to
     A   control the board of directors
     B   control a specific area of work
     C   represent the Trade Unions
     D   maintain the security of the buildings

3   Employers have introduced team working MAINLY to
     A   prevent absenteeism
     B   encourage sport at the workplace
     C   increase efficiency and productivity
     D   restrict pay rises

For questions 4 to 6, match the types of decisions required in the situations set out
at the bottom of the page with the job roles listed below

     A   director
     B   manager
     C   supervisor
     D   support staff

4   the business needs to decide whether to export its goods

5   a department needs to recruit a new employee

6   one of the cashiers takes a longer than normal coffe break

7 Employment or self-employment?

what this chapter covers

This chapter will enable you to find out what types of job there are and to discover what type of job best suits *you*.

what you will learn from this chapter

- the different types of job available – for both the employed and self-employed

- where to find information about jobs

- the job opportunities that are available in your area

- the skills that are needed for employment and self-employment

- the skills that you have or could develop

- how to make a personal plan for the type of job that would best suit you in both the short-term and the long-term

employment and self-employment

definitions – what is employment?

Being *employed* means that you work for someone else; being *self-employed* means that you are in business on your own, running your own enterprise, making the decisions, running the risks and taking the profit.

types of employment

If you are considering getting a job – being 'employed' – there is a wide range of opportunities available:

- *private sector* jobs – working in industry, financial services, travel and tourism,for example, or in the voluntary sector (for a charity)
- *public sector* jobs – working for government agencies and public corporations, the Civil Service or Local Government

types of self-employment

If you want to work for yourself, there are again many options available:

- being a *sole trader* – eg opening a music shop
- becoming a *partner* – eg going into practice as an accountant
- taking a *franchise* – eg opening a branch of the Body Shop

Becoming self-employed can involve starting a *new* business (the shop), buying *into* a business (the accountant) or buying an *existing* business or business name (the franchise). In some cases people are self-employed if they carry on the *family business*, eg the corner shop. If you are not clear about the differences between these types of business, refer back to Chapter 1.

employment or self-employment?

It is most likely when you leave school or college that you will be going on to do another course, or that you will be getting a job. It is not likely that you will be self-employed straightaway. Being self-employed normally requires two things:

- money
- 'know how' – the experience and knowledge of how to run a business

These are usually in short supply when you are a student! One organisation, however, the Prince's Youth Business Trust (PYBT), provides grants, loans and training to people between 18 and 25 who have a good business idea but little money or 'know-how'. If you do want to become self-employed you should investigate the PYBT as well as your local Careers Office, TEC (Training and Enterprise Councils), and Business Link office.

Now read the Case Studies on the next page and carry out the Activities.

CASE STUDIES

pc 2.4.1

Jane Willis – self-employed decorator

I set up my own decorating business two years ago on an Enterprise Allowance Scheme funded by the local TEC. My family has always been in decorating, so it seemed a natural step to take. I do all sorts of painting indoors and outdoors. It has been hard work – long hours and little holiday – but it is very satisfying working for yourself, especially when you get new business from existing clients recommending you to friends. If anyone asked me what it takes to be self-employed, I would say determination, good health, the ability to deal with people, and having a sense of humour!

John Hunt – bank employee

I joined Albion Bank five years ago having done a Business Studies course at the local College. People said that working in a bank would be boring. There is a lot of routine work to be done, and computer input, but I also get the chance to meet the public – we are encouraged to sell as many financial services as possible – personal loans, credit cards and so on. I work from 9.00 until 5.00 most days and can get more money by working Saturdays. I like the job because I am in contact with people all the time. There are better promotion prospects now that I am studying for my professional exams. I also play a lot of sport, so I like being able to get away at 5.00 or soon after. We also get good holidays and staff perks, and although there are boring times, we normally have a good laugh in the office.

STUDENT ACTIVITY 7.1
performance criterion 2.4.1

employed or self-employed?

Core Skill 2.2

Core Skill 2.3

Study the figures set out below and carry out the tasks that follow. If you can, use a computer charting facility to help you present your findings.

employment and self-employment

Self-employed people	3.3 million
People employed in the private sector	15.6 million
People employed in the public sector	5.9 million

average weekly hours worked by employed and self-employed people

employed men	40.7
self-employed men	46.8
employed women	34.6
self-employed women	43.9

Source: Employment Department

tasks

1 Draw a pie chart showing the number of self-employed people, and people employed in the public and private sectors. Calculate percentages and show them as labels. What conclusions do you draw from your result?

2 Comment on the differences in the average working hours of employed and self-employed people? Show your results in the form of a bar chart.

3 Arrange with your tutor for a self-employed person (or an adviser from a TEC or similar body) to come to talk to the class about the advantages and disadvantages of being self-employed. Draw up for your files a list of advantages and disadvantages. Also refer to the Case Studies on the previous page for ideas for this.

4 Choose a job in employment and self-employment which *you* would like to do. Write a paragraph on each, outlining the advantages and disadvantages.

sources of information about jobs

pcs 2.4.2 & 3

Sources of information about jobs can be divided into two types:

- advice about the *type* of job you are looking for
- information about *actual* job vacancies (local, national and overseas)

career guidance – *types* of job available

One of the most difficult choices to make is what *type* of job you want to do. There are many people and organisations who will help with career guidance:

- school or college Careers teachers and resource centres
- local authority Careers Officers and Careers Centres

In addition, it is always worthwhile talking to people – family, friends, relatives – to see what they think about their jobs. You may also have the opportunity of going on work experience or work-shadowing (working alongside someone in a job). Another source of guidance is the computer: many Careers Centres and some schools and colleges have interactive computer programs such as 'Kudos'. These enable students to sit in front of a computer screen and answer questions about their likes and dislikes; the program then analyses the type(s) of job that would suit them and will print out a report.

resources available at a Careers Office

job advertisements

job vacancies – employment opportunities

Job vacancies are advertised and publicised in a number of places:

- Job Centres
- recruitment agencies
- newspapers – local and national
- local authority employment officers

In addition, training vacancies are offered through the Training and Enterprise Councils (TECs) and local Chambers of Commerce.

information about self-employment

If you are looking for information about self-employment – setting up on your own – there are various sources of assistance and information:

- your local office of the Department of Trade and Industry (DTI)
- your local Training and Enterprise Council (TECs)
- Business Link offices
- booklets produced by the banks
- Chambers of Commerce
- Federation of the Self-Employed

the need for skills

pc 2.4.4

Employers sometimes value skills more than knowledge. A student that can show initiative, solve problems, and take responsibility for his or her actions is often worth more than a student with any number of academic qualifications. Skills can be:

- *occupational* skills – particular skills *relating to the job being done*
- *core* skills – *general* skills which can be applied in any job

occupational/vocational skills

An *occupational* or *vocational* skill is a skill which can be used in a particular job. The following jobs, for example, all require very specific skills:

- accountant
- car mechanic
- brain surgeon

The skills required for these jobs are normally acquired 'on the job' – the employee is trained while working. Practical vocational skills will be acquired in the workplace, and the theoretical knowledge which backs up these skills will be acquired through college or correspondence courses. The important point about vocational skills is that they cannot easily be transferred from one profession to another: you would not be happy if your brain surgeon had trained as a car mechanic!

core skills

Core skills, on the other hand, are general skills which can be used in any job context. They therefore form a compulsory part of many educational courses such as GNVQs. They include:

Application of Number
This skill involves the use of *numbers*: gathering them, making sense of them, using them to solve problems, and presenting them.

Communication
This skill involves taking part in discussions, being able to prepare written documents, using illustrations and images, and being able to understand and respond to them.

Information Technology
This skill enables employees to be familiar with computers and to be able to use them for a variety of business tasks: word-processing, storing and handling data, and tackling business calculations.

Other skills which will be used in the workplace include:

- working with others
- working independently
- planning
- time management
- decision making
- problem solving
- collecting information and evaluating it

EVIDENCE COLLECTION ASSIGNMENT 7

employment or self-employment?

Element 2.4

introduction
This assignment prepares you for getting a job or for becoming self-employed. It involves:

- charts showing the skills needed for self-employment and employment and an assessment of how you rate in these skills
- interviewing people who are in employment
- an investigation into *three* jobs which interest you

task 1 – qualities needed for self-employment

pc 4.2.4

Read through the list of personal qualities needed by someone who is considering becoming self-employed. In each box put either:

- a tick for "yes"
- a cross for "no"
- a question mark for "not sure"

You might find it useful to discuss the questions with someone who knows you very well – a close friend or a member of your family who will give you an honest opinion about your personal qualities!

1.	I can work long hours.	☐
2.	I am prepared to work seven days a week if necessary.	☐
3.	I am in good health.	☐
4.	I can cope under stress.	☐
5.	I am a good decision maker.	☐
6.	I am self-disciplined and organised.	☐
7.	I am good at dealing with other people.	☐
8.	I have a positive outlook and know my aims in life.	☐
9.	I can learn from mistakes and take advice from others.	☐
10.	I do not give up easily.	☐

task 2 – assessing your skills   pc 2.4.4

Read through the following list of skills needed in employment and self-employment and tick the box which you think applies to you.

	excellent	good	satisfactory	less than satisfactory
Communicating – speaking	☐	☐	☐	☐
Communicating – writing	☐	☐	☐	☐
Using numbers	☐	☐	☐	☐
Using information technology	☐	☐	☐	☐
Working with others	☐	☐	☐	☐
Working on your own	☐	☐	☐	☐
Planning your work	☐	☐	☐	☐
Managing your time	☐	☐	☐	☐
Making decisions	☐	☐	☐	☐
Solving problems	☐	☐	☐	☐
Collecting information	☐	☐	☐	☐

 task 3 – discussing your qualities and skills   pc 2.4.5

Discuss the results of Task 1 and 2 with your tutor and decide

(a)   whether or not you would be better suited to employment or self-employment – look at your strengths and weaknesses

(b)   your current level of skills development, and how this could affect the type of job to which you might be suited

You should then write a summary of what decisions you came to in the discussion. The summary should be seen and approved by the tutor and signed by the tutor and the student.

task 4 – interviewing people with jobs   pc 2.4.4

Interview three people who have jobs. Try and choose jobs which are very different from each other, eg finance officer, teacher, gardener (you may find all three working at your school or college). Write a short report describing each job in turn and covering:

(a)   what the job is

(b)   how the person got that job (eg where was it advertised?)

(c)   the skills that are needed for the job

The survey sheet below is a suggestion of how you could carry out (c)

---

the importance of skills in a job

person interviewed... date...........................

job...

	very important	important	sometimes used	never used
Communicating – speaking	☐	☐	☐	☐
Communicating – writing	☐	☐	☐	☐
Using numbers	☐	☐	☐	☐
Using information technology	☐	☐	☐	☐
Working with others	☐	☐	☐	☐
Working on your own	☐	☐	☐	☐
Planning your work	☐	☐	☐	☐
Managing your time	☐	☐	☐	☐
Making decisions	☐	☐	☐	☐
Solving problems	☐	☐	☐	☐
Collecting information	☐	☐	☐	☐
Evaluating information	☐	☐	☐	☐

task 5 – investigating job opportunities   pcs 2.4. 2 & 3

(a) Select three job vacancies which interest you. At least one should be for a job which you can do on leaving school or college, and at least one should be for a job which you would like do when you have been in work for a few years, ie higher up the promotion ladder.

The job opportunities can be for employment or self-employment, and at local, national, or international levels.

(b) Collect information about the jobs from a variety of sources including:
* the newspaper adverts (if this is where the job was advertised)
* careers offices
* visiting careers officers
* job centres
* recruitment and employment agencies
* the Federation of Self-Employed

(c) Write a summary about each job opportunity, explaining in the form of notes:
* the title of the job
* what the job involves
* the likely pay
* details of any qualifications needed

Include with your summary a copy of any newspaper advert and careers information leaflets (from the careers office or from the body which supervises the qualification for the job, eg a RSA NVQ in Business Administration). State in each case where the information came from.

chapter summary and key terms

- ■ There are many different types of employment opportunities in the public sector (eg in local government) and the private sector (eg in financial services, leisure and tourism).

- ■ If you want to become self-employed you can become a sole trader, a partner, or take up a franchise.

- ■ There are many sources of information about jobs: careers offices, newspapers, employment and recruitment agencies, and local advisory bodies such as TECs and Business Link offices.

- ■ Core Skills are essential in a job. You will already be developing these as part of your GNVQ course: communication, application of number and information technology, working with others, working independently, time management and planning, decision making and problem solving, gathering and evaluating information.

- ■ Jobs also involve 'occupational skills' which relate to the job itself.

key terms

self-employment	working for yourself as opposed to working for an employer
employment	working for an employer
public sector	organisations which are owned or controlled by government
private sector	organisations which are owned by private individuals
occupational skills	skills which relate to the nature of the job itself (car mechanic, brain surgeon), also known as 'vocational skills'
core skills	general skills – such as communication, application of number, information technology, – which apply in any job area and are developed by your GNVQ course

multiple-choice questions

1   The definition of a public sector job is that it
  A   is open to anyone
  B   involves dealing with the public
  C   involves working for a government-controlled organisation
  D   means staying in the same department

2   The following type of job means that the person is self-employed
  A   a sole trader
  B   a company director
  C   a careers officer
  D   a policeman

3   A person wanting to become self-employed is MOST likely to approach
  A   an employment agency
  B   a recruitment agency
  C   a TEC
  D   a charity

For questions 4 to 6, match the core skills listed at the bottom of the page to the occupations listed below

  A   accountant
  B   computer programmer
  C   journalist

4   Information technology

5   Communication

6   Application of number

GNVQ UNIT 3
CONSUMERS AND CUSTOMERS

8 Consumers and customers

GNVQ SPECIFICATIONS
Element 3.1
Explain the importance of consumers and customers
performance criteria – a student must
1   describe the effect of consumers on sales of goods and services
2   identify and explain the buying habits of consumers with different characteristics
3   identify trends in consumer demand
4   produce graphics to illustrate the trends
5   explain causes of change in consumer demand for consumer goods and services
6   explain and give examples of the importance of customers to business organisations

what this chapter covers

This chapter shows you how consumers' buying habits affect what businesses produce, and the way those buying habits change over time.

what you will learn from this chapter

- consumers create demand for goods and services – they dictate to a major extent what businesses will produce

- consumers have many different characteristics – eg age, sex, where they live – and these will affect what they buy

- consumer demand will change over time as a result of a variety of factors, including the amount of income available and advertising pressure

- it is possible to trace trends in what consumers want and will buy – this helps businesses to make decisions about what to produce

- because customers (the people who buy) are essential to the survival of a business, they are given high priority in business objectives

the effects of consumers on businesses

consumers and customers

In this chapter we will be referring to *consumers* and *customers*, so we must first distinguish between these two words.

A *consumer* is a member of the general public who receives and makes use of goods and services. The *customer* is the individual who has to pay for the goods or services. These are not necessarily the same person. Take, for example, the child who is subjected to a barrage of TV advertisements for toys at weekend breakfast-time viewing. The child is the *consumer*, the poor parent who has to go off to buy the Barbie Doll is the *customer*.

creating consumer demand

As we saw in Chapter 2, businesses sell their products because there is a *demand* for them. We defined *demand* as:

the amount of a product that consumers want over a period of time

In the example given above the toy company has carefully classified a particular type of consumer (by age) and stimulated a *demand* for its product.

A business selling a product will need to be sure there is a *demand* for it. Demand can be for

- a consumer's *needs* – items that are essential, eg lavatory paper, bread
- a consumer's *wants* – items that the consumer can be persuaded to want to buy, eg luxury biscuits, a video

It is straightforward enough for a business to sell products that are needed. The skill lies in a business promoting products which the consumer can be *persuaded to want* and to buy.

consumer preferences

What the consumer wants will affect what businesses produce ...

- *weak demand* for a product will lead to a reduction in supply by businesses – there has been a dramatic fall in demand for fur goods, for example, because of campaigns against the killing of wild animals
- *strong demand*, on the other hand, leads to a rise in supply; fashion goods are a good example here – designer watches and designer jeans are sold at high prices and profit because businesses know the demand exists

Those same businesses will be watching consumer buying habits carefully for *changes* in demand, and will use advertising to *stimulate* demand.

STUDENT ACTIVITY 8.1
performance criterion 3.1.1

consumers and demand

Divide into small groups of three or four within the class and think of

(a)   products for which there is strong consumer demand

(b)   products for which there is weak consumer demand

(c)   reasons for strength and weakness in demand in these products

Report your findings back to the class for discussion.

reasons for changes in consumer demand

pc 3.1.5

Why should consumer demand change? We have already seen how preferences and fashion affect buying decisions. We now look at this area in more detail.

money to spend

'*Disposable income*' is the money households in the UK have available to spend after deduction of taxes (income tax and National Insurance) and pension contributions. This is a critical figure for producers of goods and services to watch. In 1993 it was £453.2 billion, an increase of £16.7 billion over the 1991 figure (see page 150).

confidence to spend

In times of economic recession (when the economy is not performing well), the confidence of consumers to spend money will decrease: they will borrow less and save more. Statistics show that from 1987 to 1989 the percentage of disposable income saved by households was negative (ie they spent more than they earned – by borrowing!), whereas in 1991 households saved over 2.5% of their disposable income. This trend should be worrying for producers.

the cost of living

Having more money to spend is not a lot of use if prices keep going up and the cost of living increases. In the UK the level of prices is measured by the Retail Prices Index (RPI) which measures the cost of a typical 'shopping basket' of goods and services. The cost is related by means of an index number to the cost in January 1987 (= 100). The RPI in January 1994 stood at 149.1. In short, on average goods cost 49.1% more in 1994 than they did in 1987, an average inflation rate of 7% per year.   If the amount of disposable income does not keep up with the cost of living, producers of goods and services are less likely to expect an increase in sales – there is less money for spending.

the population

Another factor affecting demand for goods and services is the number of people wanting to purchase them – the population. Producers pay a great deal of attention to not only the size of the population, but also the way it is made up, and where it lives. The different factors involved include:

population size

The growth in population size is slowing significantly: the population of the UK has grown by 50% since 1900 to over 57 million people, but since 1970 a lower birth rate has slowed the rate of growth.

an older population

The UK population is getting older: By 2021 nearly one in five of the population will be over 65 (compare this with only one in ten in 1951).

employment

It is clear that if the level of employment is high – ie people have jobs – then the amount of spending on consumer goods will be more than if there is high unemployment. Producers will also note that in times of high unemployment there will be an increase in demand for products and services which will occupy the time of the unemployed, for example videos and sports gear.

changing needs and wants

We have already seen that a consumer's 'need' is a basic necessity which must be fulfilled: food, housing, clothing. A 'want' is a desire which can be stimulated and fulfilled by a producer. For example a Barbie Doll and a Porsche are both 'toys' – their owners could hardly say that their purchase was an absolute necessity, however much they were *wanted*.

advertising

Producers not only react to the trends of taste and fashion, they also help to create them. Fashion is an unpredictable feature of consumer behaviour: you will know how dreadful people look in the clothes and hair-styles of ten years ago. Lifestyle can also be subject to fashion: healthy food, vegetarian diets, jogging are all part of the healthy person's lifestyle. No doubt some people would welcome back fish and chips and cream cakes if they were fashionable. The successful business not only follows fashion, it sets the trend by carefully planned advertising campaigns in the media. In this sense, businesses create demand.

STUDENT ACTIVITY 8.2
performance criterion 3.1.5

changing demand for goods and services

What effect would the trends listed below have on demand for goods and services? In each case state the reason for the change.

(a) a rise in population

(b) a rise in unemployment

(c) a rise in the inflation rate

(d) an increase in the amount of disposable income saved by households

(e) a health scare related to the consumption of pasta

(f) a report stating that the moderate consumption of red wine decreases the risk of heart disease

(g) a rise in the number of people aged over 65

(h) an economic recession

Your income/allowance is cut by 50%. Without conferring with your fellow-students,

(i) what items would you continue to buy?

(j) what items would you sacrifice?

(k) what does this say about your needs and your wants?

Now compare your findings with those of your fellow students. Would you change your mind about any items? What does this say about your behaviour as a consumer?

consumer classification and buying habits

pc 3.1.2

Consumers are interesting because they vary so much, both in their *type* and also in their *buying habits* – what they will buy. Producers spend much time and resources in *classifying* consumers into *market segments* so that they can direct their marketing effort towards the right people. There would little point, for example, trying to sell expensive holidays to people who are unemployed. Common classifications of consumers are by

• age

• sex/gender (him/her)

• geographical area

• lifestyle (fashion, taste and preferences)

We will look at all these in turn.

classification by age

Producers of goods carefully distinguish between different age groups when marketing their products, as we saw in the case of the Barbie doll. Commonly accepted age groups include:

age	buying group
0 – 10	child
11 – 17	teenager
18 – 35	young working person
36 – 59	mature working person
60 – 100	retired person

You may well be able to add to these classifications, or you may wish to change them.

STUDENT ACTIVITY 8.3
performance criterion 3.1.2

Core Skill 2.1

customer age groups

Divide into groups of three or four students and make lists of the products which are specifically aimed at the following age groups (for example – types of footwear, types of holiday, drinks):

(a) 11 - 17 years

(b) 18 - 35 years

(c) 60 + years

Then ...

(d) make a list of shops which sell products (eg clothes) for these age groups

Compile your results on a word processor and circulate copies to the rest of the class for discussion.

classification by sex (gender)

Although we apparently live in an age of sexual equality, there will always be differences between male and female consumer demand, and producers will always exploit those differences by marketing products 'for him' and products 'for her'. These differences can be obvious as in the clothing, cosmetics and perfumes industries. They can also be more subtle, as you should be able to find out in the next Student Activity.

products for him and for her

Divide again into groups of three or four students and find examples of the following products which are more attractive to one sex than to the other. Try not to argue too much! Compare your findings with those of other groups.

(a) models of small car, eg Nissan Micra, Vauxhall Corsa, the Mini

(b) brands of drink

(c) types of food

classification by social class

A common way of segmenting the market is by social class. Each group will have its own product needs and pattern of income and expenditure. The UK social classes are divided into letter groupings (A to E) as shown below. This classification has been drawn up by the National Readership Survey.

Social grouping and % of population	Social class	occupation type
A (4%)	Upper/upper middle class	higher managerial, professional, eg director of a large company, barrister
B (20%)	Middle class	intermediate managerial, professional, eg commercial manager, salaried accountant, health service manager
C1 (21%)	Lower middle class	junior managerial and supervisory, eg insurance clerk, nurse, shop manager
C2 (30%)	Skilled working class	skilled manual workers, eg electrician, fitter
D (17%)	Working class	semi-skilled and unskilled workers, eg warehouseman, driver, shop assistant
E (8%)	Subsistence level	the lowest paid and the unemployed

Normally these social groupings coincide with income groups, and are used extensively by organisations marketing different types of product.

classification by lifestyle

This type of classification is less specific than the examples of segmentation already given, and there are a number of different lifestyle classifications, most of them originating in the USA. The basis of this type of classification is to view each consumer as a 'type' which will combine elements of social class, personality and attitude. One example is the 'Values and Lifestyle' (VALS) approach which classes various types of adult into groups, including:

survivors & sustainers	driven by need – just managing to buy the basic commodities
belongers & achievers	driven by outside forces – influenced by others' opinions
individualists	driven by inside forces – they buy to satisfy their own inner needs

taste and fashion

Classification by *taste* is related to lifestyle. Taste is what you as an individual prefer when you are faced with a choice. You will know your own taste in music, clothes, food and drink. It is clearly the aim of any producer of goods and services to influence taste so that their products are purchased. Many producers of 'brand name' goods will even charge extra for their products when they become fashionable (think of the cost of some footwear!)

STUDENT ACTIVITY 8.5
performance criterion 3.1.2

taste and lifestyle

Write down under separate headings your own tastes in – be honest with yourself! –

* clothes
* food
* drink
* music

Now answer the following questions:

(a) To what extent are you influenced by what other people (friends, fellow students) like, and to what extent are you different?

(b) To what extent are you influenced by advertising?

(c) If you were faced with the choice between a brand name pair of jeans and a cheaper alternative from a cut-price store, which would you choose, and why?

(d) How would you define your lifestyle? Are you a survivor/sustainer, a belonger/achiever or an individualist?

classification by geographical area

Businesses are able to classify customers according to the type of area in which they live. Country and city areas will clearly have different types of consumer living in them. Classification is also possible by postcode. You will know that in your locality certain areas are better than others. One form of computer database classification is ACORN (<u>A</u> <u>C</u>lassification <u>O</u>f <u>R</u>esidential <u>N</u>eighbourhoods). As a postcode covers a relatively small number of households, it is possible to classify each postcode area into a specific neighbourhood "type". There are eleven basic ACORN types, for example: older housing of intermediate status, modern family housing (higher incomes), poor quality older terraced housing, better-off council estates, and so on ...

ACORN is one of many postcode analysis systems used by businesses that mail direct to the customer. One of the very latest developments is "Portrait," the result of a collaboration between lifestyle database company NDL International, and specialist financial information provider, Infolink Decision Services. In what both companies describe as a "revolutionary breakthrough," "Portrait" will combine, at postcode level, different types of data including credit searches, household types, unemployment statistics, births and deaths, with lifestyle data from 11 million households.

consumer classifications – the UK regions

Producers also look carefully at the statistics relating to regional differences in consumption of goods. Some examples are obvious: tripe sells better in the North of England than in the Home Counties, haggis sells better in Scotland than in Surrey. The following table shows the percentage a household spends on various commodities and services in the different regions

percentages of household expenditure by commodity, service and region (1990-1991)

area	housing	alcohol & tobacco	leisure activities
South East	20.0	5.2	14.3
East Anglia	20.2	4.9	12.9
South West	19.4	5.2	13.6
West Midlands	20.0	6.1	11.1
East Midlands	18.6	5.8	13.1
Yorkshire & Humberside	17.8	7.1	12.8
North West	17.9	7.5	13.5
North	17.2	7.7	11.6
England (average)	19.3	6.0	13.0
Wales	16.3	6.8	12.9
Scotland	15.4	7.3	13.0
Northern Ireland	15.3	6.0	11.0

SOURCE: Family Expenditure Survey – extract

STUDENT ACTIVITY 8.6
performance criterion 3.1.2

regional differences in consumer spending

Study the figures set out in the table on the previous page.

(a) Examine the spending pattern on housing in the UK. Account for the differences between:
   • the North and the South of England
   • England, Wales, Scotland and Northern Ireland

(b) If you were a producer of cigarettes or alcoholic drink, where would you do best? Why?

(c) Find out from another source which country in the UK has the highest incidence of heart disease. How could you explain this from the table set out above?

trends in consumer demand

`pc 3.1.2`

a changing market – marketing research

Producers clearly have to be very aware of the different classifications of consumer – the *segmentation* of the market. Different types of consumer will require different types of product, eg different types of car, clothing, holidays. Producers are also aware of changing patterns of consumer behaviour: certain products will stop selling well, other products will suddenly 'take off'. The successful producer will be able to anticipate these trends by finding out what the consumer needs (or no longer needs), and changing his product range accordingly. Information about what is happening in the mind of the consumer is gathered in two ways – a process known as market research:

• *primary research* is communicating with the consumers – in the street, over the telephone, through the post – by means of questionnaires

• *secondary research*, sometimes known as desk research, involves looking at published material – reference books, statistics such as the tables on the previous page – and gaining an insight into trends relating to consumers' income and expenditure

sources of information

One source of statistical information is the Government's Central Statistical Office which publishes through HMSO a number of annual reports, including:

• *Regional Trends*

- *Family Spending* (a publication compiled from the annual Family Expenditure Survey)
- *Social Trends*

These publications are kept in most college and reference libraries, and make fascinating reading about the nation's habits. *Social Trends* in particular is essential reading if you want to understand the patterns of income and consumer spending. It runs to over 200 pages and covers areas such as population changes, household and family income and spending and leisure activities.

We will now look at the consumer trends which are important to producers of goods and services – the trends relating to income and spending.

household income

In the table set out below we show how household income (the money earned or received by households in the UK) has changed from 1971 to 1993. The important figure is disposable income: this is the amount of money households have left after deduction of taxes and pensions. This is the money which is available for spending on goods and services. The figures quoted are billions of pounds (note that 1 billion = 1,000 million).

Remember that over this period inflation reduced the value of money, so the increases are not as dramatic as they might at first sight appear.

UK household income (1971 - 1993) (£bn)				
	1971	*1981*	*1991*	*1993*
Income received	44.7	202.1	502.1	546.8
Disposable income	36.4	162.4	409.4	453.2

SOURCE: Social Trends 25, 1995 © Crown Copyright

STUDENT ACTIVITY 8.7
performance criterion 3.1.3

Core Skill 2.3

Using a spreadsheet charting facility:

(a) construct a line graph or bar chart showing the change in total household income from 1971 to 1993

(b) construct a line graph or bar chart showing the change in total disposable income from 1971 to 1993

What do the charts show? What are the implications for consumer spending?

consumer spending

Producers will also take note of consumer *spending* patterns. Apart from the basic products such as bread and toilet paper, where demand remains fairly steady, demand can fluctuate:

- in the *short-term* – say over six months for items such as Cup Final tickets, CD singles, or the current year's fashion in swimwear

- in the *long-term* for items such as consumer goods, eg a decline in demand for black vinyl LPs and a rise in demand for microwave ovens

Producers will have to find out about these changes in demand by looking at statistics and carrying out customer surveys. They can then change the range of products they *supply*. The Student Activity which follows illustrates the difference between short and long-term trends in consumer demand for music.

STUDENT ACTIVITY 8.8
performance criterion 3.1.3

the demand for music

Study the three charts and answer the questions on the next page.

SINGLES – THE TOP TEN

1	Boom Boom Boom	Outhere Brothers
2	Shy Guy	Diana King
3	Alright/Time	Supergrass
4	Kiss from a Rose/I'm Alive	Seal
5	In the Summertime	Shaggy
6	Hold me,Thrill me, Kiss me, Kill me	U2
7	A Girl like You	Edwyn Collins
8	3 is Family	Dana Dawson
9	I'll be there for You - You are all I Need to get by	Method Man
10	You do Something to Me	Paul Weller

ALBUMS – THE TOP TEN

1	These Days	Bon Jovi
2	I Should Coco	Supergrass
3	History: Past Present & Future Book1	Michael Jackson
4	The Show, the Afterparty, the Hotel	Jodeci
5	Stanley Road	Paul Weller
6	The Colour of my Love	Celine Dion
7	Picture this	Wet Wet Wet
8	Singles	Alison Moyet
9	Definitely Maybe	Oasis
10	No need to Argue	Cranberries

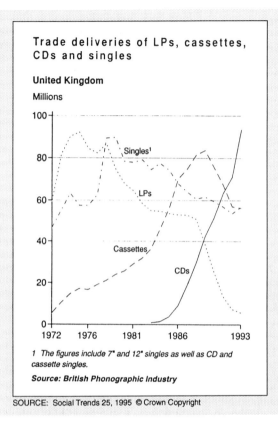

Trade deliveries of LPs, cassettes, CDs and singles

United Kingdom

Millions

1 The figures include 7" and 12" singles as well as CD and cassette singles.

Source: British Phonographic Industry

SOURCE: Social Trends 25, 1995 © Crown Copyright

questions

1 Which chart shows the shortest period of consumer demand? How long do you estimate the demand will last? What are the implications for the producer of these products?

2 Which chart shows long-term consumer trends? What are the reasons for the trends shown? How will the producers of these goods react to this trend?

3 How does the remaining chart fit into the picture of consumer demand? Why is it different from the first?

STUDENT ACTIVITY 8.10
performance criterion 3.1.4

Core Skill 2.3

producing graphics to illustrate trends

Consumer trends can be best seen if they are shown in the form of graphs or charts. The chart shown above is a good example. If you have access to a computer graphing package or a spreadsheet which will produce charts, show the following figures in graphical form. Comment on the consumer trends shown by the graph or chart you produce – what do they say about changes in disposable income and lifestyle?

percentage of total household expenditure			
	1971	*1981*	*1991*
Tobacco	4.8	3.6	2.7
Entertainment/education/recreation	8.8	9.4	10.0

SOURCE: Social Trends 25, 1995 © Crown Copyright

the importance of customers

pc 3.1.6

'the customer is king'

One of the current current 'buzz-words' in business is the saying that "the customer is king." Many business organisations now realise that a 'customer focus' is essential for a number of reasons:

income

Customers bring *income* to a business – without sales a business cannot *survive*, as it will not be able to make a *profit*!

keeping customers – repeat sales

It is important that a business keeps its customers, and that they come back again and again. A recent trend for some shops is to issue 'loyalty cards' (eg the Tesco Club Card) which accumulate 'points' each time a sale is made and provide discounts for loyal customers.

providing information

Customers are also important to businesses because they provide information about what customers want in the way of products. They also provide valuable feedback about product quality and customer service (see page 199). Businesses will often give questionnaires to customers or encourage them to fill in comment forms.

STUDENT ACTIVITY 8.10
performance criterion 3.1.6

the customer is king – a true story

Someone recently telephoned the customer services department of a well-known public power supply company to arrange a fitter to come to mend a faulty appliance. The girl on the telephone was clearly not fully trained for the job and was rude and impatient. When the fitter arrived, this was mentioned to him and he replied "I'm not surprised – we employ monkeys and we pay peanuts!"

Write down in numbered points what is wrong with the attitude of the company. Why do you think that customers are so important to a business?

EVIDENCE COLLECTION ASSIGNMENT 8

consumers and customers

Element 3.1

introduction

This assignment investigates how consumers create demand for goods and services, and why customers are so important for a business. It also investigates and illustrates trends in the demand for three products. The assignment should be presented as a word-processed report and use computer-generated graphs and charts where appropriate.

tasks

pcs 3.1.1 & 6

1   **Write** an introductory section stating

(a) why customers are so important to a business

(b) how consumers can create demand and cause changes in demand for goods and services

This introduction should be short and simple, but should use examples of products (goods *and* services) wherever possible to illustrate the points made.

pcs 3.1.2 - 5

2   **Choose** THREE products from the tables shown below

Households with consumer durables

Great Britain   Percentages

	1972	1981	1991	1993
Colour television	} 93	{ 74	95	96
Black and white television only		23	4	3
Telephone	42	75	88	90
Washing machine	66	78	87	88
Deep-freezer/fridge freezer	..	49	83	87
Video recorder	..	..	68	73
Microwave	..	..	55	62
Tumble drier	..	23	48	49
Compact disc player	..	..	27	39
Dishwasher	..	4	14	16

Source: Office of Population Censuses and Surveys.

SOURCE: Social Trends 25, 1995 © Crown Copyright

Cinema attendance[1]: by age

Great Britain				Percentages
	1984	1986	1991	1993
7-14	73	87	80	93
15-24	59	82	88	90
25-34	49	65	70	82
35-44	45	60	70	73
45 and over	13	25	39	46
All aged 7 and over	38	53	61	69

1 Percentage claiming to 'ever go' to the cinema.

Source: Cinema Advertising Association; Cinema and Video Industry Audience Research

SOURCE: Social Trends 25, 1995 © Crown Copyright

Write a summary which:

• describes the three chosen products
• describes the changes in buying habits of consumers
• describes the characteristics of the consumers (their types)
• gives reasons for the changes in buying habits and changes in demand
• suggests how demand for the three products may change over the next two to three years
• uses graphs and charts to illustrate the trends

Note that the figures given here present only part of the picture. You will need to do further research into the products themselves and obtain further statistics to support the figures you have here. Your tutor will give you credit for gathering and evaluating information from other written sources and for carrying out interviews with people who work in the relevant industries.

chapter summary and key terms

- Consumers create demand for goods and services; changes in their buying habits cause changes in demand.

- The causes of change in consumer demand include the amount of income consumers have to spend, their confidence in spending it, the cost of living, changing needs and wants, and the pressures of advertising.

- Consumers can be classified in their buying habits in terms of their age, sex, where they live, and their lifestyle.

- Producers of goods and services have to be very aware of trends in consumer demand. They achieve this through marketing research, looking at consumer income and both short-term and long-term spending patterns.

- Customers are essential to the survival and profitability of a business: they provide income, and information in the form of feedback about product quality and customer service.

key terms

consumer	a person who uses a product
customer	a person who buys a product
demand	the amount of a product that consumers want over a period of time
disposable income	the money households in the UK have to spend after the deduction of taxes and pensions
market segment	a group of consumers in the population classified according to various types, eg by age and lifestyle
lifestyle	a 'type' of consumer in terms of personality, attitude and taste
postcode classification	consumers grouped according to postcode, ie by the type of area in which they live
marketing research	research into market trends and consumer behaviour by means of customer questionnaires and analysis of statistics

multiple-choice questions

1   A supplier of a product is likely to increase production if
    A   demand is weak
    B   demand is strong
    C   disposable income falls
    D   taxes rise

2   Demand for a product is likely to increase if
    A   disposable income falls
    B   the cost of living rises
    C   unemployment rises
    D   advertising increases

3   Market segmentation can best be described as
    A   research by questionnaire
    B   research into statistics
    C   classification of producers into types
    D   division of consumers into types

For questions 4 to 6, match the products listed at the bottom of the page to the consumer classifications listed below

    A   age
    B   sex
    C   social class

4   exotic holidays

5   exotic perfumes

6   baby buggies

9 Promotional material

GNVQ SPECIFICATIONS
Element 3.2
Plan, design and produce promotional material
performance criteria – a student must
1   identify and give examples of types of promotions used in marketing goods and services
2   describe constraints on the content of promotional materials
3   plan to produce promotional materials to promote particular goods or services
4   explain the purpose of the planned promtional materials
5   design and produce promotiona materials and use them to promote goods or services
6   evaluate how successful the promotional materials were in achieving the stated purpose

what this chapter covers

This chapter looks at the ways business organisations promote their goods and services; the assignment analyses promotional materials and gets you to plan and design your own.

what you will learn from this chapter

- promotion of a product is not just advertising in the media, it also includes point of sale (in the shop) presentation, sponsorship and running competitions

- the purpose of promoting products is to create sales by communicating a message, influencing customers' perceptions of a product and providing information

- a plan for promoting products will deal with the timescale , the people needed, the materials and equipment involved and the overall cost

- there are various constraints on the content of promotional materials, some laid down in law, and some exercised by bodies such as Trading Standards

promotion

Promotion is communicating the benefits of a product to the consumer

Promotion is an essential element of marketing; it is one of the four 'Ps' which make up the marketing process, the others being Product, Price and Place. It is sometimes assumed that promotion is the same as advertising. People often think of a major product promotion as being a combination of TV commercials, roadside hoardings, and newspaper adverts. Advertising is, in fact, only part of the process of promotion which brings the product to the attention of the consumer. The overall promotion process involves:

- advertising – informing the public about your product
- branding – creating an image of your product at the point of sale
- packaging – presenting the product in an attractive way at the point of sale
- media publicity
- special promotions
- sponsorship
- competitions for consumers

advertising

Advertising may be defined as:

a selling message for a product directed at the consumer

Advertising involves :

- identifying the right market segment(s) for the product – as discussed in the last chapter – and making sure that the group(s) of consumers targeted need or want the product
- identifying the right media – newspapers, magazines, TV, radio, cinema, leaflets
- creating the right message
- getting the timing right (eg advertising sunshine holidays in winter!)
- getting the cost right – making sure that you are getting value for money for your promotion

We will look at the advertising process in more detail later in the chapter.

point of sale presentation – branding

Branding may be defined as:

identifying a product in the minds of consumers by creating a name or logo for that product which will persuade the consumer to buy it

Examples of branding include:

- a product name which has achieved wide recognition, eg Coca-Cola, Persil, Andrex, Whiskas

- using the manufacturer's name as a byword for quality , eg Kelloggs, Heinz, BMW

- using the retailer's name to denote quality or value for money, eg St Michael products from Marks & Spencer, Sainsburys and Tescos 'own brands'

People buy branded goods because they know what they are getting. There have been bitter disputes about branding, particularly when 'own brands' from the supermarkets have copied the packaging (colour and shape) of the major independent brands. Next time you are shopping in a supermarket such as Tescos or Sainsburys, compare 'Head and Shoulders' shampoo, instant coffee or Cola drink with the shop brand.

whose brands are these?

point of sale presentation – packaging

Packaging may be defined as:

the way a product is packed and presented

Packaging therefore means more than just the box or wrapper a product is sold in – it involves all aspects of presentation. Packaging is an essential part of promotion in that it gives to the consumer the right image of the product. This can involve:

- the shape and size and general appearance

- colour (look at the use of white for hygiene products)

- ease of use (can it be opened easily – sometimes a problem with modern packaging!)

- environmental factors – is the material biodegradable?

STUDENT ACTIVITY 9.1
performance criterion 3.2.1

promotion at the point of sale

Investigate your local supermarket for evidence of the use of branding and packaging as means of promoting goods. Choose two products which are available both as:

* brand names – ie of the producer or the product
* 'own brand' names, ie the product bears the name of the supermarket

Suitable examples might include oven chips, breakfast cereals, shampoos, instant coffee, ketchup, Cola

In each case:

(a) state how the use of the brand name helps to promote the product

(b) note the similarities between the brand name and the 'own brand' products

(c) explain how the packaging of the product helps to promote it – eg shape, colour, design

(d) say whether you think it is right that a brand name product should be 'copied' in this way

publicity and public relations

Publicity means appearing in the news. Good publicity is always the objective of any producer of goods and services, and will help greatly with promotion – for example, the lady climber rescued in the Scottish Highlands, who when dug out of the snow, said 'I could just do with a glass of Guinness.'

Public relations, on the other hand, is the function within a business which looks after its public image. It is expensive to run, but is essential for the promotion of its products.

promotions and competitions

Promotions involve a business marketing a specific product, or range of products, by using special offers and techniques which will attract the interest of the consumer. These methods can include:

* money off – two for the price of one, coupons, bulk packs

* competitions – always attractive to the public – for example completing a slogan

* extra benefits – eg 'air miles'

sponsorship

Sponsorship is a well-known means of promoting the name of an organisation. Many sports and arts organisations rely on support from sponsors: in return for a money payment, the name of the sponsor is mentioned prominently on publicity material and at the sponsored event. The best form of sponsorship for a business is where there is TV coverage. Many televised sports events carry the sponsor's name prominently. Many football teams are sponsored, for example:

- Liverpool, sponsored by Carlsberg
- Manchester United, sponsored by Sharp
- Arsenal, sponsored by JVC

Famous sports personalities are also sponsored, and as part of the deal wear clothes printed with the sponsor's name, or use equipment made by the sponsor: for example Boris Becker and Puma racquets, Andre Agassi and Nike footwear and clothing. Arts organisations also receive generous sponsorship.

Not all sponsorship receives such prominent publicity. Many businesses have budgets for sponsoring small local events: concerts, plays, fetes and fun runs. The sponsorship principle remains the same.

STUDENT ACTIVITY 9.2
performance criterion 3.2.1

promotions and sponsorship

task 1

Investigate examples of sales promotions in local shops and the local and national press. Collect two examples each of:

- free gifts (with the product, or sendaway gifts, or benefits, eg 'airmiles')
- 'money off' or '15% extra' type promotions
- competitions

State how effective you think each type of promotion is in promoting the product or producer.

task 2

Investigate examples of local and national sponsorship. Divide into pairs in the class. Each pair will choose one sponsored event. Without conferring:

- one student will assume the role of sponsor and draw up a list of the benefits he or she expects to receive from sponsoring a specific event
- the other student will assume the role of the sponsored organisation and prepare a list of the advantages that can be gained from sponsoring that organisation

the purposes of promotion

What are the purposes of promoting a product? This may seem an obvious question, but it is an important one. The purposes include:

- communicating a message to consumers
- providing information
- influencing consumers' perceptions of the product (ie persuading them it is what they want)
- to get them to buy the product!

communicating a message – creating demand

If you observe a child watching TV adverts for toys, or see adults standing around in W H Smith reading specialist magazines off the racks, you will appreciate that both groups are being fed images which create a demand. The child will say 'I want that' after each advert, and the adult will think something similar. The methods of creating demand include:

- suggesting that purchase of the product will enhance the owner's image – eg sexy adverts for cars
- stressing all the benefits of a product – the AA man who will rescue you, the insurance company which will act so swiftly when you have a disaster, the Yellow Pages which will get you out of a fix, and so on
- striking ways of bringing the producer to the attention of the public – animals (Dulux dog, Lloyds Bank horse); shocking images (Benetton messy new-born babies, kissing nuns, AIDS victims)

providing information

It is essential that the message given to consumers contains enough information about the product. The amount of information can vary with public awareness of the product. If a product is very well-known, such as some brands of drink, very little information is necessary – the brand name sells itself. If the product is less well-known, more product information (eg price, where it can be bought) will be necessary.

influencing consumer perceptions

The consumer must be shown through advertising and other promotional methods, such as sponsorship that the producer has a 'good' image in the eyes of the public:

- it must provide a quality product
- it must offer a high standard of customer service
- it must show that it 'cares' for society and for the environment

creating sales

Translating demand for a product into an actual sale is a prime objective of a promotional campaign. Large businesses which promote brand names, eg Persil, Kit Kat, monitor very closely the success of their advertising by comparing the amount they spend on promotion and the level of sales. Demand can only be translated into sales if:

- the public know where to obtain the product
- the product is actually in stock and prominently displayed
- the product is of a consistently good quality

purposes of promotion

Investigate promotional campaigns by watching TV adverts and reading the newspapers. Find and write down examples of:

(a) Adverts which create demand for a specific product – what means do they use, how will the products benefit the consumer?

(b) Shocking adverts which catch your attention because they are odd – how successful are they?

(c) Adverts which promote the name of the organisation rather than any specific product – have you heard of the organisation in every case?

(d) Adverts which affect consumer perceptions and give the organisation a specific image, eg of quality, friendliness, environmental or social concern.

promotion through the media

pc 3.2.1

how big is the business?

Before you read the next few pages, it is essential to appreciate that few businesses can afford all the promotion methods outlined. Take for example, the small business. The majority of businesses in the UK are small businesses, and clearly will not be able to afford TV, cinema, national newpaper or magazine advertising. They will not have marketing departments – the sole trader, for example will be the marketing department! Businesses such as these will have to use all their ingenuity to obtain maximum results from limited resources, eg computer databases, publishing programs, free publicity. This aspect of promotion is explored further in the Evidence Collection Assignment which follows this chapter. The Exercise will enable you as a small business owner to plan your own promotional campaign.

the range of the media

In this section we look at the use of the different media to promote goods and services. *Media means 'the means for getting your message across.'* The media include:

- paper-based material: newspapers and magazines, posters, leaflets
- visual and broadcast – TV and radio

The business planning a promotion campaign will either carry out the exercise itself – if it is a small or medium-sized business – or employ an agency to handle the advertising. An advertising agency is a specialist business which will research, design and arrange the advertising.

It is the job of the planner to obtain the right 'mix' of advertising media. The planner will research the type of customer targeted and use the appropriate media. For example if the product and target customer is 'up-market', an up-market newspaper would be used for an advertisement. The planner can work out how best to reach the target market by referring to directories such as BRAD (British Rate and Data) which sets out what type of consumers read which newspapers, watch certain TV programmes, and so on. It also sets out the cost of the advertising.

We will now explain the various methods of media promotion and discuss their advantages and disadvantages.

newspapers

Newspapers, despite the influence of TV, are still widely read. It is estimated that 60% of the population reads a daily newspaper. Newspapers are published both on a daily basis and on a Sunday. National newspapers are normally subdivided in two categories, all with different readerships.

tabloids

Newspapers such as The Sun and The Daily Mirror cater for the mass market and include many articles on personalities and sport. The name tabloid refers to their size: they are smaller than the 'up-market' broadsheets.

broadsheets

The larger newspapers such as The Times and The Independent cater for the reader who is more interested in politics, economics and business developments, although these newspapers are not without their sports pages and gossip columns.

It should not be forgotten that many newspapers are local, and are widely read in the locality in which they are distributed. Some are distributed free of charge, and rely on advertisers for their income.

advantages of newspapers	disadvantages of newspapers
many people read them	people ignore the advertisements
they are cheap	they are thrown away
different papers are published for different consumer groups	people tend to forget what they see very quickly

magazines

If you walk into a large stationery store you will be faced by racks and racks of different magazines; it can sometimes be a major task to find the one you want. If you consider that in addition to these titles there are many magazines which are mailed direct to the consumer, you will appreciate that magazines and journals represent a major opportunity to advertisers. Magazines fall into a number of categories:

general interest
Many general interest magazines are targeted at market segments differentiated by sex or age, eg Woman, Just Seventeen, 19.

specialist
The bulk of the racks at W H Smith are taken up by magazines for car enthusiasts, gardeners, hi-fi buffs, wine drinkers, stamp collectors and so on. These magazines are ideal for the advertiser of specialist products.

advantages of magazines	disadvantages of magazines
they are not thrown away so quickly	they are not published so frequently
better for reaching a specialist market	fewer people read them
they look better – more glossy	they are more expensive

posters

A poster is essentially a sheet of paper with a message. Posters come in different sizes and appear on roadside hoardings, where they gain maximum impact, on buses, trains, stations and generally any flat surface the bill poster can find.

advantages of posters	disadvantages of posters
high impact	seen for only a short space of time
many people see them	people get fed up with them
placed in locations where people wait (eg tube station)	they can be defaced easily

TV

Television advertising has become a sophisticated art form, and also very expensive. It is seen by millions of viewers every day. It has a major impact: advertising catch phrases pass into the language ('I know a man who does') and tunes from adverts are whistled and hummed nationwide.

advantages of TV	disadvantages of TV
mass viewing	people get up and make a cup of coffee when the adverts come on
high impact	very expensive to produce and screen
repetition of message	fast-forwarding on video'd programmes (think of the times you have wanted to fast forward adverts during a *live* programme!)

commercial radio

Radio is a very effective advertising medium. People can listen to the radio while doing a wide variety of things – eating, driving, lying in bed, working on school or college assignments! Adverts may be broadcast on any of the commercial radio stations which operate either on a national basis or on a local basis. The BBC's five channels, of course, do not carry advertising (except for their own programmes). You will know how many commercial radio stations are available by tuning acros the different wavebands. Local radio is particularly useful for promoting local products and events, while national commercial radio is an excellent medium for reaching a particular market segment. Classic FM, for example, has been very successful in reaching and increasing the market segment which listens to classical music. Picture in your mind the sort of person (ie social class, income bracket, age) who enjoys Mozart, and you will appreciate what we mean by market segmentation.

advantages of radio	disadvantages of radio
large number of listeners	people listen to the radio as a background
cheap to produce and broadcast	recall by the listener may be difficult (eg trying to remember a telephone number quoted)
easy to target consumer groups	limitations of using specialist stations (eg heavy metal music lover is unlikely to listen to Classic FM)

media promotion

Investigate the methods of media promotion used for one or more of the following products or services (in each case choose a specific product):

(a) a soft drink

(b) a local fast food outlet

(c) car insurance

(d) a type of doll

In each case analyse the types of consumer (market segments) the product/service is designed for, and state how successful the chosen methods of promotion are in reaching the consumer.

planning the promotion

pc 3.2.3

resources needed

Any organisation, however small or large, needs resources in order to produce promotional materals. These resources are:

time and people

Any business will need to allocate time and people to plan and produce its promotional materials. The larger business, eg a public limited company, will have marketing and advertising departments to research what consumers need and to advertise products. These departments are clearly expensive to run, and the staff hours allocated must be justified in terms of sales and profits from the products. A sole trader, on the other hand, may already be working 12 hours a day on production and sales, and the promotional side of the business may suffer as a result. The solution is either the business owner giving himself/ herself time to think out how to promote the product, or the use of outside help, eg a design or advertising bureau.

materials and equipment

As we have already mentioned, the extent of the resources available for promoting products and services will vary with the size of the business. A large business will have design facilities, computers, video equipment and all the resources necessary for making presentations and staging exhibitions. A small business will have fewer resources, but can make up for these shortcomings with the use of computer technology. The fall in price of office computers, printers and software mean that a sole trader, given the necessary skill, can easily produce paper-based promotional materials and can post it out.

financial resources

Any business planning its expenditure will draw up budgets – estimates of costs for various areas of operation – production, manpower and sales/advertising. A business will also allocate a certain sum each year for sales and advertising. The larger the business, the more sophisticated the planning will be, and the greater the return expected on each type of media used. After any advertising campaign a business will monitor its sales closely to see if the advertising is effective – whether it results in a rise in sales.

making the most of resources

A business does not necessarily have to rely on an expensive advertising campaign in order to maximise its sales. It may not, in any event, be able to afford such a campaign. Many small businesses (and most businesses *are* small businesses) use promotional techniques which cost little or even nothing. Here are some suggestions for a promotional 'checklist' for someone running a small business – you will see how important 'image' is:

- have a professionally produced business card which will impress

- ensure that your stationery (letterhead, invoices etc) is professionally produced

- print leaflets which can be posted through letterboxes, left at the local Enterprise Agency etc

- make contacts to spread knowledge of your product/service in the local community (try local Chambers of Commerce, TECs, Business Clubs)

- arrange for the local newspaper to publish an article about you when you launch a new product or open new premises – it will not cost you anything

- hand out 'giveaways', eg scratchpads, coffee mats (see right)

- ensure you are in directories such as the local Yellow Pages, and Thompsons

- help with the sponsorship of local events

a promotional coffee mat produced by a mailing house

constraints on promotional materials

legal and ethical issues

Advertisers are very influential. When consumers watch TV adverts or look at roadside hoardings

* they tend to believe what they see – they assume the facts given are correct, eg a car will accelerate from 0 to 60 mph in 10 seconds

* they are affected emotionally by what they see – they can be distressed or offended by what they consider to be an unpleasant picture, eg a dying AIDS victim

Advertisers therefore have a dual responsibility not to mislead and not to offend. In the UK the law sets out legal constraints on the way facts are presented, while voluntary codes of practice adopted by the advertising industry cover both the factual content and the emotional content by means of ethical constraints. 'Ethical' means relating to generally accepted standards of what is right and what is wrong. Most people would consider that the following were not ethical:

* whisky adverts for children

* adverts promoting cigarettes for a healthy lifestyle

* a poster showing a nun wearing a bikini

These adverts would not be against the law, but would be prohibited by the voluntary codes of conduct of the advertising industry. We will now look at both these areas in more detail.

legal constraints

If an advertiser is found to have broken the law, the advertiser can be taken to court and prosecuted, normally through the Trading Standards Departments operated through the local authorities, and controlled by the Office of Fair Trading (set up by the Government). Examples of legal constraints include:

* the *Trades Descriptions Acts* 1968 and 1972 – these make it an offence for anyone to give a false description of goods or to give a false indication as to price

* the *Consumer Protection Act* 1987 makes it an offence for a business to give a misleading statement about the price of goods or services

* the *Sale of Goods Act* 1979 states that the goods sold must be 'as described', ie as stated by the shop or as advertised

You will see that all these legal constraints refer to factual content of an advertisement. If a consumer or consumer group objects to an advertisement on any other grounds, eg that they find it morally offensive, they will have no legal basis to their claim.

voluntary codes of conduct

There are various codes of conduct which cover different types of advertising. A code of conduct is essentially a series of rules which advertisers have agreed amongst themselves. The rules are not legally binding, but any advertiser that broke them would find it difficult to get the advert published or broadcast. Voluntary controlof advertising is carried out as follows:

- the *Advertising Standards Authority* (ASA) monitors press and poster advertisements for legality, decency, honesty and truthfulness
- the *British Code of Advertising Practice* is a voluntary agreement by advertisers supervised by the ASA
- broadcast adverts are controlled by three statutory bodies – the *Broadcast Complaints Commission, the Broadcasting Standards Council* and the *Independent Television Commission*
- the *Broadcast Advertising Clearance Centre* 'vets' all advertising copy before it can be screened

In an attempt to clarify its position, the Committee of Advertising Practice issued a new *Code of Advertising Practice* (CAP) in February 1995. The new rules covered alcohol, children, decency, distance selling, environmental claims, health and beauty, motoring, sales promotions and slimming. The code comes under the ASA for supervision.

Despite these codes of conduct there are advertisements which always manage to offend people. Complaints about these advertisements may be sent to the Advertising Standards Authority (ASA) an independent body which investigates the offending advertisements and takes action if it thinks it necessary.

STUDENT ACTIVITY 9.5
performance criterion 3.2.2

control of advertising

task 1

What law (or laws) would protect you in the following situations?

(a) You order a pair of jeans from a mail order catalogue. You ask for a light blue pair. They send you a dark blue pair.

(b) You buy a watch from a shop. The display information says it is waterproof. You wear it in the shower and it stops.

(c) You buy a walkman advertised as being 'half-price at £49.99 – previously £94.99'.

Advertisers' health claims provoke flood of complaints

BY ALEXANDRA FREAN, MEDIA CORRESPONDENT

ADVERTISEMENTS which make dubious and unfounded health claims for slimming pills, nicotine patches or muscle-building capsules last year attracted the most complaints to the Advertising Standards Authority.

In its annual report, published today, the ASA said complaints about the portrayal of women in advertisements had also increased, reversing a general decline over the previous three years in "sexy" poster, television and press campaigns.

Launching the report, Sir Timothy Raison, the authority's chairman, said: "Our main concern now is that there are still some media which have been willing to publish advertisements that ought not to be published.

"It would be regrettable if willingness to breach the rules in a few areas damaged the generally very good name of the industry's self-regulatory system as a whole," Sir Timothy said.

Despite a rigorous campaign by the advertising authority and a crackdown by the Office of Fair Trading against manufacturers making spurious and untested claims for health-related products, these advertisements persist, he said. According to the report, complaints in this area rose 6 per cent to 569 last year.

In a survey of 20 national press titles last July, the ASA found 202 advertisments for so-called health products which broke its code.

One advertisement for muscle-building capsules promised "big arms, firm chest defined abdominals, powerful legs".

Another advertisement suggested that lying on a vibrating table could help people to lose weight.

A series of advertisments early in the year for nicotine patches, which claimed to help people to give up smoking, but which had not been licensed or tested, prompted scores of complaints. These gave rise to advertisements for several similar "alternative" products, such as slimming, vitamin C and primrose oil patches, all of which were untested.

"The fact is, none of these products can make people thin overnight or stop them smoking on their own and that needs to be made clear," a spokeswoman for the authority said.

Complaints about the portrayal of women rose by nearly 200 per cent to 536, although only 111 were upheld. These included a campaign for the Vauxhall Corsa car featuring supermodels and an advertisement for Andrex moist toilet tissue, which pictured a woman's buttocks.

A spokeswoman said that while there appeared to be less gratuitous female nudity in advertisements, there was a growing use of sexual innuendo, which many women found offensive.

Many women found the press campaign for Linn Hi Fi patronising.

The authority said that more attention needed to be paid to direct mail promotions, to prevent mailshots being sent to people who had died, and to promotions on the front pages of newspapers to attract new readers which failed to indicate substantial conditions before purchase.

There was a small drop, however, in the total number of complaints in 1993, from 10,688 to 9,603.

task 2 Core Skill 2.4

Read carefully the press cutting (taken from The Times, 7 March 1994), refer to the text in this chapter where necessary, and answer the following questions:

(a) how many complaints did the ASA receive in 1992 and in 1993?

(b) what were the two main subjects for complaint?

(c) What particular products were involved?

(d) How were the products promoted?

(e) Would you agree with the objections? If not, why not?

(f) how many adverts in July's survey were found to have broken the code?

(g) What other body can control advertising, and what are its powers?

task 3 Core Skill 2.1

Devise a simple questionnaire and conduct a survey of current advertising among your fellow students and friends. Find out:

(a) what percentage of people find some advertising offensive

(b) what they find offensive

(c) what they think should be done about it

Write a short report summarising your findings.

EVIDENCE COLLECTION ASSIGNMENT 9

a promotional plan

Element 3.2

introduction

In this assignment you should investigate individually three different types of promotion and then as a member of a team plan a promotion and present it to an audience.

task 1
pcs 3.2.1-2

Choose THREE different types of promotion including an advert and a sponsored event *and* a point of sale promotion or a competition. You are to produce a short word-processed report analysing the three promotions. Remember the promotion could be for a manufactured item or a service. Your report should describe:

- each product (item or service)
- how it is being promoted (try and give a timescale and geographical coverage)
- how the promotion is controlled both by law (eg Trades Descriptions Acts) and by voluntary code of practice (eg the 1995 Code of Advertising Practice)
- a brief evaluation of how effective you think the promotion is

task 2
pcs 3.2.3-6

In this task you are to form teams of three or four to draft a plan for the promotion of ONE product (a manufactured item or a service), and then carry out a presentation of the plan to the whole class or to the tutor. The plan could involve:

- an advertising campaign for a product
- a sponsored event
- a competition to promote goods or services

The plan should:

- state the purpose of the promotion
- set out a timescale
- state the resources required – people, materials and equipment
- estimate the cost of the promotion
- include the materials you are going to use – posters, leaflets, video tapes, audio tapes, computer-generated material – as appropriate to the type of promotion

After the presentation each team should hold a discussion to evaluate the success of the promotional material:

- as the *team* saw it
- as the *audience* saw it (the audience could be given comment sheets to complete)

The success should be measured in terms of how well it achieved its purpose and made an impact on the audience. After the discussion each student should write a summary (in the form of numbered notes) of the conclusions of the discussion.

chapter summary and key terms

■ Promotion is an essential part of the marketing process; it involves communicating the benefits of a product to the consumer.

■ The main forms of promotion used by businesses are point of sale promotions (branding and packaging), advertisements in various media, sponsorship and competitions.

■ The purpose of promotion is to communicate a message to consumers, to provide them with information, to influence what they think of the product and to encourage them to buy it.

■ There are constraints on advertising imposed by law (eg the Sale of Goods Act) and also by voluntary codes (eg the Code of Advertising Practice)

key terms

promotion	communicating the benefits of a product to the consumer
advertising	a selling message for a product directed at the consumer
branding	creating an image for a product which will encourage the consumer to buy it
packaging	the way a product is packed and presented
publicity	appearing in the news
public relations	the function in a business which deals with its public image
sponsorship	providing money to an individual or an event which receives public attention in return for the individual or event publicising the name of the sponsor
customer perception	the image of a product imprinted in the mind of a consumer as the result of a promotion
advertising constraints	laws or voluntary codes of conduct which prevent advertising misleading or offending the consumer

multiple-choice questions

1   Point of sale promotions are
   A   incentives to buy displayed in shops
   B   TV adverts for a particular product
   C   newspaper adverts for sales reductions
   D   sponsorship of race meetings

2   Branding involves
   A   copying someone else's product
   B   a special 'money-off' promotion
   C   promoting a specific image of a product
   D   heat-sealing a product in a plastic wrapper

3   Public relations is
   A   getting your product mentioned in the news
   B   the function in a business which deals with public image
   C   publicising the products of government enterprises
   D   encouraging families to visit shops

For questions 4 to 6, match the types of complaint set out at the bottom of the page with the laws or bodies listed below.

   A   Health & Safety at Work Act
   B   Advertising Standards Authority
   C   Consumer Protection Act
   D   Sale of Goods Act

4   someone finds a poster offensive

5   someone complains that a product is "not like it was in the advert"

6   someone says that the price they were charged was "not the same as in the advert"

10 Customer service

GNVQ SPECIFICATIONS
Element 3.3
Providing customer service
performance criteria – a student must

1   identify an organisation's customers and its customer needs
2   identify and describe customer service in an organisation
3   identify business communications which meet customer needs
4   demonstrate business communications which meet customer needs
5   describe procedures in one business organisation for dealing with customer complaints
6   identify relevant legislation to protect customers

---

what this chapter covers
This chapter concentrates on the customers of a business organisation – who they are, what their needs are and how those needs are met by 'customer service.'

what you will learn from this chapter
- customer service involves meeting the needs of customers from outside the business and also within the business – it also means dealing with special needs customers

- customer needs include wanting to buy something, information, making a complaint, requesting a refund, exchanging goods and being provided with an 'honest' service

- dealing with customers involves communications inside and outside the business, eg telephone calls, letters, memos and product information

- dealing with customers also involves knowing about the law which protects the consumer – in cases of queries and disputes about prices charged, product quality, refunds, and exchanges

what is customer service?

pc 3.3.2

The initial impression of a customer dealing with an organisation – whether as a shopper, a visitor or when speaking over the telephone – is based on the level of *customer service* he or she receives. Is the person who deals with the customer polite and helpful, or is the person unhelpful and not interested in the customer's request? The result will be a good impression – or a bad impression – of the whole organisation. If the impression is good, the person will want to do business again; if the impression is bad, the organisation will probably have lost a customer for good. Many organisations have a customer services department, and shops often have a customer services desk, as in the picture below.

a customer services desk

customer care

Customer care is the application of *customer service*. If you get a part-time job in an organisation or a work placement, you may have to deal with customers, over a counter, at a reception desk, over the telephone, or elsewhere on the premises. Many business organisations run special customer care training programmes, spending much time and money ensuring that their staff provide a high level of customer service. What is a customer care scheme? It is a focussing of the whole business on the needs of the *customer* rather than the needs of the *business*. It is an attitude which should run through the whole organisation from the Chief Executive to the most junior Sales Assistant.

customer service at work – external customers

Customer service should be provided wherever the customer meets the business organisation: over the counter, or on the telephone. There are many examples of job roles involving customer service:

- shop assistants

- doctors' receptionists

- bank assistants

- bus drivers

- swimming pool attendants

- telephone sales staff (mail order firms)

customer service at work – internal customers

Many business organisations train their staff to think of other employees as 'customers' and treat them as such. For example a person in charge of the stationery stores or photocopier should provide materials and copying promptly and with the same courtesy that they would give to an outside customer.

The same principal applies to quality in production – many Japanese companies train production line workers to treat the people in the *next* stage in production as their customers.

STUDENT ACTIVITY 10.1
performance criterion 3.3.2

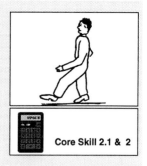

Core Skill 2.1 & 2

assessing customer service

Over a period of two or three days (a weekend for example) carry out a survey of the situations where you were a customer of a business organisation (eg a taxi ride, a disco, buying a cup of coffee). Draw up a survey sheet to cover the following:

(a) Was the impression you received good or bad? Why?

(c) Were you aware of a customer care scheme in operation?

(d) Did you see evidence of 'internal' customer care in operation, ie employees treating other employees like customers?

Write a brief summary of the findings from your survey. Use approximate ratios and percentages to illustrate your points. Conclude with an estimate of the *probability* of getting good customer service in your area.

customer needs

pc 3.3.2

If you deal with customers, you will know that no two customers are the same – that is what makes them so interesting – they all have different needs. Having already looked at the situation of a receptionist, we will now look at the common situation of a customer in a shop. When reading the text, remember that the same needs will apply in other selling situations – at a travel agent or a bank, for example. Customers' requirements may be categorised as follows:

making a purchase – the need for information
Many customers need information. They may be about to make a purchase, or they may just be 'shopping around' for a product and looking for the best price or after-sales service. Whatever the situation the shop assistant must:

know the product range
Know the price, product description, availability, and details of after-sales service (guarantees and policy on 'money back'). Knowing the product ideally also means knowing the competitor's product: 'Oh yes, I know they are cheaper at Woolwood's, but look at the quality we have here – this will last a long time.' The assistant must, however, beware of making false or over-ambitious claims: the customer will soon see through them.

know other sources of information
If the assistant is unable to provide all the information required, someone else in (or outside) the organisation may be able to help the customer. For example the question may be very technical: 'Will this hair dryer work off the mains electricity supply in Kuwait?' The question may have to be referred to the technical department of the manufacturer. The customer will not necessarily expect the shop assistant to know the answer, but may be very unhappy if the assistant does not know how to find out.

the need for help
Some customers do not just need information, they need very specific assistance. Consider the following customer requests and comments:

'Where is the nearest loo?'

'I am dying for a cup of coffee!'

'What can I do with the kids when I go shopping? It's a nightmare!'

The shop assistant in these cases could point out where the toilets are, where the coffee shop is, or where the childrens' play area is located.

the need for care

Apart from the obvious general application of customer care skills, one of the factors which motivates staff is the fulfilment of a customer's need for 'care' in a very specific sense. 'Care' is more than 'help,' it means anticipating a customer's needs. Consider the following examples:

- a sales assistant sees that a pregnant woman is exhausted with tramping around the shops and provides her with a chair to sit down on

- a sales assistant sees that an elderly lady is confused and tired, and spends more time serving the lady and helping her to make simple decisions

- a sales assistant calms a screaming child by giving him or her something as a distraction

In all these cases, the employee goes out of his or her way to provide care for the shopper, who will remember the incident and think of the organisation in a good light.

the need to complain

There will always be customers who will complain. Sometimes they will be justified, sometimes they just like complaining and will 'winge' about anything – you will know the type! It is the job of the employee of the organisation to deal with complaints. Put yourself in the shoes of the employee – what would you do in the circumstances?

listen	You should let the angry person explain the problem, however rude and aggressive they are in the process. By showing their anger and frustration they will start to get the problem out of their system. You should listen and sympathise.
be detached	Do not get drawn into an argument, otherwise a 'slanging match' will result which gets nobody anywhere, least of all your organisation.
assess the situation	Can you deal with the situation yourself, or does the situation require the customer speaking to a more senior colleague? If the customer is abusive, will you need to get help?
take action	Be decisive. If you can deal with the problem yourself, do so calmly and efficiently; if you need to pass the person to a colleague or supervisor, ensure that they are adequately briefed about the situation.

refunds/replacements

You should ensure that you know your organisation's procedures for refunds and replacements. The law states that a customer who buys faulty goods has a right to a refund rather than just a credit note. Some retailers, as part of their customer service policy, allow a refund even if the customer does not like the product – Marks & Spencer and Argos are well-known examples.

the need for honesty - ethical standards

It almost goes without saying that customers expect the employee to be honest and trustworthy. This is especially the case where the employee is dealing with valuables or cash. Nobody likes being short-changed!

STUDENT ACTIVITY 10.2
performance criterion 3.3.1

meeting customer needs

You work as a shop assistant in the stationery department of a large store. What would you do in the following circumstances? In each case state what type of need – information, help, care, complaint – you are satisfying.

(a) A customer wants to know how much 'The Times' and 'The Independent' newspapers cost.

(b) A German tourist comes in and asks for 'Die Welt' You are not sure what she means.

(c) An irate customer comes in with a pencil he has bought; he complains that the lead keeps breaking. He cannot remember when he bought it.

(d) A customer comes in very distressed asking for a copy of this month's issue of the magazine 'Which'. She says that she has bought a faulty washing machine from a discount warehouse, and they are refusing to replace it. A friend has told her that there is an article about consumer rights in the magazine. You do not stock 'Which' – it is only available by mail order.

(e) A pregnant woman comes in with two screaming children who are demanding all the sweets and toys that they can see. She looks very pale and anxious.

(f) A customer asks to change a book which she bought last week; the book looks rather grubby. Your company policy does not allow exchange of goods, unless the original was faulty.

(g) A drunk comes into the store and starts singing.

customer types

pc 3.3.1

In the last section we saw how different customers have different needs. Every employee providing customer service should be able to anticipate these needs. One way of doing this is by categorising customers into different types, for example:

- the enquirer who needs information

- the complainer who needs pacifying

- the child

- customers with 'special needs', eg people in wheelchairs, blind customers

We have dealt with the enquirer and the complainer in the last section. We will now look at the child and the special needs customer.

the child

Ask any parent, nanny or child-minder and you will find that taking children shopping, or placing them in any situation which involves waiting, can be a considerable problem! Of course, some children are not a problem, and a smiling face normally means that everyone can relax.

Employees dealing with the public may encounter the following problems with children:

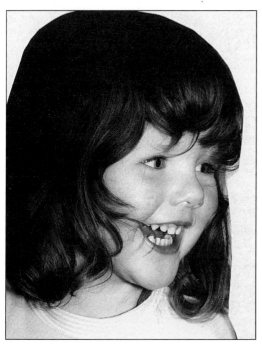

- children disrupting the course of business – creating a disturbance, destroying displays of goods

- children helping themselves to goods, tampering with telephone equipment

- lost children

- children trying to pay for goods

Whatever the situation, remember that it is the person in charge of the child who is primarily responsible and who will have to be approached in the first instance if there is a problem. Only if there is a threat to safety – eg a lost child or a collapsing display – should direct action be taken by employees.

A sympathetic employee may sense situations where 'care' is needed – eg a distressed or bored child – and may be able to help the parent in a difficult situation.

special needs customers

Customers with special needs include:

the physically handicapped and disabled

People in wheelchairs and with walking frames will need special treatment and patience; the organisation should already be equipped with suitable lifts and ramps.

the mentally handicapped

People who are slower than normal in carrying out the simplest transaction will need a high degree of care and understanding. Do not treat them like idiots.

the deaf ('hearing-impaired')

Some customers may be completely or partially deaf and will be skilled in lip reading and may be equipped with hearing aids. Do not shout at them.

the blind ('visually-impaired')

Blind people will be used to getting about in public, so ask them if they need help. Talk to them. There is nothing more frightening than being grabbed unexpectedly by a complete stranger, however well-meaning that person may be.

STUDENT ACTIVITY 10.3
performance criterion 3.3.1

dealing with special situations

You work as a shop assistant on the till in the stationery department of a large store. How would you deal with the following customer types?

(a) You suspect a three year-old child of slipping a Mars bar into her mother's shopping bag.

(b) A toddler is swinging from a card rack, threatening to bring it crashing to the floor; you cannot see the child's father or mother.

(c) A six year-old girl offers you 25p in payment for a chocolate bar costing 28p.

(d) A blind person approaches you and asks for a Bing Crosby CD. The music department is on the next floor.

(e) A customer in a wheelchair asks for this month's issue of 'Cosmopolitan'.

(f) A customer wearing a hearing aid brings you a greetings card and offers to pay with a Scottish £10 note; your store does not accept Scottish bank notes.

communicating with customers

pc 3.3.4

Communication skills form part of your Core Skills assessment in the GNVQ Intermediate course, and are covered in full on page 274. In this chapter we summarise the skills needed when providing customer service. They include:

- verbal communication – talking to people face-to-face or over the telephone
- non-verbal communication – the use of body language (gestures and facial expressions)
- written communication – letters, memos and product information

verbal (oral) communication

Verbal (oral) communication is used with customers in two contexts:

- speaking to a person face-to-face
- speaking to a person over the telephone

Speaking to a person face-to-face also involves body language (see below) whereas speaking over the telephone relies solely on the voice. How can the voice be used effectively for communication?

tone

The tone of voice you use – the mood of your voice – shows your emotions and attitude very clearly. The important point is that whatever you may be thinking personally, you should not allow it to colour the communication process. For example:

- if a customer is speaking for too long, you should not sound bored
- if a customer gets angry, you should not start shouting at the caller

manner

The manner in which you speak will depend on the person to whom you are speaking. If you are dealing with a customer you will speak in a more formal manner, unless of course the caller is well known to you.

language

The words and phrases you use will depend, of course, on the person to whom you are speaking. These are some general guidelines:

- do not use slang, eg 'Can you hang on a sec?'
- do not use long 'posh sounding' words where short simple ones will do
- avoid workplace jargon at all times when speaking to customers – they will not understand what you are talking about

technique

An organisation will have a standard technique – the house style – for greeting and dealing with customers face-to-face and over the telephone, for example:

'National Bank, good morning, may I help you?'

Employees should make sure they know what the house style is.

non-verbal communication - body language

Non-verbal communication involves the use of body language – gestures, facial expressions, and body posture – which confirm our links with the animal kingdom! When you deal with a customer you should first interpret his or her body language to establish whether you have a complaint or an enquiry on your hands, and then you should respond using appropriate body signals.

STUDENT ACTIVITY 10.4
performance criterion 3.3.3

communicating through body language

Set out below are pictures of two customers with very different attitudes. Examine the body language – the facial expressions, the gestures and the posture. What do they tell you? How would you deal with these customers?

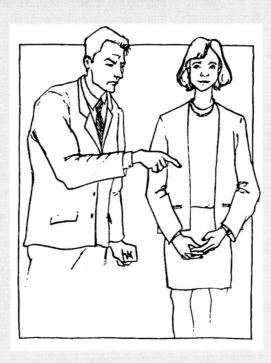

written communications

Written communications (see also Chapter 14) include:

- *external communications* with customers – eg letters, quotations, prices, notices
- *internal communications* with other employees – eg notes and memoranda

Some examples are shown below ...

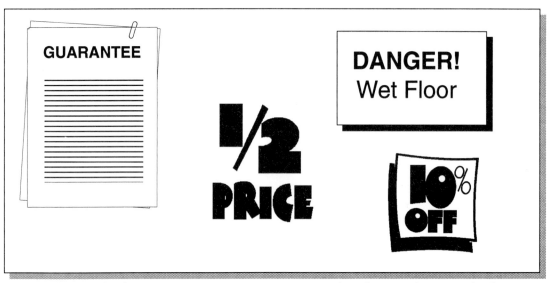

notices and written messages to customers – examples of external communications

MEMORANDUM

To Tim Blake, Sales Manager

From K Roach, Finance Manager   **Ref.** KR/AC/1098

Copies to Departmental Managers   **Date** 7 July 1996

Subject COMPUTERISATION OF ACCOUNTING RECORDS

Please attend a meeting on 14 July in the Conference Room. Attendance is
vital as the new system comes on line on 1 September. Summary details of
the new system are attached.

enc

a memorandum – an internal communication – see page 259

Wyvern Electrical Services
107 High Street
Mereford MR1 9SZ

Tel 01605 675365 Fax 01605 675576

Ref DH/SB/69

14 December 1996

J D Sutton Esq
23 Windermere Close
Crofters Green
Mereford MR6 7ER

Dear Mr Sutton

Rewiring: 23 Windermere Close

Thank you for your letter of enquiry dated 10 December.

We are pleased to enclose a brochure detailing our services and will be pleased to give you a quotation for rewiring your new extension. In order to do this we will need to send our estimator to see your property, and shall be grateful if you will telephone us to arrange a visit at a time which is convenient to you.

We look forward to hearing from you.

Yours sincerely

D Hunt

Derek Hunt
Sales Manager

enc

a letter to a customer – an external communication – see page 257

customers and the law

pc 3.3.6

We have seen earlier in the chapter what happens when customers complain about faulty goods and confusion arises over prices. It is essential that employees have a reasonable idea of what the *law* says about each situation. They will not be required to have a *detailed* knowledge of the law – they will need to know how to answer customers' questions and avoid saying the wrong thing! What are the main laws?

Trade Descriptions Acts

The Trade Descriptions Acts make it a *criminal offence:*

- to make false statements about goods offered for sale
- to make misleading statements about services

Examples of offences therefore include:

- stating that a car for sale has clocked up 15,000 miles, when in fact the figure is 25,000 miles
- making a misleading statement about the price of goods, eg saying 'Now only £49.95, was £99.95' when it has only ever sold for £69.95
- making a misleading statement about a service, eg 'our dry cleaning is guaranteed to remove every stain' when it does not, or 'our apartments are within easy reach of the sea' when they are fifteen miles away

Sale of Goods Act

This Act states that you are entitled to expect any goods that you buy from a shop to be:

of 'satisfactory quality'
This means they must meet the standard that a 'reasonable' person would expect given the description and the price

'fit for the purpose'
The goods must do what they are supposed to do, or what the shop claims they can do: an umbrella should keep the rain out, a watch should keep accurate time.

'as described'
The goods must be what they are claimed to be: a 'leather coat' must be made of leather, a 'stereo TV' must provide stereo sound.

If any of these three conditions is not met, the consumer is entitled to a full or a part refund, depending on how soon the fault appears, how serious it is and how quickly the matter is taken up. Note also the following practical points:

- the buyer can accept a replacement, but can also insist on a refund if a replacement is not wanted
- the buyer does not have to accept a credit note for spending on other purchases
- a shop is not entitled to put up a notice saying "No Refunds!"

Consumer Protection Act

The Act falls into three parts:

- a manufacturer or importer who supplies a defective product which causes loss or damage (eg a dangerous teddy bear) can be sued
- it is a criminal offence for a trader to sell unsafe goods – 'unsafe' means in breach of the safety regulations which apply to that product (eg to pushchairs, food) and also in relation to what is reasonably expected of the product (you would expect an air gun to shoot, for example)
- it is a criminal offence for a trader to mislead consumers about the price of goods or services, eg saying '£50 off' when there is no reduction

Health & Safety at Work Act

This Act has been covered earlier in the book (see page 91). As far as customers are concerned, the business must make its public areas safe.

STUDENT ACTIVITY 10.5
performance criterion 3.3.6

customers and the law

What are your rights in the following situations? Quote the relevant Act(s) of Parliament in your answer.

(a) You buy a tape of your favourite band. When you open the box at home you find a tape of Cliff Richard songs. The shop has run out of the tape you want and offers you a credit note.

(b) You buy a new pair of jeans and the next day find that the zip is faulty. You take them back to the shop, but the assistant points to a notice saying 'No refunds'.

(c) You buy a new pair of shoes which are sold as 'leather effect'. A friend tells you that they are not real leather. You take them back to the shop and demand a refund.

(d) You buy a teddy bear for your young brother at Christmas from your local store, and get a real bargain. On Boxing Day your brother is admitted to hospital having swallowed both the teddy's eyes.

EVIDENCE COLLECTION ASSIGNMENT 10

customer service in action

Element 3.3

introduction

This assignment involves a practical investigation into the range of customers of one business organisation and the legal implications of dealing with the customers. It gives you the opportunity to put customer care into action in a practical way.

 tasks

pcs 3.3.1-5	**1** You are to investigate customer service in ONE organisation, preferably a large one. This organisation can be one with which your school or college has a link, a work placement, or a business where you have a part-time job. Your investigation should take the form of a short word-processed report. It should contain:

- a description of the different types of customer (including other businesses)
- a description of how it administers its customer services (ie who deals with the customers and where)
- an example of an oral communication (a description of what happened and what was said)
- an example of a written communication (a photocopy if possible)
- a description of the procedure for dealing with customer complaints (include any documentation which you can use)

pc 3.3.6	**2** Prepare a word-processed factsheet for the staff setting out how the four Acts of Parliament on pages 188 and 189 affect dealings with customers. Try to make the factsheet relate to situations, eg with headings such as 'When refunds are due . . Faulty goods' etc rather than just a list of legal points.

pc 3.3.4	**3** The student should carry out an interview with customers face-to-face in two or more situations along the lines of those set out on the next page.

If it is not possible to carry out this task with real customers (as is probably the case), students should *simulate* the situations. They can do this by writing out between them on cards a series of situations based on the ones on the next page (2 copies of each will be needed). The cards can then be allocated to pairs of students for role play. The interviews could be recorded on audio or video tape and played back to the students for assessment.

Each interview should be structured so that it involves the following stages:
- greeting the customer
- finding out the needs of the customer
- meeting those needs
- concluding the interview

The interviews should run along the following lines ...

INTERVIEW SCENARIOS

1 A customer calls to purchase a product.

2 A customer calls to ask for information about a product because he or she is thinking of buying it.

3 A customer is very unhappy with a purchase – it does not seem to work – he or she wants a refund.

4 A customer wants to change a product because he or she is not happy with it – either it is faulty, or it may be that the customer does not like the colour ...

5 A customer calls to make a complaint about some aspect of a product or customer service.

6 The customer may have a special need – he or she may be visually or hearing-impaired, in a wheelchair, or may be heavily pregnant.

chapter summary and key terms

- Customer service involves meeting the needs of customers from outside the business and also within the business – it aso means dealing with special needs customers.

- Customer needs include wanting to buy something, information, making a complaint, requesting a refund, exchanging goods and being provided with an 'honest' service.

- Customer service involves communications both inside and outside the business, eg telephone calls, letters, memos and product information.

- Dealing with customers also involves knowing about the law which protects the consumer – in cases of queries and disputes about prices charged, product quality, refunds, and exchanged goods.

key terms

customer service	meeting customer needs
customer care	focussing the business on customer needs rather than the needs of the business organisation
external customers	members of the public and businesses which deal with the organisation
care	anticipation of customer needs
ethical standards	the expected level of honesty of the employees dealing with the customers
special needs	customers who are either in a difficult situation (eg parents with upset children) or who have a specific disability
oral communication	commuication by word of mouth, ie face-to-face or by telephone
body language	using facial expressions and gestures to convey a message
satisfactory quality	the standard expected by a reasonable person, given the price and descriptionof the product

multiple-choice questions

1   The following is an example of an internal customer:
    A   another business
    B   another employee
    C   a consumer on the premises
    D   a visiting salesman

2   A customer care scheme involves:
    A   all employees of a business
    B   only the sales force
    C   only the personnel department
    D   the Consumer Protection Act

3   A refund should always be given:
    A   for all sales transactions
    B   where the goods are faulty
    C   when the customer does not like the colour of a product
    D   to people in wheelchairs

For questions 4 to 6, match the types of complaint or problem set out at the bottom of the page with the laws listed below.

    A   Health & Safety at Work Act
    B   Sales of Goods Act
    C   Consumer Protection Act
    D   Trades Descriptions Act

4   a garage sells a used car claiming it has only done 35,000 miles; the buyer finds out from the previous owner that it has done 55,000 miles

5   someone buys a pair of jeans which fall to bits after the first wash

6   someone slips over on a wet floor in a shop and fractures her pelvis

11 Improving customer service

what this chapter covers
This chapter prepares you for an assignment which looks at how customer service can be improved in a business organisation.

what you will learn from this chapter
- the importance of customer service to a business organisation

- how businesses can judge how effective their customer service is – by asking customers, by looking at the sales levels, seeing if they are getting fewer or more complaints and gaining or losing customers

- customer services can be improved in a number of areas: reliability, availability of goods or services, speed of delivery, policy for exchanges and refunds, access to the building (particularly for people with special needs), customer safety, care for the environment

the importance of customer service

pc 3.4.1

needs of the business

We saw in the last chapter how *customer service* is provided to satisfy customers' needs. It is also essential for the business too, for a number of reasons:

- customer service enables a business to *keep* existing customers (sometimes through *'loyalty schemes'* such as Club Cards)

- customer service enables a business to *gain* new customers – often through 'word of mouth' recommendation – "You ought to go there, they have such a good range of stock, and the staff are really helpful. You can always get your money back if you don't like what you buy."

- customer service *enhances the image* of an organisation – it will increase sales when people say "I like shopping at Browns – you really ought to go there."

STUDENT ACTIVITY 11.1
performance criterion 3.4.1

customer service and needs

Head up an A4 sheet "the Importance of Customer Service" and make two lists of points:

(a) a list on the left-hand side of the paper headed "Customer Needs for Customer Service"

(b) a list on the right-hand side of the paper headed "Business Needs for Customer Service"

Try ands make the lists as long as you can.

customer care schemes

pc 3.4.2

codes of practice and customer charters

Some large businesses in the private sector operate a *code of practice* for customer service. They may publish a document (sometimes called a 'charter') which sets out for the public its objectives for customer service and the basis of the business/customer relationship. On the next page is an illustration of a page from 'Good Banking', a code of practice adopted by banks, building societies and card issuers, and produced by the British Bankers Association, the Building Societies Association and the Association for Payment Clearing Services.

**GOOD
BANKING**

5.0   **CHARGES AND DEBIT INTEREST
(PAYABLE BY CUSTOMERS)**

5.1   Banks and building societies will provide customers with details of the basis of charges, if any, payable in connection with the operation of their accounts. These will be in the form of published tariffs covering basic account services which will

– be given or sent to customers:

(a) when accounts are opened;

(b) at any time on request;

– and be available in branches.

Details of any changes will also be given or sent to customers and be available in branches before the changes are implemented.

5.2   Charges for services outside the tariff will be advised on request or at the time the service is offered.

5.3   Banks and building societies will introduce systems to come into effect by 31 December 1996 to ensure that they will give no less than 14 days' notice of the amount to be deducted from their customers' current and savings accounts in respect of interest and charges for account activity that have accumulated during the charging period.

Banks and building societies which have not introduced such systems will disregard the charges to be applied to customers' accounts for any charging period if those were incurred solely as a result of the application of charges for the previous charging period.

5.4   Banks and building societies will tell customers the interest rates applicable to their accounts, the basis on which interest is calculated and when it will be charged to their accounts. These will include the rates applicable when accounts are overdrawn without prior agreement or exceed the agreed borrowing limit. Banks and building societies will explain also the basis on which they may vary interest rates.

5.5   When banks and building societies change interest rates with immediate effect they will effectively publicise those changes, for example by notices in their branches, if any, or in the press, or on statements.

6.0   **CREDIT INTEREST
(PAYABLE TO CUSTOMERS)**

6.1   Banks and building societies will make information about the rates on interest bearing accounts which they offer (whether or not these are open to new customers) freely available and accessible to customers by one or more effective means, for example:

(a) notices and/or leaflets in branches;

(b) press advertisements;

(c) personal notice;

(d) a branch/central telephone service.

extract from 'Good Banking'

the public sector and customer service

The public sector contains all Government-owned and Government-controlled businesses. At the time of writing the public sector includes health, education and welfare services and public corporations such as British Rail and the Post Office. Many public sector businesses have already been privatised (ie turned into private sector businesses), for example British Telecom (BT) and British

Petroleum (BP). Other public sector businesses will or may become privatised (eg British Rail, parts of the Post Office) and so it is common to find a private sector approach to customer services in public sector businesses; for example customer care schemes and performance targets.

the Citizen's Charter

In July 1991 the Prime Minister, John Major, introduced the Citizen's Charter with the intention of improving the level of public service in the areas of transport, health, education, welfare and the privatised utilities (gas, electricity, telecommunications, water). This improvement was to be achieved by the publication of individual service charters setting out the rights of the customer, targets for services, and procedures for obtaining compensation if the targets are not met. Services which carry out this procedure can use the Chartermark (see below), the public service equivalent of the quality kitemark.

Since the introduction of the Citizen's Charter, a Cabinet Minister for Public Service has been appointed and a number of public service charters have been issued, the best known of which are probably British Rail's 'Passenger's Charter' and the National Health Service's 'Patient's Charter'. In 1993 British Rail paid out almost £5 million to customers whose trains were late or cancelled, and in the same year the NHS was able to treat three out of four patients in hospital within three months of being put on a waiting list. An extract from a 1994 'Customer information' leaflet produced by Severn Trent Water is illustrated below: it shows details of the company's own internal service targets.

Our own service targets

We aim to prove our commitment to top-class service by measuring performance against our own, tougher standards. We'll publish details of how we're doing:

Our own targets are:

Answering phone calls: We aim to answer calls within 15 seconds and make 30 seconds the maximum wait. However, for billing queries at peak times we will try to limit the maximum wait to 45 seconds.

Letters: We'll respond to your letters in writing, by phone or face-to-face within five working days 75 per cent of the time, and certainly within ten working days.

Appointments: Whenever we make an appointment to meet you we will agree to come either in the morning or the afternoon.

Customers who visit our offices: We always aim to make sure you see the right person within five minutes.

the chartermark   *extract from a Severn Trent Water information leaflet*

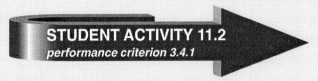

STUDENT ACTIVITY 11.2
performance criterion 3.4.1

private and public sector customer services

Obtain a copy of a customer charter from:

- a private sector business, eg 'Good Banking' the Code of Practice available from banks

  and

- a public sector service, eg the Passenger's Charter, the Patient's Charter (note that some doctors' practices produce their own 'Charter')

(a) Produce a *summary* of the contents of both documents (do not go into specific details).

(b) Compare the two documents. How are they similar, and how do they differ in terms of content and presentation?

(c) Will the documents improve customer service? How?

monitoring the success of customer service

`pc 3.4.1`

how businesses measure success

Business organisations can measure the success of their customer service by collecting statistics, for example:

positive signs (customer service is successful)

- an increase in the number of customers who approach them with an enquiry
- an increase in the number of customers who buy their products
- repeat business – an increase in the number of customers who come back again to buy their products
- an increase in the overall sales figures
- a reduction in the number of complaints and returned products

negative signs (customer service is not successful)

- an increase in the number of complaints
- an increase in the number of products returned as faulty
- a reduction in the number of customers
- a reduction in the sales figure

means of monitoring success

Businesses in the private and public sectors spend much time and money in monitoring the results of their campaigns in order to identify and solve problems that occur. Statistics should be treated with care, and supplemented with other forms of information gathering, such as questionnaires.

Monitoring can take a number of forms:

sales performance

As we have seen, an improvement in customer services for a profit-making organisation should result in an increase in the number of customers, and a better sales performance. This will happen in an ideal world, but in reality other factors may operate which will depress sales performance:

- strong competition in the industry, eg the food supermarkets all have prominent customer service campaigns, but because of price-cutting and competition, they have to work hard to maintain the same level of sales

- a declining market where the number of customers will actually be falling anyway

feedback

Many organisations organise customer questionnaires to find out what is right and what is wrong with the customer service. Shops often put questionnaires by the checkout and holiday companies circulate them on return charter flights. See the next page for an extract of a W H Smith questionnaire on service. Feedback can also be achieved simply by staff talking to customers about their needs and the level of service provided.

complaints

Businesses generally process complaints through a Customer Services department, or if they are not large enough for such a department, through the management. Whatever the situation, the management will be able to monitor complaints and analyse exactly what is wrong. For example a bank may get complaints that there are long queues at lunchtime; the answer may be simply to change the duty roster and staff lunchbreaks, in consultation with the staff, of course.

marketing research

Businesses may carry out their own marketing research by issuing questionnaires (see next page). They can also 'buy in' market research through agencies which will carry out surveys of a wide range of products. This can prove an expensive option for the individual business. There is no better way of finding out about your customers than by talking to them yourself.

Q5 Below is a list of statements about service. Can you please indicate whether you strongly agree, agree, disagree or strongly disagree with each statement for this shopping occasion at W H Smith. If the comment is not applicable to this trip please tick the 'not applicable' box. **Please tick the box which applies to each statement** (✓)

	Strongly Agree	Agree	Disagree	Strongly Disagree	Not Applicable	
Staff had time to help with my enquiry	❏	❏	❏	❏	❏	(9)
Staff were friendly	❏	❏	❏	❏	❏	(10)
Staff were approachable	❏	❏	❏	❏	❏	(11)
I did not have to queue to seek assistance	❏	❏	❏	❏	❏	(12)
Staff wanted to help me	❏	❏	❏	❏	❏	(13)
Staff were happy	❏	❏	❏	❏	❏	(14)
Staff were interested in serving me	❏	❏	❏	❏	❏	(15)
I did not have to queue too long to pay	❏	❏	❏	❏	❏	(16)
Staff were knowledgeable	❏	❏	❏	❏	❏	(17)
Staff were understanding	❏	❏	❏	❏	❏	(18)
Staff helped me make my decision	❏	❏	❏	❏	❏	(19)
I enjoyed shopping at W H Smith	❏	❏	❏	❏	❏	(20)
Staff were there if I needed them	❏	❏	❏	❏	❏	(21)
It was easy to find what I was looking for	❏	❏	❏	❏	❏	(22)
The shop is well laid out	❏	❏	❏	❏	❏	(23)
The signs helped me find my way around	❏	❏	❏	❏	❏	(24)
I could browse in peace	❏	❏	❏	❏	❏	(25)
It was fun to shop there	❏	❏	❏	❏	❏	(26)
I knew I could exchange goods easily	❏	❏	❏	❏	❏	(27)

Q 6 Was there any member of staff you thought offered a very high level of service? Can you remember their name?

Please write in _____

W H Smith – "Customer First" questionnaire
Reproduced by kind permission of W H Smith Ltd and David Young & Associates

Improving customer service 201

STUDENT ACTIVITY 11.3
performance criterion 3.4.2

Core Skill 2.2

the 'Students Charter'

Using the Charters examined in Activity 2 as a model, devise your own 'Student's Charter' setting out the standards of service you would expect from your school or college.

When you have established the standards of service, devise two ways of monitoring the standards. Set out your proposals in the form of a memorandum to your teacher/lecturer.

Note: you could also ask your teacher/lecturer to devise a short 'Tutor's Charter' setting out the standards expected of students, eg work handed in on time, attendance in class!

improving customer service

pc 3.4.3

areas for improvement
The areas of customer service which should be monitored and where improvements could be made if appropriate include:

- the *reliability* of products or services – do they perform?

- the *friendliness* of staff – do they smile or not?

- the *availability* of goods and services – are the opening hours satisfactory? are the goods in stock when needed?

- *speed of delivery* – are the goods delivered on time and to the right address?

- *exchanges and refunds* – is the policy made clear to customers? is it fair and legal?

- *access to buildings* (where appropriate) – can you get a wheelchair or a baby buggy in?

- *customer safety* – do the premises and working practices comply with Health & Safety regulations?

- *environmental policy* – customers like 'environmentally friendly' businesses – does the business have a published policy?

In addition to monitoring customer opinion and behaviour, businesses can ask their *staff* to suggest improvements to customer service by means of *staff suggestion schemes* and *quality circles*.

EVIDENCE COLLECTION ASSIGNMENT 11

improving customer service

Element 3.4

introduction

This assignment involves a practical exercise in assessing the level of customer service in an organisation, and suggesting improvements which could be implemented.

 tasks

pcs 3.4.1-3 **1** **Investigate** the way customer service is implemented in ONE large business organisation – a well-known chain of shops or a bank or building society would be ideal. You should look at :

(a) the way staff are trained

(b) how the business monitors the effectiveness of its customer service– it may for example issue customer questionnaires, it may 'log' the number and types of sales transactions on its electronic tills

Word-process a short report entitled "Customer Service in ....(the name of the business.)" The report should :

- describe briefly how customer service is monitored

- list any ways customer service *is* being improved, or *could* be improved

This report should be written *individually* by students, although it would be a good idea for students to carry out their *investigations* in groups, eg ten students look at Marks & Spencer, ten go to Midland Bank, and so on.

pcs 3.4.3-4 **2** Using your observations of the business in Task 1, you should form groups of three or four students and prepare and give a presentation suitable for delivery to new businesses. The presentation should be assessed by the tutor and possibly also by outside advisers, eg customer service personnel from the businesses investigated. The presentation should be entitled "Improving your Customer Service" and cover three of the following areas:

- friendliness of staff

- availability of goods or services

- speed of delivery

- policies for exchanges or refunds

- access to the buildings for people with special needs

- customer safety

- the need for an environmental policy

chapter summary and key terms

■ Customer service involves meeting the needs of customers.

■ Customer service also involves meeting the needs of the business – to keep customers' loyalty, to gain new customers and to enhance the image of the organisation.

■ Larger businesses in the private sector issue codes of practice containing their targets for customer service; public sector organisations issue 'charters' containing their customer service targets.

■ Businesses monitor the success of their customer service campaigns by sending questionnaires to customers and also by looking at statistics such as the level of sales and the number of customers.

■ Improvements may be made to customer service in a number of areas: reliability, availability of goods or services, speed of delivery, policy for exchanges and refunds, access to the building (particularly for people with special needs), customer safety, care for the environment.

key terms

loyalty schemes	schemes for retaining customers, eg Club Cards which give discounts on purchases
code of practice	a document containing targets for achievement of customer service targets for private sector businesses
service charter	a document containing targets for achievement of customer service targets for public sector businesses
feedback	information gathered from customers both formally (eg by questionnaire) or informally (talking to them and noting their views)
marketing research	gathering information from a specified group of people to provide a business with information about customer satisfaction

multiple-choice questions

1   Customer service is important for a business because it
   A   helps customers pay up on time
   B   encourages customers to deal with the business
   C   the business does not have to do marketing research
   D   keeps sales staff's pay in line with competing businesses

2   The chartermark is given to
   A   businesses which obtain Quality Assurance certification
   B   private sector businesses with codes of practice
   C   public sector businesses which achieve customer service targets
   D   encourage businesses to obtain new customers

3   A business may consider its customer services a success if it increases
   A   its sales figures
   B   the number of customer complaints
   C   the number of returned products
   D   the number of customers who trade with its competitors

For questions 4 to 6, match the methods set out at the bottom of the page with the
the types of monitoring listed below.

   A   sales performance
   B   customer feedback
   C   customer complaints
   D   marketing research

4   a business buys information from an outside body about the sales trends for
   a particular product in the UK

5   a business looks at how many items of its own product have been purchased
   over the last six months

6   a travel company gives each of its clients a questionnaire to complete

SECTION

4

GNVQ UNIT 4
FINANCIAL AND ADMINISTRATIVE SUPPORT

AUTHOR'S NOTE

contents of Chapters 12 and 13
As Elements 4.1 and 4.2 overlap so much as far as the *Range* is concerned, the first two chapters have been designed to deal with *both* Elements. Chapter 12 therefore deals with purchases and sales, Chapter 13 with payments and receipts. This provides students with a much more logical progression through what is at times a very technical area.

Assignments 12 and 13
The type of evidence required for Elements 4.1 and 4.2 is, however, very different. This is reflected in Assignments 12 and 13 which are placed after the chapters, starting on page 247. Tutors may wish to base the work for Elements 4.1 and 4.2 around these assignments, using the chapter text for reference and Student Activities for reinforcing learning. In passing, it should be noted that the term 'income and expenditure account' (which is the financial statement of a club or society) has been replaced throughout by the term 'profit statement' which is the term and statement generally used in business.

Chapter 14 and Assignment 14
Element 4.3, which deals with business documents, is not intended as an area of separate study, covering, as it does, so many of the Communication Core Skill requirements. The approach in this book has been to provide an assignment to 'hang the documents on' (page 253). This is followed by a 'document bank' in which the more important documents (including the report) are illustrated and explained.

12 Financial transactions and documents

GNVQ SPECIFICATIONS

This chapter covers performance criteria from two 'overlapping' elements:

Element 4.1: Identify and explain financial transactions and documents
performance criteria – a student must:

1   explain financial transactions which take place regularly in an organisation and explain why records of transactions are kept

2   explain and give examples of purchases and purchases documents

3   explain and give examples of sales transactions and sales documents

Element 4.2: Complete financial documents and explain financial recording
performance criteria – a student must:

1   complete purchase and sales documents clearly and correctly and calculate totals

3   record income and expenditure over time periods

4   explain why financial information must be recorded

5   identify and give examples of information technology which businesses use to record and monitor financial information

Note: the remaining performance criteria from these elements – which deal with payments and receipts – will be covered in the next chapter.

what you will learn from this chapter

- the recording of **financial transactions** (income and expenditure) enables the owner of a business to see whether it has made a profit or a loss

- the **purchases documents** used by a business buying goods include:
    - the *purchase order,* which places the order with the supplier
    - the *invoice*, which lists the goods and tells you what you owe
    - the *credit note*, which is sent to you if you are due a refund
    - the *goods received note*, which records the goods when they arrive

- the **sales documents** used by a business selling goods include the purchase order and invoice mentioned above – they also include:
    - the *order received note*, an internal record of the receipt of the order
    - the *delivery note*, which is sent with the goods
    - the *statement of account,* sent to the buyer summarising what is owed
    - the *remittance advice* which is sent when payment is made

financial transactions

pc 4.1.1
pcs 4.2.3-5

Financial transactions are transactions which involve money:

outward transactions – making payments – expenditure

Business payments include settling up for:

- *purchases* of materials used in the manufacturing process (if the business is a manufacturer)
- *wages and salaries* for its employees
- *overheads* – running expenses such as electricity bills, rates, insurance

inward transactions – receiving money – income

These are the transactions every business owner likes. The money comes in from:

- *sales income* (from goods and services which the business provides)
- *loans received*

As we will see in the next section of this chapter, financial transactions generate *documents* such as invoices.

production of accounts – accounting systems

Financial transactions are recorded in the *accounting system* of a business. An accounting system is simply the set of records kept by the business to record its income and expenses, and other financial details. Each type of transaction will be entered in a record known as an *account*. The accounting records may be handwritten and kept in books, they may be input onto a computer, using a commercial program such as Sage™. They may be complex or they may be simple, depending on the size and nature of the business.

monitoring business performance

A business needs to record financial transactions for very practical reasons. It will need to *monitor its performance*. It wants to know, for example:

- what its sales performance is – how much has it sold?
- what is its profit?

This information is available from the accounting records and also from financial statements extracted from the accounting records. Some of the accounting information will be used internally, some will be used for annual financial statements which may be made available outside the business if it is a limited company. If accounting information is *not* readily available, the owner or manager of a business will not have much idea as to what is going on, and may run into serious problems.

income and expenditure – profit or loss?

By looking at the amount of money received over a given time period (eg monthly, quarterly or yearly) and the amount paid out, a business can work out whether it has made a profit or loss. The formula is:

income *less* **expenditure** *equals* **profit** (or **loss**)

and so ...

- a *profit* is made when income is greater than expenditure
- a *loss* is made when income is less than expenditure
- if income and expenditure are equal, *no* profit or loss is made

income and expenditure – the profit statement

It is possible to set out the income and expenditure of a business over a period of time in the form of a profit statement which will calculate the profit or loss made. If you are familiar with computer spreadsheets, it is easy to set up a file which performs this calculation.

Look at the format shown below, and work through the calculations. Note that the total from the left-hand money column is shown in the right-hand money column so that it can be deducted from the sales figure. Note also that if a loss had been made it would have been shown in brackets.

---

profit statement for J Assam for August 1996

	£	£
income		
sales		50,000
less expenditure		
materials	20,000	
wages	5,000	
overheads	10,000	
		35,000
profit /(loss)		15,000

STUDENT ACTIVITY 12.1
performance criteria 4.1.1, 4.2.3 - 5

financial transactions

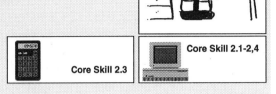

Core Skill 2.3

Core Skill 2.1-2,4

task 1

You are talking to a group of people starting up in business for the first time. Write replies in the form of short notes in response to the following questions:

(a) "What type of transactions are financial transactions?"

(b) "What sort of information can I get from my accounting records?"

(c) "Do I really need to keep accounting records?"

task 2

J Assam has recorded the following figures for the next three months.

	September	October	November
	£	£	£
Sales	50,000	50,000	40,000
Materials purchased	20,000	30,000	30,000
Wages	10,000	10,000	9,000
Overheads	10,000	10,000	8,000

(a) Draw up profit statements for J Assam for the three months shown. Use the format on the previous page.

(b) If you have the facilities, construct a spreadsheet for the profit statement and input the figures shown above – save as separate files and obtain printouts. Check your own figures from (a).

(c) What has happened to J Assam's profit? Draw a line graph to show his profitability over the *four* months from August to November (note: August's profit statement is shown on the previous page)

task 3

Investigate three different computer accounting systems for an up-to-date IBM compatible system in terms of cost and what the packages will do. Use computer magazines, computer firms and your own college or school IT centre to help you. Write a short (one page) report of your findings and recommend a suitable package for a small business.

purchases and sales documents

pcs 4.1.2 - 3
pc 4.2.1

documents and transactions

When a business buys and sells goods or services it will use a number of different *financial documents*.

The financial transactions referred to earlier in the chapter will all involve financial documents which will be used to enter the transactions into the accounting system of the business.

A single sales transaction of course involves *both* seller *and* buyer, and therefore in this chapter we taken the view that it makes sense to look at the purchases and documents *together*. A purchase invoice and a sales invoice are of course the same document – it just depends whether you are doing the purchasing or the selling!

We will look at a whole range of financial documents by means of a Case Study involving the buyer and seller of fashion socks.

Documents involved in the purchasing process include:
- the *purchase order,* which the buyer sends to the seller
- the *order received note* on which the seller records receipt of the order
- the *delivery note* which goes with the goods from the seller to the buyer
- the *goods received note*, which the buyer uses to record the goods when they arrive
- the *invoice*, which lists the goods and tells the buyer what is owed
- the *credit note*, which is sent to the buyer if any refund is due
- the *statement,* sent by the seller to remind the buyer what is owed
- the *remittance advice*, sent by the buyer when the goods are paid for

the flow of documents

Before you read the Case Study, examine the diagram set out on the next page. Down the columns representing the buyer and the seller are various activities which lead to transactions, which in turn generate documents.

You should appreciate that not all the activities happen all the time – the goods received note and order received note are not used by all organisations, and of course a credit note is only used when an adjustment is needed. Most of the time things run smoothly and the invoice is paid following receipt of a statement.

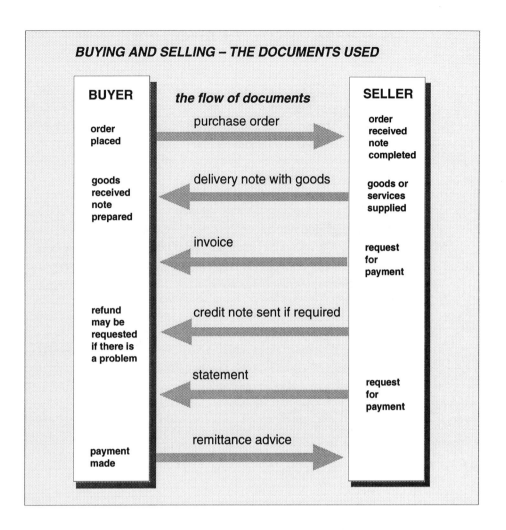

BUYING AND SELLING – THE DOCUMENTS USED

BUYER	the flow of documents	SELLER
order placed	purchase order →	order received note completed
goods received note prepared	← delivery note with goods	goods or services supplied
	← invoice	request for payment
refund may be requested if there is a problem	← credit note sent if required	
	← statement	request for payment
payment made	remittance advice →	

CASE STUDY

pcs 4.1.2 - 3
pc 4.2.1

Cool Socks – a purchase and sales transaction

situation

Cool Socks Limited manufactures fashion socks in a variety of colours. It supplies a number of different customers, including Trends, a fashion store in Broadfield.

In this Case Study we see an order for 100 pairs of socks placed by Trends with Cool Socks. The socks are delivered, but some are found to be faulty, so a refund has to be made. Finally, payment has to be made for the socks.

The Case Study looks in detail at the purchase and sales documents involved. Now read on.

purchase order – *the goods are ordered*

In this Case Study, Trends orders some socks from Cool Socks. The buyer at Trends will post or fax the authorised purchase order shown below. The order will have been typed out in the office, or produced on a computer accounting program. The details of the socks will have been obtained from Cool Socks' catalogue, or possibly by means of a written or telephoned enquiry.

Note the following details:
- each purchase order has a specific reference number – this is useful for filing and quoting on later documents such as invoices and statements
- the catalogue number of the goods required is stated in the product code column – this number can be obtained from the supplier's catalogue
- the quantity of the goods required is stated in the quantity column – socks are obviously supplied in pairs!
- the description of the goods is set out in full
- the price does not need to be stated, although some purchase orders will include a price
- the purchase order is signed and dated by the person in charge of purchasing – without this authorisation the supplier is unlikely to supply the goods (the order will probably be returned!)

Trends   PURCHASE ORDER

4 Friar Street
Broadfield
BR1 3RF
Tel 01908 761234 Fax 01908 761987
VAT REG GB 0745 8383 56

Cool Socks Limited,	purchase order no	47609
Unit 45 Elgar Estate,	date	25 09 95
Broadfield,		
BR7 4ER		

product code	quantity	description
45B	100 pairs	Blue Toebar socks

AUTHORISED signature... *D Signer* ...date... *25/09/95*

order received note – *the order is recorded*

Some organisations will record an incoming purchase order when it is received on a separate internal form – a *sales order received note*; some organisations will merely put a rubber stamp on the purchase order when it is received. Some organisations do not bother with either! The details noted if this system is used are likely to be: the date of receipt, the initials of the person checking the order, and an indication that the order has been passed for processing. It may be, for example, that the goods will have to be manufactured to order.

delivery note – *the goods are delivered*

A delivery note is despatched with the goods when the order is ready. It is normally either typed in the office or printed out by a computer accounting program. In this case, the delivery note travels with the socks, and a copy will be signed by Trends on receipt. Note the following details:

- the delivery note has a numerical reference, useful for filing and later reference if there is a query
- the method of delivery is stated – here the delivery is by parcel carrier
- the delivery note quotes the purchase order number – this enables the buyer to 'tie up' the delivery with the original order
- the delivery note quotes Cool Socks' catalogue reference, the quantity supplied and the description of the goods – these details will be checked against the goods themselves and the invoice when it is received
- no price is quoted on the delivery note
- the delivery note will be signed and dated by the person receiving the goods

---

——— DELIVERY NOTE ———

COOL SOCKS LIMITED

Unit 45 Elgar Estate, Broadfield, BR7 4ER
Tel 01908 765314 Fax 01908 765951
VAT REG GB 0745 4672 76

Trends 4 Friar Street Broadfield BR1 3RF	delivery note no delivery method your order date	68873 Lynx Parcels 47609 01 10 95

product code	quantity	description
45B	100 pairs	Blue Toebar socks

Received

signature..........*V Williams*..........name (capitals)..........*V WILLIAMS*..........date......*5/10/95*......

goods received note – *the goods are checked*

A goods received note (GRN) will be completed by the person in Trends who looks after the stock. Not all businesses keep GRNs, but when used they act as a useful 'checklist' that the goods received tally with the goods ordered, and are in good condition. In the case of this delivery, ten pairs of the socks have been received damaged – in this case Trends want a refund.

Note the following details:

- the document is an internal one, it will not be sent anywhere but kept within Trends
- details of the goods are noted, together with the purchase order number (which will be on the delivery note)
- the details of the carrier are noted, the consignment reference is the reference number given by the carrier to the parcel of socks
- the person at Trends examining the goods and the person double-checking them will both sign the form
- the condition of the goods – the damage to the socks – is recorded
- the document is in three copies – the one shown is the Accounts Department copy; there will also be copies for the buyer and the stockroom

---

Trends   GOODS RECEIVED NOTE

Supplier

Cool Socks Limited, Unit 45 Elgar Estate, Broadfield, BR7 4ER	GRN no date	1871 05 10 95

quantity	description	order number
100 pairs	Blue Toebar socks	47609

carrier   Lynx Parcels   consignment no   8479347

received by *V Williams*	checked by *R Patel*

condition of goods good condition damaged ✓ (10 pairs) shortages	**copies to** Buyer Accounts ✓ Stockroom

invoice – *payment is requested by the seller*

The invoice is the trading document which is sent by the seller to the buyer stating how much is owed by the buyer for a particular delivery of goods.

The invoice, like the delivery note, is prepared in the supplier's office, and is either typed or produced on a computer printer using a computer accounting program. Invoices produced by different organisations will vary to some extent in terms of detail, but their basic layout will always be the same. The invoice prepared by Cool Socks Ltd – illustrated on page 216 – is typical of a modern typed or computer printed document.

Note the following details, and refer to the invoice on the opposite page.

addresses
The invoice shows the address:
• of the seller/supplier of the goods – Cool Socks Limited
• where the invoice should be sent – to Trends
• where the goods are to be sent – if it is different from the invoice address

references
There are a number of important references on the invoice:
• the numerical reference of the invoice itself – 787923
• the account number allocated to Trends by the seller – 3993 – possibly for use in the seller's computer accounting program
• the original reference number on the purchase order sent by Trends – 47609 – which will enable the shop to 'tie up' the invoice with the original order

date
The date on the invoice is important because the payment date (here one month) is calculated from it. The invoice date is often described as the 'tax point' because it is the transaction date as far as VAT calculations are concerned, ie it is when the sale took place and the VAT was charged.

Note: VAT (Value Added Tax) is a tax on the supply of goods and services. At the time of writing the VAT rate is 17.5%.

Turn to page 217 for further explanation of the invoice.

INVOICE
COOL SOCKS LIMITED
Unit 45 Elgar Estate, Broadfield, BR7 4ER
Tel 01908 765314 Fax 01908 765951
VAT REG GB 0745 4672 76

invoice to

| Trends |
| 4 Friar Street |
| Broadfield |
| BR1 3RF |

invoice no	787923
account	3993
your reference	47609

deliver to

| as above |

date/tax point   01 10 95

product code	description	quantity	price	unit	total	discount %	net
45B	Blue Toebar socks	100	2.36	pair	236.00	0.00	236.00

terms
Net monthly
Carriage paid
E & OE

GOODS TOTAL	236.00
CASH DISCOUNT	0.00
SUBTOTAL	236.00
VAT	41.30
TOTAL	277.30

---

points to remember– the procedure for working out the invoice total is:

1.	*CALCULATE THE TOTAL COST:*	*QUANTITY x PRICE = TOTAL COST*
2.	*CALCULATE THE VAT:*	*TOTAL COST x 17.5% = VAT*
3.	*CALCULATE THE FINAL TOTAL:*	*TOTAL COST + VAT = FINAL TOTAL*

the goods

As the invoice states the amount owing, it must specify accurately the goods supplied. The details – set out in columns in the body of the invoice – include:

- *product code* – this is the catalogue number which appeared on the original purchase order and on the delivery note
- *description* – the goods must be specified precisely
- *quantity* – this should agree with the quantity ordered
- *price* – this is the price of each unit shown in the next column
- *unit* is the way in which the unit is counted and charged for, eg
  – boxes of tights
  – single items, eg designer dresses
- *total* is the unit price multiplied by the number of units
- *discount %* is the percentage allowance (known as trade discount) given to customers who regularly deal with the supplier ie they receive a certain percentage (eg 10%) deducted from their bill
- *net* is the amount due to the seller after deduction of trade discount, and before VAT is added on

cash discount and VAT

Further calculations are made in the box at the bottom of the invoice:

- *Goods Total* is the net amount due to the seller (the total of the net column)
- *Cash Discount* is a percentage of the Goods Total (often a 2.5% discount) which the buyer can deduct if he or she pays straightaway rather than waiting the month allowed on the invoice – there is no cash discount in this example
- *Value Added Tax* (VAT), here calculated as 17.5% of the total after deduction of any cash discount. VAT is added to produce the invoice final total.

terms

The terms for payment are stated on the invoice. In this case these include:

- *Net monthly* – this means that full payment of the invoice (without cash discount) should be made within a month of the invoice date
- *Carriage paid* means that the price of the goods includes delivery
- *E & OE* stands for 'errors and omissions excepted' which means that if there is a error or something left off the invoice by mistake, resulting in an incorrect final price, the supplier has the right to rectify the mistake and demand the correct amount

credit note – *a refund is due to the buyer*

A credit note is a 'refund' document. It reduces the amount owed by the buyer. The goods, remember, have not yet been paid for. The credit note is prepared by the supplier and sent to the buyer. For example:
- the goods may have been damaged, lost in transit or are faulty
- not all the goods have been sent – this is referred to as 'shortages'
- the unit price on the invoice may be too high

In the case of the socks, Trends has received 10 damaged pairs. These will be sent back to Cool Socks with a *returns note* (not shown here) asking for *credit* – ie a reduction in the bill for the 10 faulty pairs. Cool Socks will have to issue the credit note for £27.73 shown below.

Note the following details:
- the invoice number of the original consignment is quoted
- the reason for the issue of the credit note is stated at the bottom of the credit note – here 'damaged' goods
- the details are otherwise exactly the same as on an invoice

---

——— CREDIT NOTE ———
COOL SOCKS LIMITED
Unit 45 Elgar Estate, Broadfield, BR7 4ER
Tel 01908 765314 Fax 01908 765951
VAT REG GB 0745 4672 76

to

Trends
4 Friar Street
Broadfield
BR1 3RF

credit note no	12157
account	3993
your reference	47609
our invoice	787923
date/tax point	10 10 95

product code	description	quantity	price	unit	total	discount %	net
45B	Blue Toebar socks	10	2.36	pair	23.60	0.00	23.60

Reason for credit
10 pairs of socks received damaged
(Your returns note no. R/N 2384)

GOODS TOTAL	23.60
CASH DISCOUNT	0.00
SUBTOTAL	23.60
VAT	4.13
TOTAL	27.73

statement – *the seller requests payment*

A supplier will not normally expect a buyer to pay each individual invoice as soon as it is received: this could result in the buyer having to make a number of payments during the month. Instead, a statement of account is sent by the supplier to the buyer *at the end of the month*. This statement, which can be typed out, or printed by the seller's computer accounting program, shows what is owed by the buyer to the seller. It contains details of:

- invoices issued for goods supplied – the full amount due, including VAT
- refunds made on credit notes – including VAT
- payments received from the buyer (if any)
- the final amount due

The statement issued by Cool Socks to Trends for the period covering the sale and refund is shown below.

STATEMENT OF ACCOUNT

COOL SOCKS LIMITED

Unit 45 Elgar Estate, Broadfield, BR7 4ER
Tel 01908 765314 Fax 01908 765951
VAT REG GB 0745 4672 76

TO

Trends 4 Friar Street Broadfield BR1 3RF	account 3993 date 31 10 95

date	details	debit £	credit £	balance £
01 10 95	Invoice 787923	277.30		277.30
10 10 95	Credit note 12157		27.73	249.57

			AMOUNT NOW DUE	249.57

remittance advice – *payment is sent*

A remittance advice is a document sent by the buyer to the seller stating that payment is being made. Very often a printed remittance advice is attached to the statement sent by the seller: the idea is that this encourages the buyer to make payment!
We will look at making payments in detail in the next chapter. You should note here that payment can be made in two completely different ways
- by *cheque*, in which case the remittance advice goes with the cheque
- by *electronic transfer* (known as a BACS payment) between the bank account of the buyer and the bank account of the seller; in this case a remittance advice will be sent by post, *but no cheque is written*

We will look at both types of remittance advice.

cheque payment

Here Trends have used a 'tear-off' remittance advice sent by Cool Socks with their statement. You will see that Trends have been asked to tick the invoice they are paying. If there were more than one invoice to pay, they would tick each one that they were paying.

Note that before payment can be authorised and made, Trends must match up the Purchase Order copy, Delivery Note, Goods Received Note, invoice and any other relevant documentation to make sure in very basic terms that they re paying for what they got!

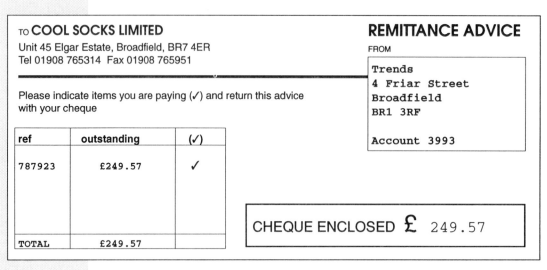

ref	outstanding	(✓)
787923	£249.57	✓
TOTAL	£249.57	

TO **COOL SOCKS LIMITED**
Unit 45 Elgar Estate, Broadfield, BR7 4ER
Tel 01908 765314 Fax 01908 765951

Please indicate items you are paying (✓) and return this advice with your cheque

REMITTANCE ADVICE
FROM

Trends
4 Friar Street
Broadfield
BR1 3RF

Account 3993

CHEQUE ENCLOSED £ 249.57

The cheque made out by Trends is shown on the next page. It will be attached to the remittance advice and will be posted to Cool Socks at the beginning of November.

Albion Bank PLC

7 The Avenue
Broadfield BR1 2AJ

Date   *5 November* 19 *95*   **90 47 17**

Pay   *Cool Socks Limited* _____

Two hundred and forty nine pounds 57p _____   **£** *249.57* ____

A/c payee only

TRENDS

V Williams

072628   90 47 17   11719512

electronic transfer payment

If Trends made regular payments to Cool Socks, Cool Socks might suggest settlement of invoices could be made by electronic transfer between their bank accounts, using BACS (Bankers Automated Clearing System) computer transfer.

If this system is used no cheque will be written, but a remittance advice will still need to be posted to Cool Socks by Trends so that Cool Socks can tally up the payment when it appears on its bank statement. A typical electronic payment remittance advice is shown below.

BACS REMITTANCE ADVICE

FROM: Trends
4 Friar Street
Broadfield
BR1 3RF

TO: Cool Socks Limited
Unit 45 Elgar Estate,
Broadfield, BR7 4ER

05 11 95

Your ref	Our ref		Amount
787923	47609	BACS TRANSFER	249.57
		Total	249.57

THIS HAS BEEN PAID BY BACS CREDIT TRANSFER DIRECTLY INTO YOUR BANK ACCOUNT
ALBION BANK NO 11451226 SORT CODE 90 47 17

Core Skill 2.2

using financial documents

Note: these tasks require you to prepare your own purchase orders and invoices. You are advised to collect samples from local businesses and to study the examples in this chapter.

task 1

Work in pairs and play the roles of buyer and seller. The buyer is a clothes shop and the seller a clothes manufacturer. You will need copies of two blank business documents: purchase order and invoice. You should use today's date and the current VAT rate, but will need to make up the following details:

• the names and addresses of buyer and seller

• catalogue numbers

• order numbers and invoice numbers

The buyer is to complete two separate purchase orders and the seller is to complete an invoice for each order. The orders are as follows:

(a)   100 pairs of tights (black) at £1.25 each
25 woollen jumpers (green) at £15 each
50 nighties (pink) at £8.50 each

(b)   25 dresses (red) at £15 each
30 pairs of denim jeans (black) at £17.50 each
50 pairs of tights (black) at £1.30 each

There is no trade discount available to the buyer. Add VAT at the current rate.

task 2

You work for Deansway Trading Company, a wholesaler of office stationery, which trades from The Modern Office, 79 Deansway, Stourminster WR1 2EJ. A customer, The Card Shop of 126 The Crescent, Marshall Green, WR4 5TX, orders the following on order number 9516:

(a)   5 boxes of assorted rubbers at £5 per box, catalogue no 26537
(b)   100 shorthand notebooks at £4 for a pack of 10, catalogue no 72625
(c)   250 ring binders at 50p each, catalogue no 72698

VAT is to be charged at the current rate on all items, and a 2.5 per cent cash discount is offered for full settlement within 14 days. Prepare invoice number 8234, under today's date, to be sent to the customer.

STUDENT ACTIVITY 12.3
performance criterion 4.2.1

Core Skill 2.2

sorting out mistakes

Examine carefully the invoice shown below and write down any errors which you can find. In each case state what the consequence of the error might be if it went undetected.

INVOICE

COOL SOCKS LIMITED

Unit 45 Elgar Estate, Broadfield, BR7 4ER
Tel 01908 765314 Fax 01908 765951
VAT REG GB 0745 4672 76

invoice to

| Trends |
| 4 Friar Street |
| Broadfield |
| BR1 3RF |

invoice no	787923
account	3993
your reference	47609

deliver to

as above

date/tax point

---

product code	description	quantity	price	unit	total	discount %	net
45R	Red Toebar socks	100	2.45	pair	254.00	10.00	279.40

GOODS TOTAL	279.40
CASH DISCOUNT	0.00
SUBTOTAL	279.40
VAT	48.89
TOTAL	230.51

chapter summary and key terms

■ Financial transactions generate documents which in turn are recorded in the accounting system of a business. They are both outward (making payments) and inwards (receiving payments).

■ The recording of financial transactions enables a business to
- monitor its performance and tell what profit (or loss) it has made
- provide accounting statements for the owner and for external use

■ The **purchases documents** used by a business buying goods include:
- the *purchase order,* which places the order with the supplier
- the *invoice*, which lists the goods and tells you what you owe
- the *credit note*, which is sent to you if you are due a refund
- the *goods received note*, which records the goods when they arrive

■ The **sales documents** used by a business selling goods include the purchase order and invoice mentioned above – they also include:
- the *order received note*, an internal record of the receipt of the order
- the *delivery note*, which is sent with the goods
- the *statement of account,* sent to the buyer summarising what is owed
- the *remittance advice* which is sent to the seller by the buyer when payment is made

■ It is important that purchases and sales documents are completed accurately. If mistakes are made, the consequences can be serious, eg
- the wrong goods supplied
- an incorrect amount charged

key terms

Value Added Tax	VAT is a tax on the supply of goods and services, ie a tax on spending; it is charged on invoices by VAT-registered businesses
trade discount	is a discount given to customers who trade regularly with the seller: it is deducted on the invoice
cash discount	is given to the buyer in some instances when payment is made by the buyer within a short period of time, ie well before the credit period expires; it is deducted on the invoice

multiple-choice questions

1   A purchase order is used to
   A   tell the purchaser how much the goods cost
   B   place an order with the seller
   C   pay the seller for the goods
   D   fix the price on a purchase of goods

2   A remittance advice is
   A   an advice note telling the buyer what goods were sent
   B   an advice note telling the seller that the wrong goods were sent
   C   a document advising the seller of payment
   D   a document advising the buyer of payment

Questions 3 – 5 relate to the following information:
   An invoice with a number of errors has resulted in the following problems:
   A   the wrong goods sent
   B   a query on the total amount payable
   C   the goods sent to the wrong person
   D   an order sent twice
   Which of these problems is likely to have been caused by the following?

3   The wrong unit price used

4   The wrong product code used

5   The wrong customer account number used

6   Decide whether each of these statements is True (T) or False (F)
   (i)   the goods received note is sent with the goods
   (ii)   the order received note is sent to the buyer
   A   (i) T   (ii) T
   B   (i) T   (ii) F
   C   (i) F   (ii) T
   D   (i) F   (ii) F

13 Documents for payments and receipts

GNVQ SPECIFICATIONS

This chapter covers performance criteria from two 'overlapping' elements:

Element 4.1: Identify and explain financial transactions and documents
performance criteria – a student must:

4   explain and give examples of payment methods and receipt documents

5   explain the importance of security and security checks for receipts and payments

Element 4.2: Complete financial documents and explain financial recording
performance criteria – a student must:

2   complete payment and receipt documents clearly and correctly and calculate totals

Note: the remaining performance criteria from these elements – which deal with financial recording, purchases and sales documents – were covered in the last chapter.

what this chapter covers

This chapter is very practical in nature: you will examine and complete the documents involved when a business makes payment and when it receives payment. You will also see why documents have to be completed accurately and you will appreciate the need for security checks.

what you will learn from this chapter

- a business can make manual payments involving cash and a petty cash voucher, or a cheque, bank giro credit, debit card or credit card

- a business can make payments by computer transfer between the banks (Bankers Automated Clearing Services – BACS) or between the businesses and the banks (Electronic data Interchange – EDI)

- a business can receive money in the form of payment by cash, cheque, debit card, or credit card

- when a business receives money it will normally pay it into the bank on a paying-in slip; the bank will regularly issue a bank statement

- when errors are made on documents, the consequences can be serious

- it is important that a business sets up a system of security checks to help avoid errors and unauthorised transactions

payments in cash

pc 4.1.4

the cashless society?

Despite the growth in the use of plastic cards, cash is the most common way of paying for goods and services – newspapers, magazines, sandwiches, cans of drink, bus fares, stationery – the list is very long.

Most cash tills will show on a screen the money amount of the purchase and also the change to be given. The till will also issue a *receipt* for *all* purchases when cash, a cheque, a debit card or a credit card is used. In the example below a customer has bought a pack of coloured paper and some biros from Mitre Stationery. A till receipt has been issued.

a till receipt for a cash transaction

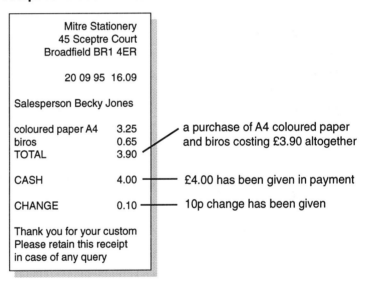

```
        Mitre Stationery
        45 Sceptre Court
        Broadfield BR1 4ER

        20 09 95  16.09

Salesperson Becky Jones

coloured paper A4    3.25
biros                0.65
TOTAL                3.90

CASH                 4.00

CHANGE               0.10

Thank you for your custom
Please retain this receipt
in case of any query
```

a purchase of A4 coloured paper and biros costing £3.90 altogether

£4.00 has been given in payment

10p change has been given

petty cash

pc 4.2.2

what is petty cash?

Sometimes businesses will make payments for small amounts in cash – known as 'petty cash'. Petty cash is a float of cash (notes and coins) kept in a locked cash box in the business under the control of someone in authority – the petty cashier. Clearly this money can only be used for *business purposes,* and not for personal items like employees' sandwiches.

petty cash voucher

In order to get petty cash from the tin, the employee will need to get a slip of paper known as a *petty cash voucher* signed by someone in authority. *To this voucher must be attached the receipt for the payment.* A petty cash voucher is illustrated below.

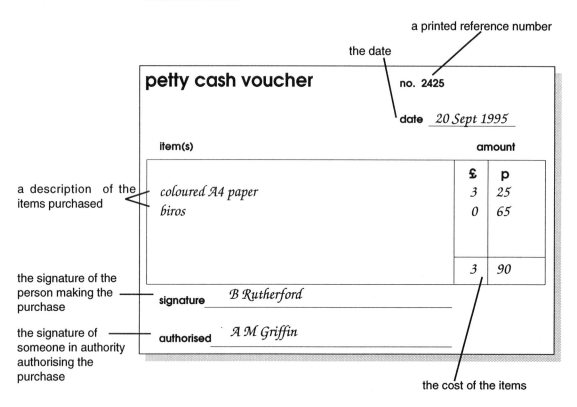

a printed reference number

the date

petty cash voucher

no. 2425

date   20 Sept 1995

item(s)   amount

a description of the items purchased

item(s)	£	p
coloured A4 paper	3	25
biros	0	65
	3	90

the signature of the person making the purchase

signature   B Rutherford

the signature of someone in authority authorising the purchase

authorised   A M Griffin

the cost of the items

payments by cheque

pc 4.2.2

what is a cheque?

a cheque is a written order to the bank signed by its customer (known as the 'drawer') to pay a specified amount to a specified person (the 'payee')

In other words a cheque is an instruction by the person writing the cheque to their bank to pay a named person a sum of money.

Cheques are commonly used in business by buyers of goods and services settling bills by post. As we saw in the last chapter, the cheque is normally accompanied by a remittance advice detailing what is being paid. Look at the illustration of a cheque on the next page.

Albion Bank PLC

7 The Avenue
Broadfield BR1 2AJ

Date _____ *1 April* 19 *95*   90 47 17

Pay   *Mitre Stationery* _____

Eighty pounds only _____ A/c payee only _____ **£** *80.00* _____

FOR AND ON BEHALF OF
BROADFIELD LEISURE LIMITED

R Patel   *N Singh*
DIRECTOR   DIRECTOR

000280   90 47 17   11787206

This cheque has been written out by two directors of Broadfield Leisure Limited in settlement of an invoice for £80 for stationery bought from Mitre Stationery. Note the following points:

drawer

The business which has issued (written) the cheque is Broadfield Leisure Limited – this company is the *drawer* of the cheque. Most limited company cheques need two or more signatures. Here two directors have signed.

payee

The business receiving the money, Mitre Stationery, will pay the cheque into the bank, and the money will go onto the bank account on the same day. The cheque will be processed in the three day bank clearing system and it will finish up at the Albion Bank in Broadfield (see the address on the cheque), where, if there is enough money on Broadfield Leisure Limited's bank account, and the cheque has no errors on it, it will be 'paid'.

amount

The amount is written in both words and figures. The amount in words and figures *must* be the same. If there is a difference, the cheque might not be 'paid' by the bank. Note here that there are lines drawn after the amount – this stops the payee from 'fiddling' by altering and increasing the amount!

date

The cheque must have a valid date. This means that the cheque cannot have a future date (be 'postdated'). Cheques go out of date after six months.

bank card?

No bank card is used to back the cheque because the cheque is being sent through the post – bank cards can only be used for 'over the counter' transactions. Also, many businesses do not have bank cards.

crossing

The two parallel lines and the words "A/c payee only" are a *crossing* – they mean that the cheque can only be paid into the bank account of Mitre Stationery (the payee), and not into any other account.

completing cheques

tasks

You are to complete the following cheques fully and accurately and add the necessary signatures. Use today's date and sign your own name if you think you need to.

1   R Singh is paying Pronto Wholesalers £4346.78 in settlement of a recent statement for goods supplied to his shop. The cheque only needs one signature. R Singh is authorised to sign.

Western Bank PLC	Date _____ 19 ____ 80 47 17
9 The Avenue	
Broadfield BR1 2AJ	

Pay _____

A/c payee only

£ _____

R SINGH STORES

083837   80 47 17   38478374

2   Mary White, Finance Officer of Wybold College is writing and signing a cheque paying Mitre Stationery for stationery supplies costing £1,250.50. The cheque needs two signatures, one of which can be Mary White's.

Albion Bank PLC	Date _____ 19 ____ 90 47 17
7 The Avenue	
Broadfield BR1 2AJ	

Pay _____

A/c payee only

£ _____

WYBOLD COLLEGE

075165   90 47 17   11719516

making payment by plastic card

pc 4.1.4

Businesss can also make payment using *plastic cards*. There are two basic types: the *debit card* and the *credit card*.

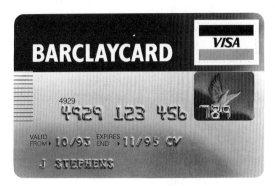

Barclays Connect – a debit card   Barclaycard – a credit card

debit card

A debit card – shown above left – is a plastic card issued by a bank or a building society to personal and business customers. It enables the customer to make payment for goods and services *without having to write out a cheque.* Common examples of debit cards include 'Switch' and 'Connect' cards. When a debit card is used in a shop, the shop receives its money either

- by electronic link through the cash till to its bank account (a process known as EFTPOS – Electronic Funds Transfer at Point Of Sale), *or*
- by the shop using a manual imprinter to produce a paper *voucher* which is then paid into the shop's bank account on a *paying-in slip*

A debit card is also commonly used to guarantee ('back') cheques issued over the counter (but not for limited company customers).

credit card

Credit cards enable the user to purchase goods over the counter, through the post and by telephone. Payment is made *at a later date* when a monthly statement listing all the purchases made is sent to the holder and payment requested. A business *accepting* a credit card payment will again receive its money *either* direct into the bank account through an electronic till (EFTPOS) *or* by paying into the bank sales vouchers processed manually. Many businesses issue credit cards to their employees to enable them to pay for *business* expenses which they incur, eg petrol used by a travelling sales rep. This helps the employee and also the business because the employee's spending can be monitored and controlled!

credit payments

cash and credit payments

When a consumer or a business buys goods or services, it will be asked either:

- to pay *cash* (ie *straightaway* – but not necessarily with notes and coins - most 'cash' payments are by cheque)

- to pay *on credit* – ie pay later

Paying on credit terms can be done in a number of ways. Either the business making the purchase will *itself* pay up, or it will *arrange finance* from elsewhere so that it can pay back over an extended period of time.

hire purchase (HP)

One method of raising finance used both by consumers and by businesses is *hire purchase (HP).* Here the person buying the goods takes possession of them straightaway and makes payments over a period of time, say up to three years, not to the seller, but to a finance company. The goods do not belong to the buyer until the payments have been completed. Hire purchase is often used for car purchases – see the advert below.

the cost of credit - APR

The law (the Consumer Credit Act) requires that lenders tell consumers the *cost* of the credit. This is shown as an APR (Annual Percentage Rate) – the annual cost of borrowing the money. So if you borrow £100 and arrange credit such as hire purchase with an APR of 10%, it will cost you £10 a year on average in interest and fees.

SPEED FINANCE – low APR%

drive this for only £850 a month!

Telephone Alun Jones for a quote – mobile 0850 193752

paying by bank giro credit

pc 4.1.4

If a business wishes to make a payment direct to a bank account it can do so by filling in a blank paper slip known as a *bank giro credit* and paying it in over the bank counter with a cheque for the same amount. The details completed by the business are shown below shaded grey – these are explained in full on page 239 where we look at the paying-in slip.

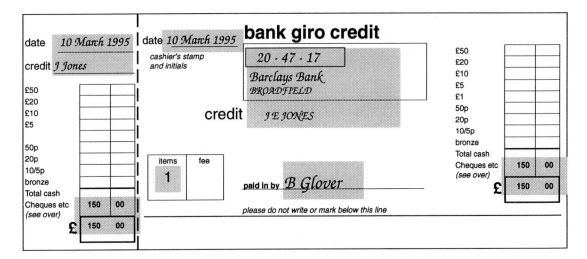

paying by computer – BACS

pc 4.1.4

from cheques to BACS

The banks and their big customers (eg British Gas) are currently encouraging businesses and private individuals to make payments using an interbank computer transfer system called BACS (Bankers Automated Clearing Services). This system enables payments to be made in two ways:

- it can send payments to other bank accounts *– direct credits*
- it can take money off bank accounts *– direct debits*

BACS direct credits – bulk payments

Suppose at the end of the month a business has to pay wages to fifty employees with bank accounts and has to settle up with twenty suppliers. Instead of writing out a large number of cheques or bank giro credits, all the customer has to do is to provide the information about the payments on computer file. This is then sent to the BACS processing centre in West London by mail, on disc or tape, *or* direct by telephone line. The information is fed into the BACS computer and three working days later the payment will leave one bank account and be received on the other bank or building society account.

direct debits

When a business collects money from someone else's account through the BACS system, it uses a *direct debit*. The direct debit system is useful for organisations such as insurance companies and credit card companies which receive a large number of payments *where the amounts can vary*. The normal procedure is for the customer who is making the payment to complete and sign a written authority (mandate) prepared by the business collecting the money – eg an insurance company. This form (see below) is then processed and input onto the computer by the bank which *receives* the money.

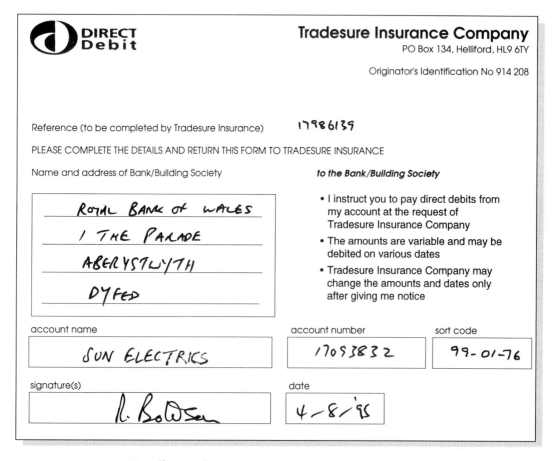

standing orders

A common example of an individual direct *credit* made through the BACS system to someone else is a *standing order*. The business that needs to make regular payments completes a written authority (a mandate), instructing the bank what payments to make, to whom, and when. The bank then sets up the instructions on its computer, and the payments are made automatically by computer link through BACS on the due dates.

the payslip

pc 4.1.4

The payslip is a document a business will have to complete when it pays its employees – it is required by law. Payslips may be completed by hand, but more commonly these days it is produced by a computer 'payroll' package which also calculates all the amounts on the slip. Now look at the illustration below and read the explanation which follows.

ALBION BANK PLC pay advice			
payments		**deductions**	
Basic pay	160.00	Income tax	32.62
Overtime	48.00	National Insurance	16.29
		Total deductions	48.91
GROSS PAY	208.00	NET PAY	159.09

date 13.05.96	employee S Barberini	ref 276327
code 352L	payment method BACS	

The payslip shows:

gross pay
This is what the employee earns *before* deductions are made – here it is basic pay of £160, plus overtime of £48. What the employee *gets* is *net pay* (£159.09).

deductions
Deductions for two 'taxes' are made by the employer through the PAYE (Pay as You Earn) system and sent direct to the Inland Revenue:

- *income tax* – a percentage of the employee's earnings, used by the Government for spending on education, health, defence etc
- *National Insurance Contributions* – also a percentage deduction, used by the Benefits Agency for state benefits such as state pensions and sick pay

In addition , the employer may deduct contributions to a pension scheme (other than the state pension) ,to savings schemes and gifts to charity.

payment details
The payslip will show how the employee is to be paid – it could be by cheque, or, as here, by BACS transfer straight to the employee's bank account.

Electronic Data Interchange (EDI)

You will have seen that the BACS system enables payments to be made by link-ups between *bank computers*. Systems now exist whereby business documents such as purchase orders and invoices are generated on computer file and the data sent between the computers of the *buyer and the seller*. This can then be followed up by a payment instruction on the due date.

This system, known as *Electronic Data Interchange (EDI)*, is extensively used in the UK, particularly by large retailing organisations which need to renew stock frequently on a Just-in-Time basis.

what is EDI ?

EDI is a system which transfers commercial and administrative instructions between computers using agreed formats for the messages. The two parties involved agree a standard format for the electronic messages which take the place of purchase orders, delivery instructions, invoices, credit notes and statements. The international standard transfer system is *UN/EDIFACT,* although there are other standards, such as *TRADACOMS* used by retailers.

EDI transfers

The transfer is normally sent from one computer to another via a third party known as a VAN (value added network). A value added network operates like an electronic post office: you deposit your information electronically in your 'post box' and the value added network transfers it to the 'postbox' of your trading partner.

The benefits of EDI include: reduced handling costs, reduced postage costs, reduced paper storage costs, fewer errors (there is less re-keying of existing computer data) and faster payment.

EDI payments

In the normal course of paper-based trading (ie using paper invoices and other business documents), settlement is usually made by cheque which is posted to the supplier or by BACS (an inter-bank computer transfer system). The banks now are developing systems whereby the buyer can use the EDI system for authorising the bank to make payment to the supplier's bank. NatWest's BankLine Interchange, for example, can be used for making payments to individual suppliers or to a number of suppliers. As the buyer's computer system already has details of each trade transaction – the parties involved and the amounts – it is a simple matter to add the banking details of the supplier, so that settlement can be made by BACS.

receipts documents

pc 4.2.2

So far in this chapter we have looked at the ways in which a business can make payment for goods and services and wages. We have examined the documents involved and in many instances learnt how to complete them.

We now 'turn the tables' and examine the process from the point of view of the business *receiving* the money and then paying it into the bank. We will examine and complete a number of different documents:

- the handwritten receipt
- the cheque (from the point of view of a business *receiving* one)
- the paying-in slip
- the bank statement

the handwritten receipt

When a business sells goods or services on a 'cash' (immediate settlement) basis, the buyer will need a *document* to provide evidence that money has been spent on those particular goods or services. It may be a travelling salesman buying petrol, or an office manager buying stationery from a shop. If there is no documentary evidence, the business (or the tax inspectors) may wonder where the money has gone – has the salesman used the money to take his wife out? Has the office manager bought himself a new briefcase? If the seller issues a formal handwritten *receipt*, there is no doubt about the transaction. Look at the example shown below.

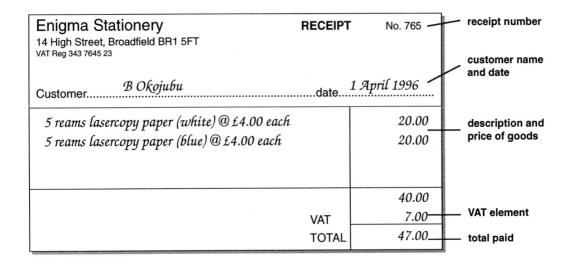

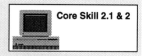

STUDENT ACTIVITY 13.2
performance criterion 4.2.2

Core Skill 2.1 & 2

completing receipts

task 1
Collect a variety of receipts – either blank ones or copies of completed receipts. Sources include local businesses (eg petrol stations) and stationers (who sell blank receipts in pads). Examine and compare them in class.

task 2
Design and draw up your own receipt. Use a computer package if you can. Invent your own business name and address for a lighting supplies firm. Remember to include a VAT registration number – you should assume that the business charges VAT.

task 3
Make (or print out) three copies of your receipt and enter the following sales transactions:
- (a) 2 flexilamps @ £13.99, plus 2 candlelight bulbs @85p each sold to George Meredith
- (b) 1 standard lamp @ £149.95, plus one 100 watt bulb @ 99p, sold to Alex Bell
- (c) 2 Georgian lamps @ £35.99 sold to Miss S Fox

Use today's date and add VAT at the current rate to the prices given.

receiving cheques

pc 4.2.2

A business can receive cheques in a variety of ways:

- a shop can receive cheques *over the counter*
- a business can receive cheques *through the post* in settlement of invoices

In both cases, the business receiving the cheque will have to *check* it carefully before paying it into the bank.

why bother to check the cheque?
If there is anything wrong with the cheque and it is paid into the bank, it may be returned *unpaid* four or five days later by the bank whose name appears on the cheque. In other words if there is anything wrong with the cheque, the money will go onto the business bank account *and then be taken off again three or four days later* and the cheque will be posted back to the business for it to sort out! Problems with cheques include: missing issuer's signature, missing payee's name, words and figures differing and corrections not signed by the issuer.

the paying-in slip

A business uses a paper paying-in slip to pay money into its bank account. The paying-in slip is also known as a 'bank giro credit' or 'credit transfer'. *Personal customers* normally have paying-in slips at the back of their chequebooks. *Business customers,* however, are normally issued with books – known as 'paying-in books' – full of paying-in slips. A paying-in slip can be used for paying in:

- cash

- cheques

- sales vouchers for debit cards and credit cards (but only where the tills of the business are *not* linked up to the bank's computer)

paying into the business account

Look at the example below which shows Sabre Stationery paying money into its bank account at Albion Bank in Broadfield on 1 April 1995. The money the business is paying in comprises:

cash
- two £20 notes
- one £5 note
- five £1 coins

cheques
- three cheques for £50.00, £30.00 and £20.00

details already printed on the paying-in slip

When a paying-in book is provided for a business, some details are already printed on the paying-in slip. These include:

- the name and branch of the bank
- the 'sort code' of the bank branch (a six digit number – 90 47 17 on the credit shown here) – a sort code is the banking equivalent of a post code – each bank branch has a different number
- the name of the account – here Sabre Stationery
- the account number of the business – here it is the eight digit number printed at the bottom of the slip

details completed by the business on the front of the slip

These include:

- a breakdown of the categories of any cash being paid in – note that it is the *amount* which is entered in each case
- the *total* of the cheques being paid in
- a grand total of the cash and the cheques
- the date
- the signature of the person paying the money into the bank
- a record of the money being paid in noted on the counterfoil

details completed by the business on the back of the slip

- a list of the individual cheques – here there are three
- a total of all the cheques – here £100

counterfoil			cheques		
	50	00	Beamish Limited	50	00
	30	00	Pronto Alarms	30	00
	20	00	D Cox	20	00
£	100	00	carried over £	100	00

Core Skill 2.2

paying-in slips

task 1

Collect a variety of paying-in slips from local banks. (Ask at the enquiry counter if there are none on display in the banking hall).

task 2

Complete a suitable paying-in slip for the following items:

CASH	CHEQUES
1 x £50 note	*H N Ford £50.00*
5 x £20 notes	*Broadfield College £1,250.50*
7 x £10 notes	*R Hanif £15.50*
25 x £1 coins	*H Smith £20.50*
25 x 50p pieces	
10 x 10p pieces	
£5.25 in bronze	

Make up your own business name and eight digit account number. Use today's date and sign your own name on the paying-in slip.

the bank statement

pc 4.2.2

The bank's record of payments in and out of the bank account will be sent to the business in the form of a bank statement. Look at the example on the next page. You will see the following details on the bank statement:

account details

The top of the statement shows the details of the bank account:

- the name and branch address of the bank
- the name and number of the account

transaction columns

There are columns for:

- the date of the transaction
- payments out of the account
- payments into the account
- the 'balance' – ie the amount left in the account after each transaction

statement of account		ALBION BANK PLC		

account: Sabre Stationery
number: 14517226

Broadfield Branch
7 The Avenue
Broadfield BR1 2AJ

date	particulars	withdrawn	paid in	balance
1996				
1 Oct	balance brought forward			1000.00 CR
1 Oct	cheque 182289	100.00		900.00 CR
9 Oct	cheque 182290	150.00		750.00 CR
11 Oct	Direct debit ABC Insurance	50.00		700.00 CR
16 Oct	Paid in		300.00	1000.00 CR
31 Oct	balance carried forward			1000.00 CR

transactions on the bank statement

The bank statement shown above sets out the transactions on the bank account of Sabre Stationery for the month of October 1996. Now look at the following details:

the date The year is shown at the top of the date column, while the date of each transaction is shown by the *day* and the *month*.

particulars
- *cheques* shown here have been written out by Sabre Stationery and passed through the banking system; note that the cheque number is shown
- *direct debits* show the name of the organisation which has collected the money from the bank account
- *paid in* shows that Sabre Stationery has paid in money on a paying-in slip
- *balance brought forward* is not a payment in or out of the account; it means 'this is the money in the account on the first day of this statement'
- *balance carried forward* is not a payment in or out of the account; it means 'this is the money in the account on the last day of this statement' – it is the figure which will be shown ('carried forward') on the first line of the November statement

balance The balance column shows the amount of money in the account after each transaction. 'CR' is short for 'credit' which means that there is money in the account. If the business has an overdraft on the account (if it owed the bank money), the balance figure would be followed by 'DR' ('debit').

STUDENT ACTIVITY 13.4
performance criterion 4.2.2

the bank statement

statement of account

ALBION BANK PLC

Broadfield Branch
7 The Avenue
Broadfield BR1 2AJ

account: Osborne Electronics Ltd
number: 01099124

date	particulars	withdrawn	paid in	balance
1995				
2 Oct	Balance brought forward			625.50 CR
9 Oct	Cheque 352817	179.30		446.20 CR
10 Oct	Paid in		485.04	931.24 CR
17 Oct	Cheque 352818	169.33		761.91 CR
23 Oct	Paid in		62.30	824.21 CR
24 Oct	Paid in		100.00	924.21 CR
26 Oct	Cheque 352819	821.80		102.41 CR
26 Oct	Unpaid cheque	250.00		147.59 DR
30 Oct	Paid in		108.00	39.59 DR
31 Oct	Balance carried forward			39.59 DR

tasks

Study the bank statement shown above and answer the following questions:

1   What do "Balance brought forward" and "Balance carried forward" mean? Why are there no figures in the withdrawn and paid in columns for these items?

2   What are the numbers following the word "cheque"? What will the business check these numbers against?

3   What do "CR" and "DR" mean?

4   What has happened to the bank account in the last week of October? Could the business have foreseen this? What can they do about the situation?

checking for errors

pc 4.1.5

Errors on documents can cause a variety of problems, and very often reflect badly on the level of customer care in a business. We have already seen in the last chapter that errors on invoices can result in the wrong goods being sent, the wrong amount being charged, and so on. Errors in payments and receipts documents also have their unfortunate consequences – for example:

- a cheque made out for the wrong amount may result in a delay in obtaining the goods or services ordered

- wrong dates on BACS instructions – a recent example is that of a bank employee who put the wrong date on the payment of several thousand employees' wages and salaries

- a mistake of addition on a paying-in slip – the business as a result could have difficulty in tallying up its records with the bank statement

- a mistake on the bank statement – again – the business could have difficulty in tallying up its records with the bank statement

The answer to these problems is careful checking of documents within a business (and the bank!). Clearly if a business was careless enough it could end up in a position of acute financial crisis because it just would not know where it stood – it could run short of cash and people to whom it owed money could start bankruptcy proceedings. This is obviously a very worse case – but it does happen occasionally.

security checks

pc 4.1.5

Businesses are vulnerable both to errors and to fraud. They can guard against both by introducing rigorous security checks to prevent one individual either perpetrating a "howler' or a "fiddle". For example:

- all purchase orders and petty cash vouchers need an *authorised signature*

- invoices should only be paid when the business is satisfied by *checking the original order and the goods received note* that the goods have been received in acceptable condition

- *cheques should be signed by the right people* – as we saw earlier a company cheque is normally signed by two or more authorised directors

- *segregation of duties* – making sure that the same person does not do two jobs where there may be opportunity for major error or a temptation to defraud the business, eg the responsibility for receiving goods and paying for goods should be given to different people

chapter summary and key terms

■ A business can make manual payments involving:
- cash and a petty cash voucher
- a cheque
- a bank giro credit
- a debit card or a credit card

■ A business can make payments by computer transfer between the banks using Bankers Automated Clearing Services (BACS).Payments can be:
- *direct credits*: individual payments (standing orders) or bulk payments
- *direct debits*: money collected from bank accounts (eg gas bills)

■ Businesses are increasingly using Electronic Data Interchange (EDI), a computer communication system between businesses to send orders, invoices and payment instructions.

■ A business can receive money in the form of payment by cash, cheque, debit card, or credit card.

■ When a business receives money it will normally pay it into the bank on a paying-in slip; the bank will regularly issue a bank statement.

■ When errors are made on documents, the consequences can be serious. It is therefore important that a business sets up a system of security checks to help avoid errors and unauthorised transactions.

key terms

petty cash	a secured 'float' of cash kept within the business for small purchases, authorised by a petty cash voucher
cheque	is a written order to the bank signed by its customer (known as the 'drawer') to pay a specified amount to a specified person (the 'payee')
BACS	Bankers Automated Clearing Services is a system of direct computer transfers between the bank accounts of businesses and individuals
EDI	Electronic Data Interchange is a computer communication system between businesses used for sending orders, invoices and payment instructions.
receipt	a document issued by a seller as evidence of a cash (immediate payment) transaction.

multiple-choice questions

1   A petty cash payment is BEST described as a
    A   cash payment to staff for personal expenses
    B   payment of notes and coins into the bank account
    C   cash payment for a small item of business expense
    D   payment made by a junior member of staff

2   A cheque can be defined as a written order from the
    A   drawer to the payee
    B   bank to the payee
    C   bank to the drawer
    D   drawer to the bank

Questions 3 – 5 relate to the following information:
    A payslip will show these details:
    A   gross pay
    B   net pay
    C   National Insurance Contributions
    D   Income tax
    Which of these relate to the following?

3   The amount of money the employee actually receives

4   A tax used for government spending in general

5   A tax used to provide money for state pensions

6   Decide whether each of these statements is True (T) or False (F)
    (i)   a BACS direct debit is used to collect money from bank accounts
    (ii) a BACS direct credit is used to pay employees' wages
    A   (i) T   (ii) T
    B   (i) T   (ii) F
    C   (i) F   (ii) T
    D   (i) F   (ii) F

EVIDENCE COLLECTION ASSIGNMENT 12

Financial transactions and documents

Element 4.1

introduction

This assignment contains a practical exercise in constructing profit statements recording the income and expenditure of a business over three months. Each profit statement will be constructed by referring to the financial documents used in the transactions. You will also collect examples of financial documents and make a list of security checks relating to the documents.

task 1 – Katy Morris and "Irresistible"

pcs 4.1.1-4

Katy Morris has set up a small business making perfume from original West Country formulas. Her main perfume is called "Irresistible". She works as a sole trader and employs three full-time assistants.

During the first three months of the year she is not sure how profitable her business has been – she has been too busy making and selling her products to keep full accounting records. She has, however, a number of box files containing financial documents. They are labelled "Sales" "Wages" "Bills" and "Bank".

The contents of the boxes are as follows:

SALES BOX

January	Copy sales invoices amounting to £8,000
February	Copy sales invoices amounting to £7,500
March	Copy sales invoices amounting to £6,500

WAGES BOX

The wages records show that payslips for each month totalled:

January	£1,500
February	£1,750
March	£1,800

BILLS BOX

Copies of paid purchase invoices and other paid bills:

January	Materials of £3,000
	Overheads (bills) of £2,000
February	Materials of £4,000
	Overheads (bills) of £1,750
March	Materials of £4,000
	Overheads (bills) of £1,500

BANK BOX   Cheque book, paying-in book, and bank statements. The bank statement for March shows two overheads items not included in the "Bills" box. They are:
* a direct debit for insurance for £400
* bank charges of £55

You are to

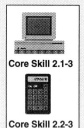

Core Skill 2.1-3

(a) Draw up profit statements for Katy for January, February and March (use the format shown on page 208 and confirm your results by setting up a suitable computer spreadsheet).

(b) Draw a graph or chart showing the profit trend (use a computer package if you can).

(c) Comment on the profit trend.

Core Skill 2.2-3

(d) What advice would you give to Katy? Why is it so important to record financial transactions?

task 2 – collecting financial documents   pcs 4.1.2-3

You are to collect examples of the following business documents:

purchases and sales documents	*receipts documents*
purchase order	receipt (handwritten and till)
sales order received note	cheque
delivery note	paying-in slip
goods received note	bank statement
invoice	
credit note	
statement of account	
remittance advice	

Ideally these documents should be obtained from local businesses. If this is not possible, examine financial documents in a number of textbooks. You should

(a)   write brief notes to accompany each document

(b)   give a brief description of four payment methods

task 3 – listing security checks   pc 4.1.5

You are to word-process on one or two A4 sheets a list of security checks a business should carry out when dealing with financial documents.You should include with your list brief comments about *why* the checks should be carried out.

Use as your source the text on page 244 and any information you can collect by talking to people working in accounts departments of businesses. Local banks may also be helpful in advising on the security checks needed when dealing with cheques. Note that practice may differ widely from business to business.

EVIDENCE COLLECTION ASSIGNMENT 13

Completing financial documents

Element 4.2

introduction

This assignment involves designing and completing a set of financial documents which will be used by Flora Jones in her business over the period of a month. They will form the basis of a profit statement showing income and expenditure and profit. You will also look into the use of information technology in accounting.

task 1 – designing the documents

pcs 4.2.1-2

You will already have collected a set of financial documents in the last Assignment, and will be familiar with the examples in this book. In order that you can do the next task in this assignment you will need a set of blank documents for Flora Jones who runs a cut-flower business called "Flora's Basket". She is a sole trader working from 1, High Road, St Johns, Worcester WR2 5HN (Tel 01905 333691, fax 01905 333693). She banks at Albion Bank, 5 Market Street, Worcester, sort code 77 88 99, account number 12392320.

For the assignment Flora will need:

purchases and sales documents

purchase order
sales invoice
delivery note
goods received note
credit note
statement of account
remittance advice

payment and receipts documents

receipt (handwritten)
cheque
paying-in slip
pay slip
petty cash voucher

Core Skill 2.1-2

You may find it helpful to use an IT package to design and produce the documents – it certainly saves time to use the same 'template' for a number of different documents. Note that Flora does not use an order received note – she just initials and dates incoming purchase orders.

task 2 – completing the documents

pcs 4.2.1-2

Core Skill 2.2

Flora's sales (income)

Flora Jones sells cut-flower arrangements both from her shop in St Johns – where she takes cash and cheques over the counter – and also to the Asco supermarket chain who pay her on the issue of a sales invoice. All her takings and payments from Asco are paid into the bank on a paying-in slip.

In May 1996 Flora's sales were as follows:

Cash sales in the shop   £4,000 (£3,000 cheques, £1,000 in mixed notes and coin) – these sales include VAT

Credit sales to Asco   £4,000 less £400 for a credit note for returned goods – these do *not* include VAT

On the 15th of the month Flora sends a statement and a remittance advice to Asco for the money due.

At the end of the month she receives a cheque for £4,230 from Asco. She then pays this cheque into the bank along with the takings from her shop.

Complete

- the appropriate invoice, delivery note, credit note, statement of account and remittance advice for the Asco transactions (note you will need to add VAT to the figures on the Asco invoice and credit note)
- a paying-in slip for the cheques and the cash paid into the bank
- a cash receipt asked for by J Clark on 15 May for a floral display costing £40.00 plus VAT

Make up any details you need to, but do not change the amounts!

Flora's expenditure

purchases of materials

Flora sends two orders to Express Flowers: £2,500 (8 May) and £500 (20 May). She is invoiced for them and pays by cheque at the end of the month.

Complete

- the appropriate purchase orders for flowers and goods received notes
- the cheque sent in settlement of both orders (note VAT will need to be added to both figures shown above)

wages

Flora's assistant Daphne Smith is paid at the end of the month. The details of her pay are as follows: gross pay (ie what the business pays) £600, income tax £80, national insurance £36, payment by cheque (the net [reduced] amount).

Complete

- a payslip for Daphne (make up any details not given here)
- the wages cheque

overheads

Flora's overheads for the month total £2,000 – they include various bills paid by cheque and direct debit. They also include a petty cash payment for some stationery costing £23.50 (including VAT) purchased on 15 May.

Complete

- a petty cash voucher for the purchase on 15 May

task 3 – completing the profit statement

pcs 4.2.3

Using the figures from Task 2, compile a profit statement setting out Flora's income and expenditure and profit for the month of May. Use a computer spreadsheet to check your figures (you should already have a suitable file set up from previous Activities). Use the following format for the profit statement:

---

profit statement for Flora Jones for May 1996

	£	£
income		
sales		
less expenditure		
materials		
wages		
overheads	————	
		————
profit /(loss)		════

Core Skill 2.4

Core Skill 2.2

task 4 – recording transactions on computer

pcs 4.2.4-5

Explain to Flora, using short notes, why she needs to record her financial transactions.

She says she is not very good with numbers and asks if it is easier to use a computer for all these complex tasks. You are to investigate computer software which could be used to help record and present financial information – eg a spreadsheet, an accounting package. Write a letter to her and recommend suitable packages, giving the price, where she can get them from, and what their main features are. Use your own name and today's date. Note: some of this information may be to hand if you have done the Activity on page 209.

14 Business documents

GNVQ SPECIFICATIONS

Element 4.3: Produce, evaluate and store business documents
performance criteria – a student must:

1   explain the purpose of routine business documents
2   produce draft and final versions of business documents
3   evaluate each business document produced
4   compare the methods of processing business documents
5   reference, correctly file and retrieve business documents
6   identify and evaluate ways to send and ways to store business documents

why this chapter is different

This chapter deals with business documents, which of course is what you have been dealing with throughout your course – so the material is not new. What we do in this chapter is to start with an Assignment – planning an exhibition – with tasks related to documents and then follow with a 'document bank' which tells you how the documents are set out and stored.

what you will learn from the Assignment

- what business documents are used for
- how to draft them in rough
- how to assess them ready for sending out
- the different ways of producing them
- the cost of producing them
- ways of sending them
- how to store them
- how to access them

EVIDENCE COLLECTION ASSIGNMENT 14

Using business documents

Element 4.3

introduction

This assignment is based on a security alarm company Rapid Alarm Limited. The business instals security alarm systems both in domestic properties and also in commercial premises.

Rapid Alarm is setting up a stand at a three day business exhibition organised by the local Chamber of Commerce. Both the general public and other businesses are expected to attend – the normal total attendance is 10,000 over the three days.

This assignment looks at how the preparations involve documents, document handling and document storage. The documents will involve people, places, addresses, telephone numbers, dates and other details which are not given here – you should make these up and relate them to your own locality.

task 1 – planning the exhibition

pcs 4.3.1-3

In these tasks you are required to produce a variety of documents. In each case you should draft them and show them to your tutor for preliminary evaluation (for style, format, punctuation, spelling, grammar) before producing the final version.

letters required

(a) The directors at a preliminary meeting decide to involve sales representatives from all over the country. You are to write a letter to be sent to all the representatives explaining briefly about the exhibition and asking them to a meeting (give the date, time and place).

(b) Write a letter from one of the representatives confirming the meeting (give the date, time and place).

(c) The sales manager receives a letter from a new customer enquiring if Rapid Alarm will be at the exhibition (the customer has heard about the exhibition in the local press). The sales manager writes a suitable reply.

Core Skill 2.2

(d) The sales manager receives a letter of complaint from Ivor Grouch who has had a domestic alarm fitted, but it keeps going off in the middle of the night. The customer writes "Why can't you come and see to my alarm, you seem too busy exhibiting your useless products elsewhere!" The sales manager makes enquiries – this is the first time Mr Grouch has complained.

memo

The Managing Director, Henry Bell, sends a memo to all directors and departmental managers, inviting them to attend a meeting in the Board Room in seven days time as a planning committee. Draft the memorandum.

notice

The committee meets as planned and it is decided to publicise the event internally by placing a notice on the staff notice board. Design a suitable A4-sized notice. Use a Desk Top Publishing package or word-processor if you can.

message

You take a telephone call from Sally Greenwell, the secretary of the Chamber of Commerce (the exhibition organiser), asking for the Sales Manager, who is out. She says that there will be mains power available for the exhibition stand. Write a suitable message for the Sales Manager

invitation

The committee also decides to send a written invitation to all Rapid Alarms's 500 existing clients to come to the exhibition. They cannot agree on the format. Should it be a letter or an invitation card? See the next task.

 ## task 2 – producing the documents   pc 4.3.4

Some decisions have to be made. Local printers will have to be contacted for quotes. Write a short report to the planning committee covering the following:

Core Skill 2.2

producing the invitation

Investigate the cost of having 500 white cards printed, 500 letters photocopied, and 500 letters printed out on the office laser printer. How long will it take? What is your recommendation?

a flyer leaflet

The committee also want to have an A4 'flyer' leaflet produced for visitors to the exhibition to pick up from the stand. They reckon on a print run of 5,000. It is to be produced in black ink on blue paper. Should it be photocopied or printed? How long will it take? What is your recommendation?

 ## task 3 – sending documents   pc 4.3.6

There is a last minute panic over getting the text of the flyer to the printer, who is some distance away. He needs it tomorrow morning. The text is stored on your computer. What are the costs and advantages of sending it by – special delivery, post, fax or e-mail? What method would you choose, and why?

task 4 – storing documents

Rapid Alarm Limited has designed a new customer enquiry form which it will circulate at the exhibition. New customers can fill it in if they are interested in having an alarm fitted. This is the form:

RAPID ALARM CUSTOMER ENQUIRY

Are you interested in having an alarm fitted?

For a quotation without obligation please complete the details below.

Please tick the appropriate box:

☐ I am interested in an alarm   ☐ I am interested in an alarm
for domestic premises   for commercial premises

Name ....

Address ....

....

....

postcode...telephone..

The Sales Manager wants to know what is the best way of storing this information, on paper or on computer database? Or both? He needs to be able to access customers by name and also by whether they are domestic or commercial customers. His present system also gives each customer an account number. Set out for him in short note form how you would:

(a)   store the completed forms in a paper-based system

(b)   set up the details on a computer database (and provide a back-up)

He states that he wants both systems in operation (ie computer database, backed up on disc and also with the paper forms).

You are to

•   set up a suitable computer database

•   enter 40 records (make up the details) and obtain a printout

DOCUMENT BANK

THE LETTER

house style
If you work in an organisation or receive letters from an organisation, you will note that the appearance and format of each letter is (or should be!) in a uniform 'house' style, a style which readily identifies that organisation. The most common way of setting out a letter is the fully-blocked style, explained on the next two pages. The example letter has been prepared by a firm of electrical contractors, Wyvern Electrical Services. A potential customer, Mr J Sutton, has enquired about the possibility of having his house rewired.

characteristics of a fully-blocked letter
- the most commonly used style of letter
- all the lines start at the left margin
- use of open punctuation, ie there is no punctuation, except in the main body of the letter, which uses normal punctuation
- a fully-blocked letter looks neat and clean (no untidy punctuation)
- a fully-blocked letter is easy to type as all the lines are set uniformly to the left margin

elements of the letter
The references to the left of the letter illustrated describe the elements of a letter. These are explained more fully below.

printed letterhead
This is always pre-printed, and must be up-to-date.

reference
The reference on the letter illustrated -DH/SB/69 - is a standard format
- DH (Derek Hunt), the writer
- SB (Sally Burgess), the typist
- 69, the number of the file where Mr Sutton's correspondence is kept

If you need to quote the reference of a letter to which you are replying, the references will be quoted as follows: Your ref. TR/FG/45 Our ref. DH/SB/69

date
The date is typed in date (number), month (word), year (number) order.

Elements of the letter	
	Wyvern Electrical Services **107 High Street** **Mereford MR1 9SZ** **Tel 01605 675365 Fax 01605 675576**
reference	Ref DH/SB/69
date	14 December 1996
name and address of recipient of letter	J D Sutton Esq 23 Windermere Close Crofters Green Mereford MR6 7ER
salutation	Dear Mr Sutton
heading	<u>Rewiring: 23 Windermere Close</u>
body of the letter	Thank you for your letter of enquiry dated 10 December. We are pleased to enclose a brochure detailing our services and will be pleased to give you a quotation for rewiring your new extension. In order to do this we will need to send our estimator to see your property, and shall be grateful if you will telephone us to arrange a visit at a time which is convenient to you. We look forward to hearing from you.
complimentary close	Yours sincerely
signature	*D Hunt*
name and job title of sender	Derek Hunt Sales Manager
enclosure indicator	enc

recipient

The name and address of the person to whom the letter is sent. This section of the letter may be displayed in the window of a window envelope, so it is essential that it is accurate. Note the difference between the open and full punctuation in the recipient section of the letters; the open punctuation in the blocked and semi-blocked styles appears much 'cleaner.'

salutation

'Dear Sir. . . Dear Madam' if you know the person's name and title (eg Mr, Mrs, Ms), use it, but check that it is spelt or applied correctly - a misspelt name or an incorrect title will ruin an otherwise competent letter.

heading

The heading sets out the subject matter of the letter - it will concentrate the reader's mind.

body

The body of the letter is an area where communications skills can be developed. The text must be:

- laid out in short precise paragraphs and short clear sentences
- start with a point of reference (e.g. thanking for a letter)
- set out the message in a logical sequence
- avoid jargon and slang expressions
- finish with a clear indication of the next step to be taken (e.g. please telephone, please arrange appointment, please buy our products, please pay our invoice).

complimentary close

The complimentary close (signing off phrase) must be consistent with the salutation:

'Dear Sir/Dear Madam' followed by 'Yours faithfully'

'Dear Mr Sutton/Dear Ms Jones' followed by 'Yours sincerely'.

name and job title

It is essential for the reader to know the name of the person who sent the letter, and that person's job title, because a reply will need to be addressed to a specific person.

enclosures

If there are enclosures with the letter, the abbreviation 'enc' or 'encl' is used.

DOCUMENT BANK

THE MEMORANDUM

format

The memorandum (plural memoranda) is a formal written note used for internal communication within an organisation. It may be typed or handwritten, and will often be produced in a number of copies which can be circulated as necessary. It can be used for situations such as:

- giving instructions
- requesting information
- making suggestions
- recording of opinions
- confirming telephone conversations

A memorandum is normally pre-printed by the organisation with all the headings in place, and can be half page or full page in size. A completed memorandum is illustrated below and explained on the next page.

MEMORANDUM

To Tim Blake, Sales Manager

From K Roach, Finance Manager   **Ref.** KR/AC/1098

Copies to Departmental Managers   **Date** 7 July 1996

Subject COMPUTERISATION OF ACCOUNTING RECORDS

Please attend a meeting on 14 July in the Conference Room. Attendance is vital as the new system comes on line on 1 September. Summary details of the new system are attached.

enc

---

elements of the memorandum

Most of the headings on the pre-printed memorandum form are self-explanatory, as they are also to be found on business letters. You should, however, note the following:

heading

The name of the organisation may be printed above the word 'Memorandum', although this is not strictly necessary, as the memorandum is an internal document.

'to' and 'from'

The name and job title of the sender and the recipient are entered in full, and as a consequence the salutation 'Dear......' and the complimentary close 'Yours ....' are not necessary.

copies to

Memoranda are frequently sent (as in the example above) to a large number of people; the recipients will be indicated in this section of the document.

reference

As in a business letter the reference indicates the writer, the typist, and the file number.

date

As in a business letter the order is day (number), month (word), year (number).

subject

The subject matter of the memorandum must be concisely stated.

text

The message of the memorandum should be clear and concise.

signature

A memorandum can be signed, initialled, or even – as is often the case – left blank.

enclosures

If material is circulated with the memorandum, the abbreviation 'enc' or 'encl' should be used.

DOCUMENT BANK

THE MESSAGE

format

There is no set format for a written message – it can be a scribbled note on the back of envelope, or it can be a printed form bought from a commercial stationer.

Shown below is a typical preprinted message form.

TELEPHONE MESSAGE

for ....

date ....time......................................

caller's name...

caller's organisation...

telephone no...

> **message**
>
>
>
>
>
>
>
>
>
>

call taken by...

DOCUMENT BANK

THE REPORT

This type of document has been included here because it is used widely in business and also by students doing assignment work.

types of report

The most common types of report are:

- the full-length formal report
- the short formal report

structure of a report

A report will normally be structured as follows:

title	the subject matter of the report – what it is about
terms of reference	the circumstances and the scope of the report: • the person(s) who commissioned it • the ground it has to cover • the date by which it has to be submitted • whether it has to make any recommendations
procedures	this section sets out how the report was compiled: • identification of source documents • interviews – details should be given • observation
findings	the information is set out in a structured way and analysed
conclusions	a summary of the analysis of the findings
recommendations	if required, specific recommendations can be made on the basis of the conclusions drawn from the findings
appendices	the inclusion of any relevant material from the findings, eg numerical data, copies of important source material

The structure set out on the previous page is the normal format for the short formal report, and should be adopted for reports which you will from time-to-time compile as part of your studies.

report layout

The report, as well as being structured in a formal way, is often laid out in a formal manner. It should normally be typed or word processed. The increasing use of laser printers and sophisticated word processing or DTP (Desk Top Publishing) systems has resulted in the more 'professional' appearance of many internal documents such as reports.

It has become common practice for reports to be divided into sections by the use of the decimal point referencing system. This divides the structure of a report (as set out above) into numbered sections, and identifies subdivisions of those sections by setting out the number of the section followed by a decimal point and a number identifying the subsection. The subsection can also be subdivided by placing a decimal point after the subsection number and incorporating a third number.

This is best understood by looking at the plan set out below of the Conclusions and Recommendations sections of a short formal report – note how the sections and subsections are indented from the left margin (ie the text starts further away from the left margin) as the sections become more subsidiary. Note also that the structure is illustrated here, not the text itself:

4.0	CONCLUSIONS
4.1	first conclusion (main heading)
4.2	second conclusion (main heading)
4.3	third conclusion (main heading)
	4.3.1 – first point of third conclusion
	4.3.2 – second point of third conclusion
5.0	RECOMMENDATIONS
5.1	first recommendation
5.2	second recommendation

Now read on the next page an extract from a short formal report submitted by an Administration Manager to the Managing Director of a small company. The matter under investigation is the introduction of a drinks machine in the staff rest room. Note carefully the format of the report, the use of sections and headings in capital letters.

CONFIDENTIAL

to	Howard Neskin, Managing Director	**ref**	DS/FT/GH6
from	David Salcombe, Administration Manager	**date**	15 February 19-9

REPORT ON PROPOSED PURCHASE OF DRINKS VENDING MACHINE FOR STAFF REST ROOM

1.0 TERMS OF REFERENCE

On 6 January 19-9 the Managing Director requested David Salcombe, Administration Manager, to investigate the feasibility of the introduction of a drinks vending machine in the first floor staff rest room. He was asked to assess demand for the machine and types of drink, to compare the cost of buying a machine with the cost of rental, and to investigate the servicing costs. He was requested to forward his written report, with recommendations, to the Managing Director by 20 February 19-9.

2.0 PROCEDURE

The following investigations were made:

2.1 A questionnaire to staff (for copy see Appendix 1) was circulated on 15 January and completed by 20 January 19-9.

2.2 Details of vending machines were requested and received from five companies. These details were:

2.2.1 The comparative costs of purchase and rental

2.2.2 The servicing and maintenance costs

3.0 FINDINGS

3.1 Questionnaire to staff

58 Staff members completed the questionnaire. The questionnaire established that the majority of staff wanted the installation of a drinks vending machine. The results showed that:

3.1.1 89% of staff wanted a machine installed

3.1.2 67% wanted *all* of the following available drinks: soup, hot chocolate, coffee, tea

extract from a short formal report

SECTION 5

Core Skills Activities

The Activities which follow are designed to cover the Performance Criteria of the 1995 NCVQ Level 2 Core Skills specifications. There is one main Activity for each mandatory Core Skill. Individual tasks within each Activity are referenced to performance criteria, and 'assessment points' are introduced from time-to-time to enable the Tutor to carry out the necessary assessment.

The authors do not recommend that these Activities be adopted as a 'stand alone' approach to Core Skills delivery. Core Skills should be delivered as an integral part of the course. Tutors should make students aware of the Core Skills symbols (see above) which appear in many of the Student Activities within the main text of the book.

Tutors should refer to the 'Core Skills Coverage' table (page 7) which sets out page references for coverage of Core Skills Elements in the Student Activities in the main text.

The three mandatory Core Skills covered in the Activities which follow are:

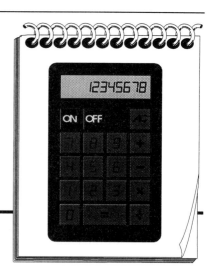

Core Skills Activity
– application of number

TO THE STUDENT

what is application of number?

"Application of number" means understanding and using numbers, and being able to solve problems involving numbers.

dealing with numbers

Some people like dealing with numbers and can handle them easily. Some people cannot cope with numbers and get a 'mental block' when calculations are called for! Your GNVQ course requires that you should be able to deal with straightforward calculations and be able to use numbers to solve problems. You have probably already made a start – you will have dealt with numbers when completing or checking invoices, setting up profit statements and spreadsheets.

Your tutor may well also arrange for time to be given to practising skills such as dealing with decimals, percentages and formulas.

what skills will the Activity develop?

The Activity is divided into a number of Tasks, each of which develops a range of skills.

The Tasks will involve you in:

- **numerical techniques** – using numbers (plus and minus numbers), fractions, percentages, ratios, estimating quantities

- **collecting and recording data** – finding out numbers from people and from written sources, writing down prices and measurements using data collection sheets

- **tackling numerical problems** – calculating numbers, dealing with shapes and sizes, converting between common units of measurement

- **interpreting and presenting data** – setting out the results of calculations in the forms of charts and drawings so that the figures can be understood

"What do people drink?"
– application of number

soft drinks
You have been asked to carry out a survey into canned soft drinks. You need to find out:

1.   what people like to drink

2.   what their buying habits are

surveys
You may have been asked by someone with a clipboard to take part in a survey – usually when you are in a hurry to get somewhere else! A survey involves:
* interviewing a number of people – known as a "sample"
* asking a series of questions with a clear range of possible answers
* analysing and presenting the results you get

survey questions
You must be careful to make sure that the questions asked require a clear answer. You can do this by giving the person you interview a choice of answers – and you then tick the box for the answer they choose. For example –

QUESTION   What is your favourite canned soft drink?

ANSWER   Coke ☐   Fruit juice ☐   Tango ✓   Other ☐

QUESTION   Where do you normally buy your drinks?

ANSWER   Small shop ☐   Supermarket ☐   Machine ✓   Other ☐

On the next page is a suggestion of how the survey could be set out. You will probably want to change and adapt the questions.

Whatever you eventually decide to do, you should check your survey with your Tutor before interviewing anyone.

SURVEY

SOFT DRINKS

name of questioner ....*Luigi Fornova*.................................... **date**.......*1 April 1996*.......

1.   Do you like soft drinks?
       Yes ☐   No ☐
       If the answer is NO, <u>no more questions should be asked.</u>

2.   What is your favourite canned soft drink?
       Coke ☐   Pepsi ☐   Lilt ☐   Tango ☐   Other ☐

       If OTHER, please state name of drink ....

3.   How often do you buy soft drinks – on average?

       Every day   ☐
       2 or 3 times a week   ☐
       Once a week   ☐
       Once a fortnight   ☐
       Once a month   ☐
       Very occasionally   ☐

4.   Do you prefer your drink chilled?
       Yes ☐   No ☐   I don't mind ☐

5.   Where do you buy your soft drinks?
       Local shop ☐   Supermarket ☐   Machine ☐   Other ☐

6.   Do you shop around for the lowest price?
       Yes ☐   No ☐

7.   What do you do with the empty can?
       Throw it away ☐   Keep it for recycling ☐

An example of a survey which you can adapt for your own use.

carrying out the survey

Your Tutor will tell you whom you can interview. It may be the public, it may be your fellow students, it may be your family and friends. Before carrying out the survey you should:

- check your survey questions with your Tutor to make sure that they are clear and won't offend people, eg NOT "Do you think soft drinks make you put on weight?" when the person interviewed may be twenty stone!

- produce the survey sheet on a word-processor

- have a trial run of the survey sheet with a friend – just to make sure it 'works'

- arrange to have a number of sheets copied (or printed off the computer)

- if possible, obtain a clipboard to hold the sheets when you are asking the questions

summarising the results

When you have finished the survey you should keep your survey sheets safely in a folder so that you can then summarise them on a separate sheet of paper.

This is an extract from a summary:

SURVEY SUMMARY name of questioner..........*Luigi Fornova*...................

number of people questioned..........*30*.........

date of survey...........*1 April 1996*................

1.   Do you like soft drinks?

Yes   29

No   1

2.   What is your favourite canned soft drink?

Coke   10,   Pepsi   5,   Lilt 5,   Tango 5,   Other   4

OTHER includes 7-up (2) Lucozade (1)   Sprite(1)

---

analysing the results

Your summary sheet provides you with the data which you can analyse.

Analysis involves asking a number of questions about your results and then showing the answers in the form of charts which can either be hand drawn or produced on a computer.

Find out if the computers you use can produce charts – either from a special 'charting' package or as part of a database or spreadsheet program.

how to do your analysis

Here are some suggested ways in which you could analyse the results from the survey shown on page 268:

1.   What percentage of people DO and DO NOT like soft drinks? Work out the figures using a calculator. What are these percentages as fractions? (Survey question 1).

2.   Draw up a pie chart showing people's preferences for types of soft drink. (Survey question 2).

3.   Draw up a bar chart showing how often people buy soft drinks. (Survey question 3).

4.   Draw up a pie chart showing peoples' preferences for chilled drinks. (Survey question 4).

5.   Draw up a bar chart showing where people buy their drinks. (Survey question 5).

6.   Work out the percentages of 'yes' and 'no' in Survey question 6. Comment on this result.

7.   Present the answers to Survey question 7 in a pie chart. What conclusions can you draw from this result?

example of a bar chart

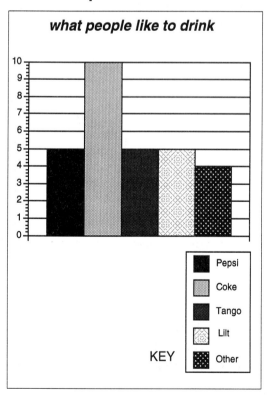

example of a pie chart

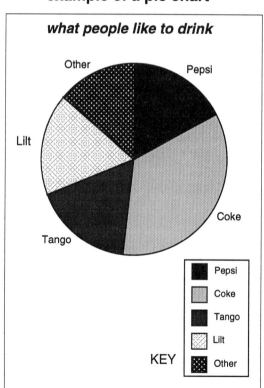

assessment point 1

Although your Tutor will have been checking your work as you have been doing Task 1, you should now hand to your Tutor for assessment:

* one copy of your original survey
* the survey summary sheet
* your analysis of the survey, together with supporting charts, graphs and calculations

You are now ready to do Task 2.

TASK 2: SOFT DRINK PACKAGING (Elements 2.1, pcs 1-6; 2.2, pcs 1-8)

different types, shapes and sizes

So far in this Activity you have looked at canned soft drinks. Of course there are many other forms of packaging – cartons, plastic bottles and so on. In this Task you will investigate:

* the different shapes and sizes of drinks containers
* how much each container holds – its 'volume'
* different ways of measuring dimensions and volume, eg pints, litres

1. **Investigate** as many different types of drinks container as you can find. Bring examples into the classroom. **Make a list of your findings** by using a table which you can rule up on an A4 sheet. Here is an extract from a suitable table:

type of drink	container	material	volume
milk	carton	cardboard	2 pints
orange juice	carton	plastic	2 litres
Coke	can	aluminium	330ml

2. **Obtain a Coke can** (or similar type of can) and note down its:
    * height in centimetres
    * diameter in centimetres (the distance across the top)
    * radius in centimetres (half the distance across the top)

    Then **work out how much the can holds in cubic centimeters** using the formulas

Area of the top of the can $= \pi r^2$

Volume of a can $=$ *area of the top of the can* $\times$ *its height*

Note:

• in the first formula the symbol 'π' (pronounced "pie") stands for the number 3.142

• 'r^2' means the radius 'squared' ie the radius multiplied by the radius (a number 'squared' is a number multiplied by itself).

• ignore any rounding in shape at the ends of the can!

Draw a diagram of the can as seen from the side, making it look as if it is three dimensional, adding labels to show its height and diameter.

3. Suppose the can you have just examined comes in a square pack of four as shown in the diagram on the right. **How much volume will the pack take up?** How does this compare with the total volume of four cans? Why do you think cans and packs are this shape?

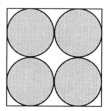

4. A supermarket stand measures 10 feet long by 4 feet high by three feet deep.

(a) Draw a diagram of this stand, labelling it with the dimensions.

(b) What is the storage volume of this stand?

(c) Approximately how many 'four packs' of Coke would fit in this space?

5. Investigate the price of a standard can of Coca Cola and 'lookalikes' eg Virgin Cola. What price range is there? Why are the prices different?

assessment point 2

Present the following evidence to your Tutor for assessment:

• your table showing the different types of container

• the diagram of the can of Coke

• your calculation of the volume of a can and the 'four-pack'

• the calculation of the storage space of the stand

• the calculation of the number of 'four packs' the stand will hold (including any conversions you may have done)

• the results of your investigation into Coke prices

You are now ready to do Task 3.

TASK 3: THE PRICE OF A PINTA (Elements 2.1, pcs 1-6; 2.2, pcs 1-8)

the cost of your daily pint of milk

Many people still drink milk, even if it is just added to coffee or poured over the cornflakes in the morning. Milk can be bought from many different sources: the dairy which delivers to the doorstep, the local cornershop, garage, 24 hour store, or the local supermarket. It can be bought by the pint bottle or carton or in large plastic containers from the supermarket.

In this task you are to:

1.   Make a list of as many different types of outlet selling milk as you can find.

2.   Investigate in those outlets the different prices of a pint of milk – to do this you will need to divide the price of each container by the number of pints it contains. Try to find at least six different prices.

3.   Arrange your findings in a table, starting with the cheapest and finishing with the most expensive. It should look something like this

outlet/shop	size of container	container price	price per pint
Safeburys	6 pint	£1.50	25p
Sainsco	4 pint	£1.20	30p
Gormleys Corner shop	1 pint	32p	32p
Western Dairies (doorstep delivery)	1 pint	35p	35p

4.   Work out from your table the **average** cost of a pint of milk.

(The average is calculated by adding up the prices found, eg 25p + 30p + 32p etc, and then dividing the result by the number of prices).

5.   Write down the reasons why you think there is such a variation in price. Why doesn't everyone just buy the cheapest milk available?

assessment point 3

Hand to your Tutor for assessment:

* your table of outlets selling milk
* your calculation of the average cost of a pint of milk
* your comments on the difference in prices

Core Skills Activity
– *communication*

TO THE STUDENT

what is communication?

"Communication" is a two-way process – it involves understanding information and messages received from others, and it means making yourself understood.

communicating in business

Working in business means working with people. Working with people means being able to send and receive messages in many different ways:

- taking part in discussions with one person or in groups

- producing written material, either filling in forms or producing a set format such as a letter

- using images to get your point across in discussions and when using written communications

- extracting and understanding information taken from written materials and from images

Already on your course you will have been practising these skills – speaking and writing to people in business, preparing written work for your Portfolio, talking and arguing about your work with your fellow students and Tutor. In this Activity you will be able to develop your Communication skills by taking part in assessed discussions, producing written materials, using images, and reading and responding to written materials and images.

GNVQ Intermediate course leaflet – communication

TASK 1: DISCUSSING THE FORMAT (Element 2.1, pcs 1-4)

what is required?
You have been asked to design and produce a leaflet about your GNVQ Intermediate course. **Each student is to produce his/her own leaflet.** The purpose of the leaflet is to give information to students who are thinking of taking the course at your school or college. The information should include:

- an explanation of what a GNVQ Intermediate course is
- a description of the Units that can be taken (mandatory and option)
- a description of the way you study
- the viewpoint of a 'typical' student – "Why I enjoy the course"
- details of your school/college (address, name of contact, telephone number, map)

discussion
You should discuss in class, under the supervision of your Tutor, what format should be used, ie what size and type of paper, and how it should be folded (if it is to be folded!)

resources?
You should also discuss with your Tutor, your class, and with people outside the class (eg IT staff, library staff) what resources are available for making the leaflet. A list of resources should be drawn up. For example, the following might be made available:

- a page make-up (DTP) program on the computer
- a Polaroid camera for taking pictures of a typical student at work
- a school or college map

assessment point 1
You will be assessed in two ways for this Task by your Tutor:
- in your contribution to class discussion and discussion with other staff
- in a face-to-face interview with your Tutor in which you tell him/her how you are going to compile your leaflet.

TASK 2: PREPARING THE TEXT (Element 2.2, pcs.1- 5)

writing the text

You are writing an introduction to your course to students of your own age. Keep the language simple, to the point and avoid using jargon or slang. Check your punctuation and spelling carefully.You may find it useful to collect examples of other course leaflets. You may find that the course is already explained in your school or college prospectus or in material from NCVQ!

We are not telling you here what you have to write or how much you have to write. You will have to sort these out with your Tutor, who will be able to help you and discuss your progress. As a guide to content, remember the points made on the previous page under the heading "what is required?"

Do not include any pictures, diagrams or photographs at this point, but be thinking about how you could introduce them.

written requests

You may find that when you are planning your resources, you will need to make formal requests to various departments within your school or college. For example you may need to request the loan of a camera, the supply of paper, a copy of a map, a picture of the school/college. In each case make your request in writing:

- *either* on a specified request form, *or*
- by means of a Memorandum (look at the example below)

Make sure you keep a copy of any written communication – you will need it for assessment purposes.

MEMORANDUM

To Ms S Drew. School Secretary   Ref. AP/F4

From A Patel, F4   Date 1 April 1996

Subject GNVQ Intermediate Business Leaflet

Please supply me with a copy of a location map of the school. I would like to use the map in a course leaflet which I am preparing as part of my GNVQ Intermediate Business Skills assessment.

assessment point 2

You should now hand to your Tutor:

- your draft text
- any copies of written requests

TASK 3: USING IMAGES (Element 2.3, pcs.1- 3)

deciding what to use

You will have been planning the use of at least two images in your leaflet. Here are some suggestions for the types of image you might use:

- a chart showing the Units that make up the Intermediate GNVQ
- a photograph of a student at work
- a map showing where the school/college is
- a picture of the school/college

Discuss the use of the images with your Tutor. Discuss with your IT staff the way the images might be imported into the text .

using images in the text

When you have decided what images to use, they should be inserted in the text of the leaflet in the appropriate place. The leaflet should now be complete.

assessment point 3

Now hand the completed draft leaflet to your Tutor for assessment.

TASK 4: RESPONDING TO WRITTEN MATERIAL (Element 2.4, pcs.1- 4)

breakdown!

Obtain an illustrated manual to some complex piece of equipment which is used in your school or college and find the section which deals with faults and breakdowns. Assume that there has been a breakdown in the production of your leaflet, for example:

- a photocopier paper jam
- a computer printer ribbon has worn out or toner has run out

Find the relevant section in the manual and study the text and diagrams carefully. If there are any points which are not clear, consult your Tutor or a technician. Jot down in numbered notes how to solve the problem. Now tell your Tutor how to rectify the fault!

assessment point 4

Your Tutor will assess you on the way in which you have understood the instructions, and have then been able to note them down and pass them on by word of mouth.

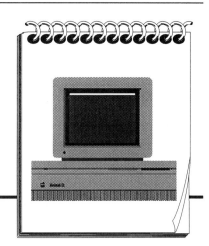

Core Skills Activity
– information technology

TO THE STUDENT

what is information technology?
"Information technology" is the technology – the equipment and 'know how' – which provides businesses with up-to-date and accurate information.

the need for up-to-date information
Businesses need up-to-date information to answer questions such as:

"Who are my customers?"

"What did we sell last month?"

"How many have we got left in stock?"

how is the information provided?
Information like this can now be made available rapidly and accurately by electronic means. This 'information technology' involves the use of computers and communication equipment such as fax machines. A business can set up systems so that information such as stock held, sales figures and customer details can easily be made available to the people who need them.

what skills will the Activity develop?
This Activity involves compiling a 'lifestyle' profile of your class, much in the way a marketing research team would find out about customer needs. The tasks develop information technology skills. When you have finished the activities you will be able to:

- enter and save information on a computer system
- organise the information the way you want it
- present the information you have been dealing with
- deal with day-to-day operating problems such as errors and breakdowns
- evaluate computer programs

A *class lifestyle profile*
– information technology

TASK 1: WHAT RESOURCES ARE NEEDED? (Element 2.4, pcs 1-5)

INTRODUCTION
You have been asked to divide into groups of three or four students and to produce a computer-based *profile* of your class and of members of your group. This profile will be useful in a number of ways:

- you will get to know each other as individuals and as a class
- you will also get an idea of the type of information needed by marketing research teams
- you will produce material which can be used to show to the general public on open days, open evenings and parents evenings

The profile will be compiled using information technology and will take the form of a presentation folder, preferably A4 in size.

the profile
The profile *could* contain (it is up to the class to plan the final contents):

- the results of a survey of the whole class, including details of age, sex, height and also details of taste (eg favourite food) – the survey will be undertaken in the form of a questionnaire
- an individual profile of each of the group members
- a profile of the tutor, produced as a result of an interview

resources needed?
The group must investigate what software and hardware they are going to need by talking to the tutor and the IT staff.

The profile will be produced using information technology, *ideally* with:

- a database in which to enter the class details
- a spreadsheet to process the results of the questionnaire and to produce charts and graphs
- a word processing package to process the basic text
- image scanning software for any pictures used
- a desk-top publishing package into which can be imported text and images and which will produce the final output

- suitable hardware – a computer to process the data, a scanner and a laser printer

This is only a suggestion – clearly not every centre will have all these resources, and not all groups will want to use this combination. The point of this task is the *evaluation* of the resources – hardware and software – available.

While still in this planning stage, students should be aware of the *Health & Safety aspects* of computer operation and think through problems they may encounter in using either the hardware or the software. They should plan how they are going to store the data and make data back-ups.

assessment point 1

Each group should discuss with the Tutor at this stage
- the resources needed
- any problems identified in using the hardware and software

TASK 2: PREPARING THE DATA (Element 2.1, pcs 1 - 4)

the lifestyle survey

The main part of the profile involves a survey of the whole class. As a class you should devise a *common* questionnaire sheet which you can fill in to provide the data. This could be done with the Tutor – compiling questions on the board as a result of discussion. Suggested data which you could collect includes:

- name of student
- sex of student
- age of student
- favourite music
- favourite food
- favourite drink
- favourite subject studied
- favourite leisure activity
- favourite holiday destination
- intended job (or course) after GNVQ

This is only a suggestion – you may well have other ideas!

Remember that in questions such as "What is your favourite band?" it is best to set the questions to *give* a choice, eg "Which of these six bands do you like best?"

When the questionnaire has been completed and analysed by the class as a whole, the results should then be distributed on a summary sheet to each group within the class.

Each group should:

1. Create a suitable database file for the survey results. Fields should be allocated to each of the significant areas – they may be text, numeric or date.

2. Work out how the input data can be output for analysis – eg how can you extract a graph to show the proportion of girls in the group – will you need a spreadsheet?

3. Ensure that the original data is kept safely and that a back-up routine has been established.

assessment point 2

Each group should discuss with the Tutor at this stage to make sure that

- the database and any other software is set up satisfactorily
- the group has a system for storage of its source information and for back-up of computer data

The data can now be input. Remember to 'save' regularly, correct errors as you go along, printout the finished file, back-up, correct any errors and back-up again.

assessment point 3

The input stage should be observed and assessed by the Tutor.

TASK 3: PROCESSING THE DATA (Element 2.2. pcs 1 - 6)

The data is now reading for accessing and using in the class lifestyle profile which you are going to compile. At this stage you will need to:

- establish how you are going to use the software to present the data – this will probably involve a combination of text, charts and numbers
- plan out the profile
- enter the text
- produce the charts

If you need to import text and graphics (the charts) into a separate program, you may need help from your Tutor or IT staff.

assessment point 4

Each group should discuss its progress with the Tutor at this stage to make sure that:

- the plans for combining data will work
- the resources are available

TASK 4: PRESENTING THE DATA (Element 2.3. pcs 1 - 5)

The lifestyle profile is now ready for production. The group should combine text and charts in whatever way the software allows.

Suggestions for areas to present include:
- the percentage split between males and females
- male eating habits
- female leisure pursuits
- proportion of students who want to get a job on finishing the course

and so on ...

additional/optional tasks

The class profile produced by each group could also contain a profile of individual members of the group and also of the tutor.

Profiles of individuals could take the form of an interview in which the individual is asked to describe how he/she spends his day – when he/she gets up, what he/she has for breakfast, what are 'pet hates' and special likes, weaknesses and strengths, evening activities, and so on ...

A suggested format for these is a one page report of an interview and a photograph of the person. The finished page could therefore include both imported text and a scanned image.

completing the profile

Each member of the group should ideally have their own copy of the profile, and an extra copy should be made for the tutor and for display within the school or college. If the profile is all on computer file, this should pose no problem. The tutor copy of the profile should be compiled in the form of a presentation folder.

assessment point 5

Each group should present and discuss their finished profile document with the Tutor. Part of the discussion should include an analysis of any problems they encountered with the hardware or software, or with Health & Safety aspects. Would they have done the project any other way?

In assessing the work, the Tutor should be aware of the contribution made by individual students.

notes

notes

comments page

If you have any comments, criticisms, or queries about this book, please write them on this page, tear it out and send it to:

The General Editor
Osborne Books
Unit 1B Everoak Estate
Bromyard Road
St Johns
Worcester WR2 5HN

your comments ...